Using 1-2-3

Geoffrey T. LeBlond
Douglas Ford Cobb

Que Corporation
Indianapolis

Library of Congress Catalog No.: LC 83-62060
ISBN 0-88022-045-7

Using 1-2-3 is an independently produced product of Que Corporation and is not endorsed by Lotus Development Corporation.

1-2-3 is a trademark of Lotus Development Corporation.

Parts of Chapter 1 of *Using 1-2-3* are excerpted from the book *Spreadsheet Software: From VisiCalc to 1-2-3*, by Thomas B. Henderson, Douglas Ford Cobb, and Gena Berg Cobb, copyright © 1983, Que Corporation.

Cover Design: Cargill Associates, Atlanta

88 87 86 85 84   12

Interpretation of the printing code: the rightmost double-digit number is the year of the book's printing: the rightmost single-digit number, the number of the book's printing. For example, a printing code of 83-4 shows that the fourth printing of the book occurred in 1983.

Dedication

To Laura
—G.L.

To my wife, Gena
—D.F.C.

Editorial Director
David F. Noble, Ph.D.

Editor
Diane F. Brown, M.A.

Managing Editor
Paul Mangin

About the Authors

Douglas Ford Cobb received his B.A., magna cum laude, from Williams College and his M.S. in accounting from New York University's Graduate School of Business Administration. He has worked for Arthur Andersen & Co. and was president of Cobb Associates, Inc., a Boston-based microcomputer consulting firm. Mr. Cobb has worked for Que Corporation as general manager of the company's business software products. He coauthored *Spreadsheet Software: From VisiCalc to 1-2-3*, *Using 1-2-3*, *1-2-3 Tips, Tricks, and Traps*, and *1-2-3 for Business*, all published by Que Corporation. He is president of The Cobb Group, Inc., a microcomputer information firm in Louisville, Kentucky.

Geoffrey T. LeBlond is manager of business software products at Que Corporation. He received his B.A. degree from Brown University and his M.B.A. in finance from Indiana University's Graduate School of Business. Mr. LeBlond is coauthor of *Using Symphony* and a contributing author to *1-2-3 for Business*, both published by Que Corporation. Mr. LeBlond is also a technical editor for the *IBM PC Update* magazine and editor-in-chief of *Absolute Reference: The Journal for 1-2-3 and Symphony Users*.

Acknowledgments

The authors would like to make the following acknowledgments:

Dr. John Boquist, for his helpful insights in comparing 1-2-3 to VisiCalc and VisiTrend/Plot.

Dr. Hugh McLaughlin, for his help in getting started with 1-2-3.

Steve Miller, Chris Morgan, and Ezra Gottheil of Lotus Development Corporation.

Rex Hancock of ComputerLand of Castleton, Indiana.

Tom Henderson, Tom Perkins, and Ann de Calonne of Que Corporation, for their assistance with this project.

Introduction

1-2-3 is the most exciting new program for microcomputers since VisiCalc. This new "all-in-one" program combines the best of the popular electronic spreadsheets, business graphics software, and personal data managers into one integrated software package. Thanks to its power and sophistication, 1-2-3 has become the hottest product in the microcomputer industry.

Although 1-2-3 is in many ways similar to VisiCalc, Multiplan, and the other electronic spreadsheet programs, 1-2-3 is a dramatic improvement on the basic concept of a spreadsheet. If 1-2-3 were only a spreadsheet, it would still be an excellent product; but 1-2-3 offers much more. It is an amazingly powerful product that combines exceptional graphics and useful data base management functions with its state-of-the-art spreadsheet.

Using 1-2-3

With the sophistication of 1-2-3 comes complexity. Although the basics of 1-2-3 are easy to learn, especially for the experienced VisiCalc user, the fine points of the program can take months to master. As a result, many users are not taking full advantage of the power of 1-2-3.

Using 1-2-3 helps solve this problem. This book explains 1-2-3's commands and functions in a clear, easy-to-understand style. It includes examples of 1-2-3's commands and functions that will help you apply 1-2-3 to your business problems. The unique elements of 1-2-3—graphics, data management, and keyboard macros—are covered in detail.

Using 1-2-3 is not a substitute for 1-2-3's very good manual, but rather a user's guide that goes beyond the basics of the manual to give examples and practical hints on using the program. This book should be used with the Lotus manual to gain a complete understanding of the power of 1-2-3.

Who Should Buy This Book?

If you own 1-2-3, you should own this book. *Using 1-2-3* picks up where the 1-2-3 manual leaves off to explain both the basics and the fine points of the program. Every chapter includes clear explanations and examples, and special care has been taken to cover in detail those topics that are not thoroughly explained in the 1-2-3 manual. For example, Chapter 6 demonstrates 1-2-3's built-in functions, and Chapter 12 covers 1-2-3's keyboard macros functions. The explanations and examples in this book help put the full power of 1-2-3 at your fingertips.

If you do not own 1-2-3 but are considering purchasing the program, this book is also for you. Chapter 1, "An Overview of 1-2-3," will help you understand the unique features of this powerful program. If you are an experienced spreadsheeter who is considering trading up to 1-2-3, you will appreciate the special attention this book pays to those elements of the program that may be unfamiliar to the VisiCalc or SuperCalc user.

About This Book

Chapter 1, "An Overview of 1-2-3," discusses 1-2-3 in the context of the spreadsheet programs that preceded it. This chapter explains the basic concepts of 1-2-3 as well as its new features that, when combined, make the program different from anything that has come before it. You will also learn the story behind the development of 1-2-3.

Chapter 2, "Getting Started," covers the process of readying 1-2-3 for your computer, the Lotus Access System, the 1-2-3 Tutorial, and the program's exceptional help screen facility.

Chapter 3, "The 1-2-3 Spreadsheet," introduces the basic element of 1-2-3—the spreadsheet. This chapter covers the size and memory capacity of the spreadsheet and teaches you the fundamentals of entering data into it.

Chapter 4, "Commands," discusses the basic 1-2-3 spreadsheet commands, including *Range*, *Worksheet*, *Move*, and *Copy*.

The process of formatting the spreadsheet is covered in Chapter 5. This chapter includes descriptions and examples of all of 1-2-3's range and global formats.

The next chapter, "Functions," explains 1-2-3's built-in spreadsheet functions, including @HLOOKUP, @VLOOKUP, and @IRR. This chapter also deals with 1-2-3's exciting date arithmetic capabilities.

Chapter 7, "File Management," covers the commands used to store and retrieve worksheets. This chapter also shows the commands that are used to merge and consolidate worksheets.

Chapter 8, "Printing Reports," provides explanations and examples of 1-2-3's report printing commands. This chapter goes beyond the 1-2-3 manual to give examples of 1-2-3's powerful report formatting features.

Chapters 9 and 10, "Creating and Displaying Graphs" and "Printing Graphs," cover 1-2-3's built-in graphics capabilites. Chapter 9 provides an example of each of 1-2-3's graph types—bar, stacked bar, line, XY, and pie—and explains all of the 1-2-3 graph display options. Chapter 10 covers the process of printing a graph, using the PrintGraph program. The examples and illustrations will help you make productive use of 1-2-3's graphics.

1-2-3's built-in data base commands are discussed in Chapter 11, "Data Management." This chapter includes all of 1-2-3's /Data commands, including the sort, query, and data table commands, as well as 1-2-3's built-in data base statistical functions.

Keyboard macros are covered in Chapter 12. This chapter explains each macro command and function and presents a number of interesting and useful example macros. If you are a 1-2-3 user, you know that the program's manual leaves much to be desired in its explanations of this exciting capability. *Using 1-2-3* gives you all the instructions you will need to begin using 1-2-3's macros.

The final chapter, "A Comprehensive Model," draws together all of the concepts developed in the earlier chapters into one comprehensive 1-2-3 application. This model includes a spreadsheet, a data base, a set of graphs, and a macro or two. The comprehensive model will show you how the knowledge you have gained from *Using 1-2-3* can be applied to your needs.

This book has one appendix that summarizes 1-2-3's built-in commands and functions and compares the program to its predecessor, VisiCalc. This section is particularly useful for VisiCalc users who are considering stepping up to 1-2-3.

A comprehensive index is also included.

More 1-2-3 Knowledge

1-2-3 for Business

Que's book *1-2-3 for Business,* by Hugh McLaughlin, Leith Anderson, and Douglas Ford Cobb, makes an excellent companion to *Using 1-2-3.* Where *Using 1-2-3* concentrates on explaining the fundamentals of 1-2-3, *1-2-3 for Business* offers more than 15 interesting and useful business applications for 1-2-3. You may be able to use many of these applications in your business. All of them will help you learn more about 1-2-3. Once you have read *Using 1-2-3,* you may want to polish further your 1-2-3 skills with *1-2-3 for Business.*

Absolute Reference

If you would like to receive a continuous flow of information about 1-2-3, you should consider subscribing to Que's new publication, *Absolute Reference: The Journal for 1-2-3 Users.* For more on this exciting opportunity, see the announcement inside the back cover of this book.

Table of Contents

Using 1-2-3

1

An Overview of 1-2-3

What Is 1-2-3?

1-2-3™ has been hailed as the most significant new software product since VisiCalc® was introduced more than five years ago. 1-2-3 required only three months to replace VisiCalc on the software best-seller lists. This program has generated more interest in its short life than any other new software product in recent years.

The excitement over 1-2-3 comes primarily from the program's tremendous power. 1-2-3 is one of the first *integrated* office management software programs. 1-2-3 means 3 in 1. It combines three of the most popular business applications programs—electronic spreadsheet, business graphics, and data management—into one sophisticated program. Unlike other programs that attempt to accomplish this feat, the various elements of 1-2-3 are not compromised to achieve this interactivity. Each element is competitive with stand-alone programs designed to accomplish the same task.

1-2-3 is also one of the first members of a new generation of microcomputer software programs designed specifically for the exciting new 16-bit computers like the IBM® Personal Computer. 1-2-3 takes full advantage of the memory capacity and speed of these new computers.

For this reason, many industry observers have hailed 1-2-3 as a revolutionary new development in software. These observers believe that 1-2-3's integrated approach to business management software makes it a totally new kind of program.

Basically, however, 1-2-3 is an electronic spreadsheet. The graphics and data management elements of the program are contained within the framework of a spreadsheet that is surprisingly like the VisiCalc sheet. Graphics are produced through the use of spreadsheet commands. Data management occurs in the standard row-column spreadsheet layout. Because 1-2-3 is primarily a spreadsheet, it owes a great deal to the spreadsheet programs that came before it—especially VisiCalc. This has led to the description of 1-2-3 as an evolutionary development of the basic features pioneered by VisiCalc. 1-2-3 is regarded as the logical next step in the development of the electronic spreadsheet.

Because 1-2-3 owes so much to the programs that came before it, an understanding of the developments that led up to the creation of 1-2-3 in 1983 is important.

The History of 1-2-3

The history of 1-2-3 begins with the history of computing. Our discussion, therefore, begins with the origins of computers.

The Beginning

The first computers were developed during World War II. They were used exclusively for military applications, such as breaking coded messages and computing shell trajectories.

During the 1950s, these large computers began to find their way into the nation's largest businesses. By the 1970s, virtually every large corporation had at least one large computer, and many small and medium-sized firms had the smaller minicomputers. These machines were used primarily for accounting and payroll applications and for specialized functions, such as processing banking records—jobs that required rapid processing of large volumes of data.

Because these computers required a carefully controlled, secure environment, they were sequestered in special computer rooms. Since the computers were expensive to purchase and operate, they were run 24 hours a day on tight schedules to achieve the highest

---

1-2-3 at a Glance

Published by:
  Lotus Development Corporation
  55 Wheeler Street
  Cambridge, Massachusetts 02138

System requirements:
  IBM Personal Computer
  Display: Color or monochrome
  Disk capacity: Two 320K double-sided disk drives
  Memory size: 128K
  Maximum usable memory size: 512K
  Operating system: PC DOS V1.1, V2.0
  Other hardware: Color/Graphics Adapter, printer (optional), plotter

Price: $495.00

Also available for:
  Compaq Portable Computer
  Victor 9000
  T.I. Professional
  Wang Professional
  Zenith Z-100
  Dynalogic Hyperion
  NEC Advanced Personal Computer

---

possible return on investment. Work on these machines was usually scheduled to make the most efficient use of the computer, but not to meet the needs of the user. These two factors combined to make the computer inaccessible to the average manager. Special requests for programming time were frequently put off until time could be found to fit them into the schedule. "You want it when?" became a popular poster in data processing departments everywhere.

The First Microcomputers

In 1974, Intel Corporation developed the first microprocessor, the 8008™. It condensed thousands of electronic circuits onto a single, tiny silicon chip. The processing power of the room-sized computers of a few years earlier could now fit onto a piece of silicon less than one inch square. Intel soon followed the 8008 with the 8080 microprocessor, which was selected by early computer hobbyists as *the* chip for many microcomputer kits.

About the same time, another integrated circuit manufacturer, MOS Technologies™ (later purchased by Commodore Business Machines), developed a more advanced processor, the 6502™. This processor was selected for several early microcomputers, including the Commodore PET™ and the Apple II®.

These microprocessors were integrated with other components to make the first commercial microcomputers. These early machines were sold as kits. The most famous computer kit was the Altair MITS™. Kit computers did not look much like the popular computers we know today. Instead of the familiar video displays and keyboards, the front panels consisted of lights and programming switches. All programming was done in machine language. Printers and disk drives were not available for these early machines. Needless to say, the first micros were as inaccessible and impractical for the average businessperson as the mainframe computers. It is not surprising that when microcomputers were first developed, they were used only by a few hardy individuals with advanced technical abilities.

Appliance Computers

In 1977, Steve Wozniak and Steve Jobs introduced a microcomputer kit called the Apple I. About 500 units of this machine were eventually sold. Wozniak and Jobs soon offered the Apple II. Unlike all of the computers that had gone before it, the Apple II was sold preassembled. It also had a disk drive and a powerful Disk Operating System (both developed by Wozniak).

Near that time, Tandy/Radio Shack® also developed a microcomputer, the TRS-80® Model I, around an advanced derivative of the 8080 chip, the Z80® (manufactured by Zilog).

These appliance microcomputers opened the doors of microcomputing to nontechnical users. Because the machines did not have to be assembled, no advanced technical knowledge was required. Both machines were shipped fully assembled and factory tested and were sold through a new kind of store, the computer store. It offered some help in acquiring the computer as well as factory-authorized service. Both computers had several *expansion slots* that could be used to attach devices like printers, disk drives, and telephone modems to the computer.

Chips inside the appliance microcomputers contained the BASIC programming language. (Occasionally, the language was provided on a floppy diskette packaged with the computer.) Because BASIC is easier to learn and use than machine or assembly language, users of these computers found it practical to write their own programs in BASIC.

Although BASIC uses English-like words to develop relationships, programs designed to accomplish simple tasks, such as multiplying two numbers, could require 8 to 10 lines of code. Imagine the complexity of using BASIC to solve sophisticated problems. A program written in BASIC to produce a financial report for a large company would be quite large, containing hundreds, or even thousands, of lines of code.

In the early days of microcomputers, little *canned* software (pre-written for a specific purpose and sold by a software publisher) was available. This left users with three choices: become experts in programming, pay a programmer, or accomplish very little with the expensive microcomputers. Because most businesspeople are too busy (or too intimidated) to learn BASIC, many of those who bought micros during this period found themselves "all dressed up with no place to go." Countless others simply avoided microcomputers altogether.

The First Generation

Enter VisiCalc

This situation changed with the introduction of VisiCalc, the first spreadsheet program for microcomputers, in 1978. Since its introduction, VisiCalc has become the most popular computer program of all time, selling well over 400,000 copies. Some observers argue that VisiCalc launched the entire microcomputer industry. There is no question that VisiCalc "wrote the rules" for all the spreadsheet programs that have followed it, including 1-2-3.

VisiCalc was created in 1978 by Robert Frankston and Dan Bricklin in Cambridge, Massachusetts. Bricklin, a student at Harvard Business School, was frustrated with the tedium of analyzing three business cases a night, five days a week. Many of these cases required the preparation of intricate financial analyses. It didn't take him long to decide that there had to be a better way to do that sort of work. Teaming up with his programmer friend Frankston, Bricklin established Software Arts and began to develop VisiCalc. Another student, Dan Fylstra, acquired the rights to market the program and founded Personal Software (now VisiCorp, after its most famous product) to do so. One year later, VisiCalc was offered to the public.

VisiCalc arrived on the scene shortly after Steve Wozniak and Steve Jobs began selling the Apple II. The combination of VisiCalc and Apple had a tremendous impact on the infant microcomputer industry. For the first time, there was a legitimate business and professional application for desktop computers. VisiCalc met a clear need in the business world for a personal analysis tool. The Apple II was an attractive, reliable, readily available vehicle for the program. For about two years, this combination ruled the market for business microcomputers.

Advantages

Although financial analysis software had been available for years on mainframe computers, VisiCalc offered several major improvements. First, VisiCalc ran on personal computers. This meant that, for the first time, a financial, sales, or production manager had a tool for numerical analysis that was his alone. He didn't have to share time with every other manager in the firm. He could play with his analysis until it suited him perfectly and did not have to worry about mainframe computer-user budgets or EDP procedures. He also did not have to wait to see the results of his analysis. He simply booted his computer, loaded the model, and went to work.

VisiCalc brought about another important change. Unlike mainframe analysis programs, which require that input be in list form, VisiCalc is a *visible calculator*. Data and assumptions are entered in the model at the intersection of rows and columns on the sheet in much the same way that the information would appear on an accountant's pad. The model flows in a logical, understandable way.

Because the appearance of the model on the computer's screen is essentially the same as on a piece of paper, the user can quickly grasp the relationships in the model. The model is, therefore, much easier to use and modify. Editing requires only a few moments with a visible processor, instead of the hours that might be needed with mainframe planning tools.

VisiCalc had one more attractive feature. Its price, less than $200 when it was first introduced, knocked the mainframe competition out of the ring.

Limitations

The earliest version of VisiCalc lacked some of the powerful features common to today's spreadsheets, including the current editions of VisiCalc itself. Although it had the ability to sum, count, average, look up, and calculate maximums, minimums, trigonometric functions, and net present values, it did not have Boolean functions (if, or, and, not). The earliest VisiCalcs also lacked the power to communicate with other software programs. Finally, the formatting capabilities of the first version were fairly limited. Despite these limitations, VisiCalc was clearly one of the most powerful and functional programs ever introduced.

As more people became experienced with VisiCalc, they attempted to expand its applications to include such things as tax computations, financial statement production, and more sophisticated budget analysis. They also began to wish for If-Then-Else logic, the ability to represent models graphically, and a tool that could transfer VisiCalc data to word processing and other software. Users also wanted more flexibility in the setup and formatting of models.

Changes

These desires led to improvements in VisiCalc itself and the introduction of companion programs that expanded the power of the product. One major improvement was the introduction of the Data Interchange Format (DIF), developed by Software Arts as an answer to the problem of transferring data among different programs. DIF allows the user to move the results of a VisiCalc planning session into a word processor, a graphics generator, or a data base manager.

The first programs to take advantage of this ability were the other members of the Visi- family: VisiTrend/Plot™ and VisiFile™. These programs are all completely interactive with VisiCalc through the DIF format. This family was, in effect, one of the first attempts at an "all-in-one" software system. Interestingly enough, the developer of VisiPlot, the graphics element of the family, was Mitch Kapor, the founder of the company that publishes 1-2-3, Lotus Development Corporation.

Other versions of VisiCalc include VisiCalc III, developed to utilize the 128K memory capacity of the Apple III®, and VisiCalc Advanced Version™, which includes some powerful new formatting and output features.

SuperCalc

VisiCalc was first introduced on the Apple II and TRS-80 Model I microcomputers. However, it soon became available for a large number of desktop computers, including the Atari 800™, the Commodore PET, the TRS-80 models II and III, the Hewlett-Packard 80™ series and 125™, and the Apple III. Personal Software (now VisiCorp), however, chose not to make its product available to the growing CP/M® market. Because many businesses were selecting CP/M micros for accounting and word processing, a large segment of potential spreadsheet users was left without a satisfactory program.

This situation left the door open for Sorcim Corporation's Super-Calc™, the first major CP/M spreadsheet and the most important spreadsheet program after VisiCalc. Sorcim Corporation (Sorcim is micros spelled backwards) introduced SuperCalc in 1980. It met with immediate success and is the second largest selling electronic spreadsheet in the world. SuperCalc is available for more than 125 different computers—by far the most of any spreadsheet program we know of. It is also "bundled" with Osborne Computer Corporation's Osborne 1™ as well as with other popular microcomputers. Almost 100,000 copies of the Osborne/SuperCalc combination have been sold.

SuperCalc was clearly designed with the intention of surpassing VisiCalc. SuperCalc contains many features and functions not found in VisiCalc. However, the experienced VisiCalc user will immediately recognize many of SuperCalc's features. Like VisiCalc, SuperCalc is a visible processor spreadsheet program with cells for entry of information or equations at the intersection of 63 columns and 254 rows. SuperCalc includes all of the basic spreadsheet functions found in VisiCalc, such as SUM, MAX, LOOKUP, and NPV. Like VisiCalc (and 1-2-3) SuperCalc uses the / symbol to activate commands. In fact, most VisiCalc functions and commands are also found in SuperCalc.

Summary

The first-generation programs were very significant when they were first introduced. VisiCalc, SuperCalc, and the other spreadsheets in this group were a vast improvement on the traditional analysis tools—the accountant's pad, pencil, and calculator. These programs were an important force in the early success of the microcomputer industry. In fact, VisiCalc helped to legitimize the industry. Its practicality and flexibility made it the most popular program in the history of microcomputing.

These programs dominated the sales of business software for the past five years and continue to be among the biggest sellers. VisiCalc and SuperCalc are powerful, flexible, and extremely useful pieces of software. Their popularity should continue for some time.

The New Generation

Recently, software packages have emerged that build on the basic spreadsheet concept, but have much more capability. This group of programs includes 1-2-3, Multiplan™, Context Management Systems' Context MBA™, and several other exciting programs.

Many factors have influenced the development of this *new generation* of spreadsheet software. First, enough people have used VisiCalc and its imitators to become aware of their limitations, thus developing a "wish list" of features and benefits to serve as the basis for these new programs. This wish list includes the desire for more memory; the ability to link individual spreadsheets together into an integrated system of sheets; the need for more powerful arithmetic and formatting functions; and the desire for more fully integrated graphics, data base management, and word processing.

A second factor driving this new software is the availability of more powerful microcomputers, led by the IBM Personal Computer. The memory capacity and processing power of these new 16-bit computers allows the new generation of spreadsheets to offer an unheard of level of power and sophistication.

These packages have also been created in response to the growing Fortune 1000 market for microcomputers and microcomputer software. As microcomputers become more pervasive in business, the market for new software is becoming increasingly more attractive.

New-Generation Programs

The new generation contains new versions of several familiar programs as well as some new names. At least three of the second-generation programs are descendants of first-generation sheets: SuperCalc² ™, VisiCalc Advanced Version, and ProCalc™. Others, like Multiplan, Context MBA, and 1-2-3, are exciting new efforts. All of the new-generation programs incorporate the features of the first generation and add many major new ones.

For example, Sorcim Corporation, responsive to the desires of SuperCalc users for a more advanced spreadsheet, introduced SuperCalc². This program offers dramatic improvements over the basic SuperCalc capabilities. SuperCalc² has a variety of new built-in functions, including date arithmetic, the ability to manipulate text entries, and a command that allows you to consolidate different sheets into summary sheets.

Microsoft's new spreadsheet Multiplan can link several different models, like pages in a book. This is an incredible step in the development of spreadsheets. For the first time, multiple departmental income statements can be built and consolidated into a company-wide statement.

Because Multiplan can run on a computer with only 64K of memory (unlike many new-generation programs), it is available to the hundreds of thousands of Apple II and CP/M owners who are looking for a new spreadsheet. This wide availability has helped Multiplan become the overall best-selling microcomputer program.

VisiCalc Advanced Version is VisiCorp's long-awaited response to the wish lists of experienced users. Its functions and formats have been designed and implemented to appeal to two audiences: former VisiCalc users, and would-be users of electronic spreadsheet programs.

The Integrated Approach

Two new-generation programs stand out from the others because they integrate graphics and data management with advanced spreadsheets: Context MBA and 1-2-3. (Context MBA also includes simple text processing and data communications.) These programs incorporate all of these applications in a single, extremely powerful package.

Context MBA, the first integrated program to be introduced, is the only program that incorporates all five applications into one package. The MBA program was the result of a long study done by the Arthur D. Little Company on the needs and desires of business-people for desktop management software.

Context MBA has suffered from some unfavorable criticisms about its speed and jack-of-all-trades orientation. But it is an impressive program backed by a serious and professional organization.

Enter 1-2-3

If VisiCalc is the grandfather of electronic spreadsheets, then 1-2-3 is the wonder child. 1-2-3 is an extremely advanced spreadsheet that combines the features of an easy-to-use spreadsheet program with graphics and data management functions. Even Context MBA does not approach the power, speed, and sophistication of 1-2-3.

1-2-3 is the brainchild of Mitch Kapor, President of Lotus Development Corporation, and Jonathan Sachs, Vice President of Research and Development at Lotus. Like so many of the early leaders of the microcomputer industry, Kapor taught himself the art of programming. He learned well. Prior to founding Lotus, Kapor scored one of the largest successes in the young microcomputer software industry with VisiTrend/Plot™, a graphics and statistical package that he sold to VisiCorp. After working for VisiCorp for a brief time following the sale, he left and founded Lotus with the intention of producing the ultimate spreadsheet software program. Sachs had been involved in three spreadsheet development projects prior to joining Lotus.

Kapor's first step was to assemble an experienced team of financiers and business managers to help launch his new product. Ben Rosen, one of the most respected businessmen in the industry (Rosen was one of the original VisiCorp investors and is the Chairman of Compaq™ Computer Corporation) was one of the first investors in Lotus and is a member of the Board of Directors of the company. Kapor also recruited Chris Morgan, previously Editor-in-Chief of *Byte Magazine* and *Popular Computing Magazine,* to be Vice President of Communications. Because every member of the Lotus team had prior experience in the microcomputer industry, Kapor calls Lotus a "second-generation" software company.

1-2-3 was designed by Kapor and Sachs to beat VisiCalc at its own game. 1-2-3's overall design, command syntax, and built-in functions are based on the conventions used by VisiCalc. In fact, according to one rumor, Kapor's experience working at VisiCorp after the VisiPlot sale was the spark that fueled his desire to create 1-2-3.

While Sachs and company worked to create the program, Kapor was working to build excitement about 1-2-3 in the marketplace. Articles praising the product appeared in *The Wall Street Journal, The New York Times, Business Week,* and other national publications. Nearly every magazine in the microcomputer industry has carried a feature story about the program. 1-2-3 is clearly the hottest program in the marketplace.

How Is 1-2-3 Like Other Spreadsheets?

As we have observed, 1-2-3 is primarily an electronic spreadsheet. Like all spreadsheet programs, 1-2-3 is an electronic replacement for the traditional financial modeling tools: the accountant's columnar pad, pencil, and calculator. In some ways, spreadsheet programs are to those tools what word processors are to typewriters.

Spreadsheets offer dramatic improvements in ease of creating, editing, and using financial models.

The typical electronic spreadsheet configures the memory of a computer to resemble an accountant's columnar pad. Because this "pad" exists in the dynamic world of the computer's memory, the pad is different from paper pads in some important ways. For one thing, electronic spreadsheets are much larger than their paper counterparts. Most electronic spreadsheets have 254 *rows* and 64 *columns*. 1-2-3 has *2,048* rows and *254* columns!

Each row in 1-2-3 is assigned a number, and each column a letter. The intersections of the rows and columns are called *cells*. Cells are identified by their row-column coordinates. For example, the cell located at the intersection of column A and row 15 would be called A15. The cell at the intersection of column X and row 55 is called X55. These cells can be filled with three kinds of information: *numbers;* mathematical *formulas,* as well as special spreadsheet *functions;* and *text* (or labels).

A *cursor* allows you to write information into the cells much as a pencil lets you write on a piece of paper. In 1-2-3, as in most spreadsheets, the cursor looks like a a bright rectangle on the computer's screen. The cursor typically is one row high and one column wide.

Because the 1-2-3 grid is so large, the entire spreadsheet cannot be viewed on the screen at one time. The screen thus serves as a window onto the worksheet. To view other parts of the sheet, you *scroll* the cursor across the worksheet with the cursor-movement keys. When the cursor reaches the edge of the current window, the window begins to shift to follow the cursor across the sheet.

To illustrate the window concept, imagine cutting a hole one inch square in a piece of cardboard. If you placed the cardboard over this page, you would be able to see only a one-inch square piece of text. Naturally, the rest of the text is still on the page; it is simply hidden from view. When you move the cardboard around the page (in much the same way that the window moves when the cursor keys are used), different parts of the page become visible.

Formulas

Electronic spreadsheets allow mathematical *relationships* to be created between cells. For example, if a cell named C1 contains the formula:

C1 = A1+B1

then C1 will display the sum of the contents of cells A1 and B1. The cell references serve as variables in the equation. No matter what numbers are entered in A1 and B1, cell C1 will always return their sum. For example, if cell A1 contained the number 5 and cell B1 contained the number 10, the formula in cell C1 would return the value 15. If the number in cell A1 were changed to 4, C1 would also change to 14. Of course, spreadsheet formulas can be much more complex than this simple example. A cell can be added to, subtracted from, or multiplied or divided by, any other cell. In addition, spreadsheet functions may be applied to the cells.

Functions

Spreadsheet *functions* are shortcuts that help the user perform common mathematical computations with a minimum of typing. Functions are like abbreviations for otherwise long and cumbersome formulas. 1-2-3 contains all of the basic functions found in the first-generation programs like VisiCalc: SUM, COUNT, AVERAGE, MAX, and MIN; the basic Boolean functions, such as IF, AND, and OR; and trigonometric functions, including SIN, COS, TAN, and PI. Newer spreadsheets like 1-2-3 include other more advanced functions.

Likewise, most sheets use an @ symbol to signal a function. For instance, the SUM function in 1-2-3 is written as @SUM(A1..C1).

Commands

Like other spreadsheet programs, 1-2-3 includes several important *commands* that manipulate the worksheet in various ways. For example, all electronic spreadsheets include a command (or commands) that can be used to *format* the appearance of the contents of cells in the sheet. These commands can alter the display to make numbers appear in a variety of forms. In most spreadsheets, commands are activated by pressing the slash (/) key. After the slash is typed, a *menu* of commands appears on the screen. The user must then select the command to be implemented.

Most electronic spreadsheets use this basic command structure pioneered by VisiCalc. Many competitive programs even use the same letters to stand for these commands. There are, however, noticeable differences between the precise effects of the commands on different sheets. Some sheets use different letters to stand for a command with an exact parallel in VisiCalc. SuperCalc, for example, uses the /C command to stand for COPY. To CLEAR a SuperCalc sheet, a /Z is used, representing the word ZAP. In 1-2-3, the worksheet is cleared by typing /WE (for Worksheet Erase).

Spreadsheet commands can be used at every phase of building and using a model. Because a spreadsheet holds in the computer's memory a model while you build it, you are not bound by the physical limitations of the printed page. Do some of your formulas repeat across across time? Use the spreadsheet's *copy* feature to project quickly your assumptions from one cell to another. Did you forget a row or a column? Simply *insert* it at the appropriate point. Is one of your assumptions or formulas incorrect, or is there a typographical error in one of your headings? Correct the error instantly with the *edit* command.

Playing "What if...?"

The act of building a model on a spreadsheet defines all of the mathematical relationships in the model. Until you decide to change them, every sum, product, division, subtraction, average, and net present value will remain the same. Each time you enter data into the model, computations will be calculated at your command with no effort on your part. All of these computations will be calculated correctly; spreadsheets don't make math errors. And next month, when you decide to use the same model again, the formulas will still be set, ready to calculate at your command.

Even more important, spreadsheet software allows you to play "What if . . . ?" with your model after it has been developed. Once a set of mathematical relationships has been built into the sheet, it can be recalculated with amazing speed, using different sets of assumptions. If you use only paper, a pencil, and a calculator to build your models, every change to the model will require recalculating every relationship in it. If the model has 100 formulas and you change the first one, you must make 100 calculations by hand to flow the change through the entire model. If, on the other hand, you use a spreadsheet, the same change requires the press of only a few keys—the program does the rest. This capability permits extensive "what if" analysis.

For example, suppose you build a financial projection for your business for the years 1983 through 1989. In building this forecast, you assume that your sales will grow at an annual rate of 10 percent. But what happens to your projections if the rate of growth is only 3 percent? What if the rate is 15 percent? If you were using a pencil and a calculator to do this analysis, it might take hours to compute the effects of these changes. With 1-2-3 or other electronic spreadsheets, all that is required is to change the growth rate you entered in the sheet and strike one key to recompute. The entire process takes just seconds.

As your models become more complex, this ability becomes more and more valuable.

What Makes 1-2-3 Different?

1-2-3 has taken the microcomputer world by storm. Within six months after its introduction, 1-2-3 had zoomed to the number one position on *Softalk*'s IBM Personal Computer best-seller list. Except for VisiCalc, no program has demonstrated such complete dominance of the software market. 1-2-3 has achieved this dominance by combining staggering performance with expertly coordinated publicity and advertising.

But what is this exciting new program? It integrates graphics and information management with a first-rate spreadsheet, but that description obviously only scratches the surface. The following discussion will help you understand more about the features and capabilities of 1-2-3.

Getting Started

It is obvious that 1-2-3 is a formidable product from the moment you open the package. The program, with tutorial and utilities, is so large that it is distributed on five diskettes. One diskette contains the basic program. The others contain a backup of the main program disk, a tutorial, a set of utilities, and the PrintGraph program. Glancing through the manual will show you just how much there is to this program.

The program also comes with a shirt-pocket summary of 1-2-3's commands, functions, and options. 1-2-3's on-line help function is so good, however, that most users will probably not use this card very much.

Hardware

1-2-3 on the IBM PC

The IBM PC, with its expandable memory and excellent video display, is the best spreadsheeting machine available today. Many corporations and individuals have found the IBM-plus-spreadsheet combination to be a terrific investment, saving time and effort while improving analysis.

For the first six months of its life, 1-2-3 was available only for the IBM Personal Computer. It was one of the first programs specifically designed for the PC. 1-2-3 is also one of the few programs that uses virtually *every key* on the PC's keyboard, including all of the function keys, the scroll key, the delete key, and the alternate key. The function keys serve several purposes. The F1 key activates 1-2-3's on-line help facility. F2 activates the program's editor. (Striking this key has essentially the same result as typing / E in VisiCalc.) The F10 key replots graphics. The PgUp key jumps the cursor up one screen, and the PgDn key moves it down one. The HOME key returns the cursor to cell A1.

The plastic function-key template included in every 1-2-3 package contains one-word explanations of the action performed by each key. It is designed to be placed over the function keys on the PC's keyboard. Unlike the template provided by Context for the MBA program, the Lotus template both looks and feels substantial. Lotus could have saved money by using a less expensive, and less impressive, template. But, in typical form, Lotus chose the best. This emphasis on quality down to the smallest detail is one of the things that has made 1-2-3 so popular.

1-2-3 on Other Computers

Lotus recently announced that 1-2-3 will be available for a variety of IBM look-alike computers in 1983. Included in this list are the Zenith Data Systems Z-100™, the DEC Rainbow™, the Texas Instruments Professional Computer™, the Victor 9000™, the Dynalogic Hyperion™, the Wang™ Professional, and the NEC Advanced Personal Computer™.

Because the first release of 1-2-3 ran only on the IBM PC, program installation was not necessary. The program was ready to run right out of the box. With the announcement of the program's availability for six new computers, however, this has changed. The newest version of 1-2-3 comes with a utilities disk that contains drivers for customizing the program to a particular computer. These drivers also allow you to take full advantage of any optional hardware, such as plotters and graphics printers, that you purchased to accompany the computer. (More information on installing 1-2-3 and drivers can be found in "The First Steps" section of Chapter 2.)

A Considerable Investment

1-2-3 requires a considerable investment in hardware to make full use of its capabilities. Two double-sided, double-density floppy disk drives are suggested. 1-2-3 will run on a system with only one double-sided disk drive, but the diskette swapping between program and data diskette that is required on a one-drive system can be confusing even for advanced users. For now, a minimum of 128K of RAM memory is required to use the program. This amount increases to 192K in version 1A of the program. In contrast, VisiCalc requires a system with only one disk drive, 64K of RAM, and only one color or monochrome display.

A color monitor is required for 1-2-3 if you want to view spectacular color graphics. If you have only a monochrome monitor, you will still be able to see the spreadsheet and data base parts of 1-2-3 and produce hard-copy graphs, but you won't be able to see the graphs on the screen.

The Access System

When you first load 1-2-3 (either by typing LOTUS from the system level or by doing a warm boot), you come into the Lotus Access System. The access system is a five-part menu that gives you the choice of entering the 1-2-3 spreadsheet or the PrintGraph program, or performing various file handling and disk maintenance operations. This handy menu system helps tie together the various elements of 1-2-3 into one neat package. (For more information on the Access System, see Chapter 2.)

Getting Help

On-line help is becoming a must for virtually all spreadsheet programs. No spreadsheet publisher takes on-line help as seriously as Lotus Development. 1-2-3 offers the most extensive on-line help facility of any program. The help screens are keyed to the user's location in the program and are accessed by typing the F1 key. The level of detail depends on how deeply the user is embedded in the commands. (See Chapter 2 for more information.)

The level of detail available in the 1-2-3 help screens is unsurpassed. The section on printing, for example, provides the control sequences required to make the IBM Printer (Epson™ MX-80) perform condensed or expanded print. Each screen offers a similar amount of detail about the command or function it explains.

The 1-2-3 Spreadsheet

The Spreadsheet Itself

As we have seen, the design of the 1-2-3 spreadsheet is much like that of VisiCalc. This should be reassuring to those with electronic spreadsheet experience. Remember, though, that the 1-2-3 sheet is much larger than VisiCalc's sheet. 1-2-3 offers 254 columns by 2,048 rows, or more than 500,000 cells. VisiCalc and SuperCalc offer just over 16,000 cells. To take advantage of all of that space, however, you'll need a great deal of memory in your machine. 1-2-3 can accommodate up to 544K of RAM memory. (See Chapter 3 for more information on the 1-2-3 worksheet and the memory requirements of the program.)

Speed

Given the staggering size of the 1-2-3 spreadsheet, it is reasonable to expect the program to be a bit slow. This is not the case, however. 1-2-3's spreadsheet is one of the fastest, if not *the* fastest, spreadsheet program available today. In some tests, 1-2-3 was 300 percent faster than VisiCalc. 1-2-3 outperformed the other "all-in-one" program, Context MBA, by a wide margin in every test. (For more information on these tests, see *Spreadsheet Software: From VisiCalc to 1-2-3,* by Thomas B. Henderson, Douglas Ford Cobb, and Gena Berg Cobb, published by Que Corporation.)

1-2-3 is written in assembly language, the closest language to the hexadecimal numbers the computer uses. Beyond that, the program is well designed. This combination allows 1-2-3 to recalculate at a speed that is unmatched by any spreadsheet.

Built-in Functions

All of the new-generation software packages have responded to the need for more powerful "built-in spreadsheet functions."

New Functions

1-2-3 offers several new financial functions. For example, whereas VisiCalc's only financial function was net present value, 1-2-3 includes functions for calculating internal rate of return, the payment amount on a loan, the net present value of an annuity, and the future value of a stream of payments.

In addition, 1-2-3 offers a new function called @MOD. This function computes the remainder of the division of two numbers. For example, @MOD(13,3) returns 1, because thirteen divided by three yields 4 with a remainder of 1.

1-2-3 also has two statistical functions, @STD and @VAR, that compute the standard deviation and variance of a range of values.

Date Functions

Probably 1-2-3's most exciting new built-in functions are its date arithmetic functions. This built-in time-keeping system allows the program to retrieve the system date from PC DOS. A date can also be entered directly from the keyboard. 1-2-3 has a series of unique date-display format options.

The @TODAY function takes the PC DOS time stamp and calculates the number of days between that date and December 31, 1899. The @DATE function can be used to enter any date into the worksheet. For example, the function:

@DATE(83,3,21)

enters into the current cell the Julian number that represents the date March 21, 1983.

1-2-3 has three other date functions. The @DAY function extracts the day of the month from a given date cell. The @MONTH function derives the month number from a date, and the @YEAR function pulls the year number from a given date.

These date functions are among 1-2-3's most advanced features. The functions can be used for tasks as simple as date stamping your worksheets or as complex as performing accounts receivable aging and managing stock and bond portfolios. (For a complete explanation of 1-2-3's built-in functions, see Chapter 6.)

Commands

Formatting the Worksheet

1-2-3 offers a wide variety of formats for numeric entries. These new formats include the ability to display or print numbers with embedded commas, dollar signs, parentheses, or percent signs, and to specify the exact number of digits that will be displayed to the right of the decimal. For example, 1-2-3 can format the number 12345 to look like $12,345.00, 12,345, 1.23E3, or 12345; the number -12345 to look like ($12,345.00) or -12,345; and the number .45 to look like 45% or $.45. (The details of all of 1-2-3's cell formats are covered in Chapter 5.)

These new formatting features allow users to create finished reports and financial statements directly from analyses. Numbers can appear as you would expect them to in a formal document, and eye-pleasing spacing can be achieved by varying column widths.

In VisiCalc, cell formats are assigned one cell at a time. To format more than one cell at once, the user must format a cell, then replicate its attributes over the desired range. In 1-2-3, formats are always assigned to a range of cells. In fact, the format command is an option of a higher level command called *Range*. A range in 1-2-3 can be as small as a single cell or as large as the entire worksheet. When you assign a format, the program prompts you to provide the appropriate range for that format by pointing to its limits with the cursor.

Naming Ranges

1-2-3 also allows a name to be assigned to a range. This feature lets you label an area for use in formulas or as the range for a command. For example, if a part of your worksheet has been named Summary, you can tell 1-2-3 to print the section of the sheet called Summary. Only the cells contained in that region will be printed. Similarly, if you have created a temporary area called SCRATCH, you can use that name with 1-2-3's /RE (for Range Erase) command to blank that part of the screen. (This exciting feature is discussed in Chapter 4.)

Copying

1-2-3 uses a Copy command, like the replicate command of VisiCalc and SuperCalc, to make replicas of values, labels, or formulas in other cells. This replication allows the user to develop quickly a model by building a few key relationships, then replicating them over the entire workspace.

Unlike Visicalc and SuperCalc, which require that the user specify whether a cell reference should be replicated relatively or with no change at the time the replication is done, 1-2-3 allows cell references to be defined as relative or absolute at the time the cell is defined. Relative cell references are entered in the normal way. Absolute references are entered with a dollar sign ($) preceding the reference. For example, in the formula:

A1+$A2+A$3+A4

the reference to cell A1 is relative. The references to cells A2 and A3 are mixed: relative in one direction and absolute in the other. The reference to A4 is absolute in both directions.

Although this method of determining absolute and relative references is difficult for experienced VisiCalc users to adjust to, it has some interesting advantages. For example, you can Copy a single cell into a block of cells without making complicated formula adjustments. (See Chapter 4 for complete details of this new feature.)

Recalculating

VisiCalc and SuperCalc use a simple linear form of recalculation. The model recalculates by starting at the upper left corner of the spreadsheet (cell A1) and proceeding either row by row or column by column through the sheet. The user must be very careful to build dependencies in the worksheet to avoid *forward references* (a cell whose value depends on other cells below it in the recalculation order) and *circular references* (two or more cells defined by each other) that can create calculation nightmares.

1-2-3 addresses these limitations by offering a *natural* mode of recalculation. Natural recalculation begins by discerning the most fundamental cell in the sheet (that is, the cell on which most other cells are based). This cell is evaluated first. Next, the program searches for the second most basic formula in the sheet and evaluates that cell. This process continues until the entire worksheet is recomputed.

Accompanying natural recalculation is the ability to perform iterative calculations. In 1-2-3, the user can specify the number of passes the program should make through the same worksheet each time it is recalculated. Iterative calculation helps to relieve the problem of circular references.

The addition of these two new features simplifies the design and use of complex spreadsheets. With the new programs, the user does not have to be as careful about planning the locations of the various model sections. Instead, the computer can manage the order of recalculation. (More details on recalculation are provided in Chapter 4.)

Printing

1-2-3 has more printing flexibility than any other spreadsheet. The user has the choice of printing the entire worksheet or any part of it. In addition, the user can alter the left, right, top, and bottom margins on the page; change the page length and width; insert page headers and footers in the text (which can even contain the date and page number); and send setup codes to the printer to alter the size and style of type used to print. (For more information on printing, see Chapter 8.)

Storing Files

1-2-3 offers the basic loading and saving commands found in other electronic spreadsheets. Three types of files can be created: normal spreadsheet files, or .WKS files; text files, or .PRN files; and graph files, called .PIC files. In addition, the program has the ability to load a text file created by another program, including a WordStar word-processing file. This feature allows you to load information from other sources into 1-2-3.

1-2-3 also has the ability to import files created by dBASE II™ and VisiCalc. Version 1.1A of 1-2-3 has a utility that translates a dBASE file into a .WKS file. The file will appear in standard 1-2-3 data base format, with each row representing a record and each column representing a field.

Finally, 1-2-3 has a utility that translates a VisiCalc file into a .WKS file. This utility converts all of the formulas and functions in the file into 1-2-3 syntax. Although there are usually some adjustments to be made after the file is loaded, this utility makes it easy for a VisiCalc user to convert existing worksheets into 1-2-3 templates. (Chapter 7 covers in detail the use of 1-2-3's storage commands.)

1-2-3 Graphics

Mitch Kapor's background in graphics software design is evident in the graphics portion of 1-2-3. The program has definitely benefited from his experience.

The ability to convert spreadsheet data into graphs is not unique to the new-generation spreadsheets. Kapor's own program, VisiPlot, makes graphics available to VisiCalc users. However, 1-2-3 ties the graphics capability directly into the spreadsheet so that there is no need to use a DIF (VisiCalc), SDI (SuperCalc), SYLK (Multiplan), or other communications file. 1-2-3's graphics capability is also remarkably versatile and easy to use. It even allows you to do "what if" analysis on the graphs.

1-2-3 has five basic graph types: bar, stacked bar, line, scatter, and pie. Up to six ranges of data can be represented on a single graph (except for pie charts and scatter diagrams). This means, for example, that a line chart with six different lines can be created.

Graphs are created with 1-2-3's /G command. Although the program has a number of options, the user need only specify a graph type and a single data range. After providing the required information, the user simply types V, for View. This will plot the graph to the screen. If the computer has both a color and a monochrome display, the graph will appear on the color screen while the spreadsheet remains on the monochrome monitor. If there is only a color monitor, the graph will replace the spreadsheet on the display until a key is typed.

1-2-3 gives the user an exceptional amount of flexibility in formatting graphs. Up to three different colors can be used to represent graphs on a color monitor. On a black-and-white monitor, the user can choose different shading patterns. The *color legend,* which defines the color or pattern for each data range, can also be displayed on the screen.

Labels can be inserted in graphs by referencing a list in the worksheet. Although 1-2-3 automatically scales the x and y axes to fit the data being plotted, users are free to adjust the scaling to suit their tastes. A grid can be placed over the worksheet. The user can specify a title and subtitle for each graph, as well as labels for both the vertical and horizontal axes. In line and scatter graphs, the user has the options of selecting the type of symbol that will represent the data on the graph and connecting the data points with a line.

Because 1-2-3 lets the user name graphs after they are created, these graphs can be replotted by typing */GNU* (for *Graph Name Use*) and supplying the graphs' names. With this feature, you can create a slide show of graphs that are recalled, one after another, and plotted.

"What If" with Graphics

The most exciting thing about 1-2-3's graphics is not the variety of graphs, but the degree to which the graphics and spreadsheet elements are interrelated. With 1-2-3, graphs can be quickly designed and altered as worksheet data changes. This means that graphs may be changed almost as fast as the data is recalculated.

True graphic "what if" analysis can be performed with 1-2-3. In fact, the F10 function key on the IBM PC allows the user to replot a graph after making changes to the worksheet, without having to redefine the graph with the /G command. This replotting immediately shows the effects of changes on the current graph.

Printing Graphics

Because the basic 1-2-3 program is not capable of producing hard-copy graphics, it is accompanied by a second program, called PrintGraph, which is used to create printed or plotted copies of graphs.

After a graph is created by 1-2-3, the graph can be saved in a file on a diskette. These files, called .PIC files, are created with the /GS (for Graph Save) command. The graph files can then be read into the PrintGraph program for additional formatting and printing. The PrintGraph program offers a number of options for further formatting of graphs before they are printed. The Color option allows parts of the graph to be assigned different colors. The Font option allows the labels and titles in the graph to be printed in one or several of eight different fonts, including a script face and a block face. The Size option allows the user to specify the size of the printed graph. A graph can be printed full size to occupy an entire printed page, or half size to fill half a page; or a manual option can be chosen. After the options have been selected, the PrintGraph program will print the graph to the specified graphics device.

The professional results that can be obtained from the PrintGraph program are another indication of the overall high quality of the 1-2-3 program. The user friendliness of 1-2-3's graphics capability is also very important. Because graphs can be quickly and easily created and changed, managers will use them more frequently both for their own insight and to communicate their analyses to others.

With previous graphics software, the time and trouble involved in creating and changing graphs often outweighed the benefit they could provide. (Chapter 9 provides more information on 1-2-3's graphics capabilities.)

1-2-3 Information Management

The column-row structure used to store data in a spreadsheet program is very similar to the structure of a relational data base. The similarity between a data base and a spreadsheet is demonstrated by the expanded LOOKUP capabilities of the new-generation spreadsheets. 1-2-3 has expanded LOOKUP like ProCalc and Multiplan, but goes one step further and provides a true data base management function as well. One important advantage of 1-2-3's data base manager over independent DBM systems is that its commands are very similar to the other commands used in the 1-2-3 program. The user can, therefore, learn how to use the 1-2-3 data base manager along with the rest of the 1-2-3 program.

Data Base Functions and Commands

Once a data base has been built in 1-2-3 (which is no different from building any other spreadsheet table), a variety of functions can be performed on it. Some of the tasks you will want to perform on a 1-2-3 data base can be accomplished with standard 1-2-3 commands. For example, records can be added to a data base with the /WIR (Worksheet Insert Row) command. Fields can be added with the /WIC (Worksheet Insert Column) command. Editing the contents of a data base cell is as easy as editing any other cell—you simply move the cursor to that location, type F2 to invoke the editor, and start typing.

The data can also be sorted. Sorts can be done with both a primary and a secondary key, in ascending or descending order, using alphabetic or numeric keys. In addition, various kinds of mathematical analyses can be performed on a field of data over a specified range of records. For example, you can count the number of items in a data base that match a set of criteria; compute a mean, variance, or standard deviation; and find the maximum or minimum value in the range. The ability to perform statistical analysis on a data base is an advanced feature for data base management systems on any microcomputer.

Other data base operations require special data base commands, such as /DQU (Data Query Unique) and /DQF (Data Query Find). A 1-2-3 data base can be queried in several ways. After specifying the criteria on which you are basing your search, you can ask the program to point to each selected record in turn, or to extract the selected records to a separate area of the spreadsheet. You can also ask the program to delete records that fit your specified criteria.

Several commands help the user make inquiries and clean the data of duplications. All of these commands are subcommands of the /DQ (Data Query) command. These commands require that the user specify one or more criteria for searching the data base. The criteria refer to a field in the data base and set the conditions that the data to be selected must meet.

1-2-3 allows a great deal of latitude in defining criteria. As many as 32 cells across, each containing multiple criteria, can be included in the criteria range. Criteria can include complex formulas as well as simple numbers and text entries. Two or more criteria in the same row are considered to be joined with an "and." Criteria in different rows are assumed to be combined with an "or." Criteria can also include "wild card" characters that stand for other characters.

1-2-3 also has a special set of statistical functions that operate only on information stored in the data base. Like the query commands, the statistics functions use criteria to determine which records they will operate on.

The following data base functions are supported: @DCOUNT, @DSUM, @DAVG, @DSTD, @DMAX, and @DMIN. These functions perform essentially the same tasks as their spreadsheet counter-parts. For example, @DMIN finds the minimum number in a given range. @DCOUNT counts all of the nonzero entries in a range. @DSTD computes the standard deviation of the items in the range.

The combination of these functions and 1-2-3's data base commands makes this program a very capable data manager. 1-2-3's data management capabilities, however, do not put it in competition with more sophisticated data base languages, such as Condor™ or dBASE II. Both of these programs use a data base language to translate the user's requests to the computer. By comparison, 1-2-3's data management is fairly simple.

When compared to less powerful data managers, however, such as VisiDex™ and Pfs:File™, 1-2-3 looks good. It is fast and has adequate capacity (at 2,048 records) for most data management tasks. Because it uses the same basic command structure as the rest of 1-2-3, the program is easy to learn. In summary, the data base function of 1-2-3 is very valuable. It sets 1-2-3 apart from the generic spreadsheet. (1-2-3's data management capabilities are covered in detail in Chapter 11.)

Data Table

Data Table is 1-2-3's most misunderstood command. A data table is simply a way to look at all of the outcomes of a set of conditions without having to enter manually each set into the equation. The command simply allows you to build a table that defines the formula you wish to evaluate and contains all of the values you wish to test. A data table is very similar to the X-Y decision grids you probably built as a math student in high school.

The Data Table command can be used to structure a variety of "what if" problems. It can also be combined with 1-2-3's data base and statistical functions to solve far more complex problems. (Chapter 11 explains in detail the data table command and gives examples that will help you master this tricky tool.)

Programming 1-2-3: Keyboard Macros

One of 1-2-3's most exciting features is its ability to use *keyboard macros*. Keyboard macros are like small user-defined programs inside the 1-2-3 spreadsheet. These programs can be used for a variety of purposes, including automating tedious repetitive tasks or creating sophisticated data input and output systems.

A keyboard macro is really just a series of normal 1-2-3 commands, text, or numbers that have been grouped together and given a name. In fact, this feature was originally called the *typing alternative* because it provided an alternative to typing commands from the computer's keyboard. The name is created by typing a backslash (\), followed by one alphabetic character. A macro is executed by typing ALT, followed by the letter name of the macro.

The implications of the ALT sequence feature are exciting. A user can create a spreadsheet program that will automatically perform complex or repetitive tasks with a single keystroke. For example, typing the names of months as column headings is a task frequently performed in budget building. This task could be programmed into an ALT sequence, thereby reducing it to a single keystroke. The typing alternative of 1-2-3 offers several significant advantages over the programs created by any other spreadsheet program. An ALT sequence in 1-2-3 can be structured to make decisions when the sequence is executed. These decisions can be based either on values found in the spreadsheet or on input from the user at the time the sequence is executed, A macro can pause in its execution and wait for user input. When an external command file is executed in SuperCalc, the entire file must be executed without additional input.

These functions are accomplished with special commands that can be embedded in macros. These commands are much like statements you would expect to see in a BASIC program. For example, the command {?} can be used to accept user input into the worksheet while the macro is processing. This is similar to BASIC's Input command. (For more information about macros, see Chapter 12.)

Conclusion

1-2-3 has become an extraordinarily popular program for many reasons. First, it combines several sought-after functions into one program. Second, and more importantly, the program is "done right." 1-2-3 is one of the first microcomputer programs ever released that is not filled with compromises. Third, the program is fun to use, especially for those who have experience with VisiCalc.

Although 1-2-3 should not be mistaken for a full-featured office automation system, the program does represent a bridge between traditional spreadsheets and the office automation environments, such as Vision™ and LISA®. Each element of the program is a full-fledged application program in its own right. Together, they offer unprecedented power and flexibility.

2

Getting Started

The First Step

The first step in getting started with 1-2-3 is to tailor the program to your particular computer system. There are three different considerations here. First, 1-2-3 has to know what kind of display hardware you have. For example, different graphics control characters are used to display color graphs on a color monitor instead of displaying regular black-and-white graphs on a monochrome display equipped with a Hercules Graphics Card.

The second consideration is the printer configuration. Depending on the particular printer model and the size and shape of the report you want to print, certain special settings must be selected. In many cases, the system defaults can be used. However, if you have a 132-character printer, for example, you will want to change some of the settings.

The third and final consideration is the preparation of data diskettes. 1-2-3 provides a special program for this purpose, or the DOS FORMAT.COM program can be used.

Installing 1-2-3 System Disks

Installing the 1-2-3 system disks is a fairly easy procedure and a necessary part of configuring the program to your system. Without this step, the program will not boot.

Five disks come in the 1-2-3 package, and all of them must be installed. They are

    System disk
    System Backup disk
    PrintGraph disk
    Utility disk
    Tutorial disk

The first step in installing these disks is to copy certain external command programs and system files from DOS by loading a copy of DOS Version 1.1 or 2.0 into the default drive.

Two-Diskette System

If you have a two-diskette system with 320K or more and intend to run 1-2-3 under DOS Version 1.1, one special step is required before you copy the external command programs. Errors in DOS' DISK-COPY.COM and DISKCOMP.COM programs must be corrected on the actual DOS diskette. A *copy* of the DOS diskette is used for this procedure. To correct the errors, you place the Utility disk in Drive B and type B:FIXDOS, followed by RETURN. If your system size is less than or equal to 320K, you needn't bother with this step.

In installing 1-2-3 for your system, the next step, which everyone with a two-diskette system must perform, is to run the INSTALL.BAT program. This program installs DOS' external command programs and system files. The programs and files concerned are listed below:

COMMAND.COM	Command processor; runs programs you enter
DISKCOPY.COM	Copies contents of diskette from source to target drive
DISKCOMP.COM	Compares contents of diskette in source drive to contents of diskette on target drive
FORMAT.COM	Initializes diskette in target drive to recording format acceptable to DOS
CHKDSK.COM	Analyzes directory and produces a memory status report

IBMBIO.COM   I/O device handler program; reads and
                    writes data to and from computer
                    memory and devices

IBMDOS.COM   Does file management and service
                    functions

INSTALL.BAT must be run for all five disks. To do this, type
B:INSTALL and hit RETURN for each disk.

The IBMBIO.COM and IBMDOS.COM files are used on all disks for
managing system devices and files and for running programs. (The
other programs are used by the Disk Manager program, which is
part of the Lotus Access System. The features of the Lotus Access
System are explained later.)

Hard Disk System

If you have a hard disk and a single diskette drive, you must copy to
the hard disk the contents of all the diskettes, except the System
disk. To do this, use the DOS COPY command after loading each
disk into the diskette drive. All of the .COM files listed above must
reside on the hard disk.

The next step is to fix the errors in DOS' DISKCOMP.COM and
programs. As with the two-diskette system, this procedure is
accomplished by placing the Utility disk in the diskette drive and
typing x:FIXDOS, where x = A, B, C, etc., for the diskette drive.

One special thing about using 1-2-3 on a hard disk system is that
whenever you start the program, the System disk must be in drive A
(the diskette drive). You can remove the System disk at any point
after 1-2-3 begins. The reason for this is that Lotus Development
wants to prevent any unauthorized copying of the 1-2-3 program. If
the program did not check for a valid System disk each time, there
would be nothing to prevent unauthorized copying.

Which Version of DOS?

As mentioned earlier, either Version 1.1 or 2.0 of DOS can be run
with 1-2-3, but not both. That is, if you run 1-2-3 under DOS 2.0, you
should not copy DOS 1.1 .COM files to the 1-2-3 disks. You must be
consistent because the two versions are not compatible in some
ways, especially with regard to the FORMAT.COM program.

To upgrade 1-2-3 from DOS 1.1 to DOS 2.0, you must reinstall 1-2-3. Be sure that you use data files created under DOS 2.0. The COPY command allows you to move files from diskettes formatted under Version 1.1 to diskettes formatted under 2.0.

Installing Drivers

Installing driver programs is the next step in tailoring 1-2-3 disks to your particular system. This step is not necessary for Version 1.0 of 1-2-3 (the original version). Lotus Development later decided, however, and wisely so, that rather than carry the overhead for all the different system configurations, it would give you a way to match the 1-2-3 program to your particular system.

The drivers are small programs that reside in files on the Utility disk. You can tell which files contain the driver programs by their .DRV extensions.

Drivers are provided for the following system choices:

MONO	Monochrome display with monochrome adapter (no graphics)
HERCULES	Monochrome display with Hercules Graphics Card
COLOR	Color monitor with graphics adapter
B&W	Black-and-white monitor with graphics adapter
BOTH	Two-screen system—monochrome and graphics displays
COMPAQ	Compaq Portable Computer

To install the appropriate drivers for your system, first place the Utility disk in a drive and assign it as the default or source drive (for example, issue A:, followed by RETURN, if you place the Utility disk in Drive A). Next, select one of the installation choices in the list above and enter it, followed by a target drive indicator in the form x:, where x = A, B, C, etc. For example,

MONO A:	Installation of MONO with drive A as target
B&W B:	Installation of B&W with drive B as target

COLOR C: Installation of COLOR with drive C
                      (usually the hard disk drive) as target

The driver programs will then instruct you to place the five 1-2-3 disks into the target drive one by one so that drivers can be copied to them. If you have a hard disk, you will have to copy the drivers to the hard disk only once. In this case, you are instructed to interrupt the driver program at a specific point.

Configuring the Printer and the Data Disk

After the drivers are installed, the configuration must be set for the printer and the default drive for disk storage. 1-2-3 helps in this process by saving certain default settings from session to session. Lotus Development provides a default configuration for all settings, but you will want to change some of their choices.

The actual settings for the printer are accessed by entering the / Worksheet Global Default Printer command (discussed later). The setting for the default drive for disk storage is accessed with the / Worksheet Global Default Disk command (also discussed later). The default drive for transferring data to and from disk storage is Drive B. This drive assignment may have to be changed if you have a hard disk system.

Preparing Data Diskettes

The final procedure in getting started in 1-2-3 is preparing data diskettes. For those who are unfamiliar with preparing diskettes, all diskettes must be properly initialized before they can be used. 1-2-3 gives you an easy way to do this without exiting from the program: the Disk Manager program, which is one of the functions of the Lotus Access System.

The Lotus Access System

Lotus Development devised the Lotus Access System as a way to tie all the different functions of 1-2-3 together in one unit. This system is a series of menus that gives you the ability to move back and forth between 1-2-3 and other Lotus programs for file and disk management, printing graphs, and transferring files between 1-2-3 and other outside programs, such as VisiCalc. One of the advantages of the system is that it gives inexperienced users access to several important DOS commands without having to stray far from 1-2-3 to execute them. Another advantage is that you can perform the DOS functions without having to boot a DOS system disk.

To enter the Lotus Access System, you must first load the System disk into drive A and enter "lotus" at the A> system prompt. An alternative is to boot the system with the System disk in the drive. The Lotus Access System command menu will appear after a few seconds. There are six different functions available in the command menu:

1-2-3 File-Manager Disk-Manager PrintGraph Translate Exit

These options should not intimidate the user. Taken individually, they are very easy to understand and use. If you have any questions when you are in the Access System, you can always get help by hitting F1, just as in 1-2-3. The help screen lists the different Access System options and their use. If you have questions about a particular option, you can press F1 to get information.

Entering and Exiting from 1-2-3

The first option in the Lotus Access System menu is to enter 1-2-3. To do this, either point to 1-2-3 in the menu and hit RETURN or enter 1. It will take several seconds for the 1-2-3 logo to appear on the screen. When it does, hit RETURN to get the 1-2-3 spreadsheet screen.

You can also enter 1-2-3 without going through the Lotus Access System by entering "123" from the DOS operating system prompt. This method saves time. You can also save more time later by not having to exit from the Access System at the end of the session.

Whatever way you choose to enter 1-2-3, you should make sure that the date and time have been entered correctly with the DOS DATE. command. 1-2-3's @TODAY function takes the date and time from the entries you make in DOS. If this function is not entered correctly, it will not work properly.

If your system has an internal clock or you don't intend to use the @TODAY function, you won't have to worry about entering the time and date. Lotus Development has created an AUTOEXEC.BAT file that automatically prompts you for the date and time and enters "lotus." If you have an internal clock, you will not have to bother with this.

To exit the 1-2-3 program, enter *Quit* from the 1-2-3 main command menu. This command is used by all the programs in the Lotus Access system. If you look at the 1-2-3 command menu, you will see the *Quit* option at the end of the list of menu items. If you enter 1-2-3 directly from DOS, without going through the Lotus Access system, the DOS command prompt A> will appear right after you select *Quit*.

If you entered 1-2-3 from the Lotus Access System, *Quit* will return you to it. To exit from the Access System, you can select either *Exit* (Version 1A) or *PC* DOS (Version 1) from the command menu.

File-Manager

The *File*-Manager program allows the user to manipulate individual files on diskette. Because this program is stored in FILEMGR.COM on the Utility disk (for Version 1A of 1-2-3), when it is entered from the Lotus Access System, you will be prompted to load the Utility disk into Drive A to run the program. In earlier versions of 1-2-3, *File*-Manager (as well as *Disk*-Manager) was stored on the System disk. Because of the growth of the 1-2-3 program, however, the location of FILEMGR.COM was shifted to the Utility disk.

After you load the Utility disk and hit RETURN, you are asked to choose which disk drive you want to perform file maintenance on—A or B. Once you select a drive, you are given the following choices:

Copy	Copies files from the disk you have selected to another disk. The new files have the same names and extensions.
Erase	Erases files on the drive you have selected
Rename	Allows you to rename files on the current disk
Archive	Creates a second copy of a file on the current disk under a new name.
Disk	Changes the current disk drive

Sort	Sorts the files on the current disk according to primary and secondary keys
Quit	Exits from the *File*-Manager program and returns to the Lotus Access System

Figure 2.1 shows a typical *File*-Manager screen with a list of files.

To show you how the File-Manager program is used, let's try two simple tasks: renaming a file and sorting a menu of files.

Suppose that you want to rename the file BUGVAR.WKS to SAYWHAT.WKS. You first select *Rename* from the command menu, then use the cursor-movement keys on the right-hand side of the keyboard to move down to BUGUAR.WKS in the file menu. The following is a list of the cursor-movement keys and how they work:

↑	Up one line
↓	Down one line
PgUp	Up one screen
PgDn	Down one screen
HOME	Move to the top of the list
END	Move to the bottom of the list

Next, stop the reverse video field, which indicates the current position, over the title name BUGVAR.WKS. To lock-in your selection, hit the space bar. More than one file can be processed at a time by locking-in another file. If you hit RETURN after making your selection, 1-2-3 will then ask you for a new file name. Now you should enter SAYWHAT.WKS (or saywhat.wks because File-Manager is not particular about capital letters) and hit RETURN. The new file name will appear in the file menu.

You should always be careful to assign an appropriate file extension. If you forget the extension, you may not be able to access your newly renamed program from 1-2-3. If you are unfamiliar with the method for naming files, see Chapter 7.

For the second example, suppose that you want to sort a file menu to select all the files with a .WKS extension and to list the file names in ascending alphabetical order. To do this, first select *Sort* from the File-Manager command menu. The program will then provide another set of options to choose from.

Primary-key   Secondary-key   Reset   Go   Quit

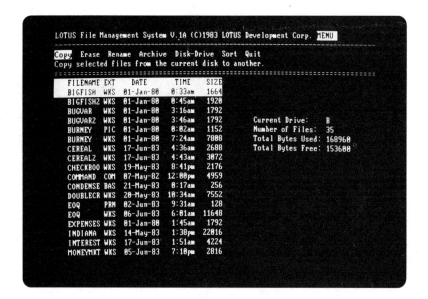

LOTUS File Management System V.1A (C)1983 LOTUS Development Corp. MENU

Copy Erase Rename Archive Disk-Drive Sort Quit
Copy selected files from the current disk to another.
==

FILENAME	EXT	DATE	TIME	SIZE
BIGFISH	WKS	01-Jan-80	8:33am	1664
BIGFISH2	WKS	01-Jan-80	8:45am	1920
BUGVAR	WKS	01-Jan-80	3:16am	1792
BUGVAR2	WKS	01-Jan-80	3:46am	1792
BURNEY	PIC	01-Jan-80	8:02am	1152
BURNEY	WKS	01-Jan-80	7:24am	7808
CEREAL	WKS	17-Jun-83	4:36am	2688
CEREAL2	WKS	17-Jun-83	4:43am	3072
CHECKBOO	WKS	19-May-83	8:41pm	2176
COMMAND	COM	07-May-82	12:00pm	4959
CONDENSE	BAS	21-May-83	8:17am	256
DOUBLECR	WKS	20-May-83	10:34am	7552
EOQ	PRN	02-Jun-83	9:31am	128
EOQ	WKS	06-Jun-83	6:01am	11648
EXPENSES	WKS	01-Jan-80	1:45am	1792
INDIANA	WKS	14-May-83	1:38pm	22016
INTEREST	WKS	17-Jun-83	1:51am	4224
MONEYMKT	WKS	05-Jun-83	7:10pm	2816

Current Drive: B
Number of Files: 35
Total Bytes Used: 168960
Total Bytes Free: 153600

Figure 2.1

In this case, both a *Primary-key* and a *Secondary-key* should be selected because two fields are important. The .WKS extension is the *Primary* key. After the *Primary* key is selected from the menu, another menu appears.

    Name   Extension   Date/Time   Size

The choices on this menu correspond to the different fields in the file menu. After *Extension* is selected from the list, you are given the choice of *Ascending* or *Descending* order. For this example, because .WKS is near the end of the alphabet, *Descending* order should be used to make sure that the .WKS files appear at the top of the list.

To set the *Secondary-key*, specify *Name* and *Ascending* order from the appropriate menus. The *Secondary* key will give you all the file names in ascending order after they have been sorted according to the *Primary-key*.

The final step is to activate the *Sort* by entering *Go* from the *Primary-key/Secondary-key* menu above. Figure 2.2 shows the results of the sort.

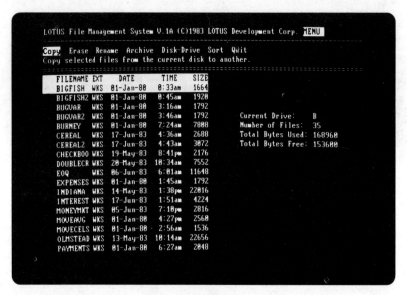

Figure 2.2

Disk-Manager

In contrast to *File*-Manager, which performs maintenance on individual files, *Disk*-Manager performs maintenance on entire diskettes. Whereas *File*-Manager is contained in a single file (FILEMGR.COM), Disk-Manager is a combination of four different DOS files on the Utility disk. These are copied directly to the Utility disk from a DOS diskette during configuration (Version 1A).

After *Disk*-Manager is selected from the Lotus Access System menu, the following choices appear:

Disk-Copy	Copies an entire diskette as is. Is restricted to copying from drive A to drive B. Uses the DOS program DISKCOPY.COM.
Compare	Compares two diskettes to see if they are exact duplicates. Uses the DOS program DISKCOMP.COM.

Prepare	Initializes a diskette to prepare it to accept data. (This is required in order to use a diskette for 1-2-3 files.) Uses the DOS program FORMAT.COM.
Status	Reports the disk utilization statistics and checks files to make sure that there are no inconsistencies. Uses the DOS program CHKDSK.COM.

Suppose, for example, that you want to make a backup copy of a data diskette and check it against the original. To do this, first select *Disk-Manager* from the Lotus Access System menu, then *Disk-Copy* to make an exact copy of the diskette.

The *Prepare* option is not needed in this case because you are copying the entire diskette. Just as FORMAT.COM is not required prior to DISKCOPY.COM in DOS, *Prepare* is not required before *Disk-Copy* in *Disk-Manager*. *Format* is required, however, for any other function. For instance, to make a copy of a single file on a new diskette, you would have to use *Prepare* to initialize the disk, followed by *Copy* in the *File-Manager* program to copy the file.

Once an exact copy of the data diskette is made, you would select the *Compare* option from the *Disk-Manager* program to verify the diskette. If there are any problems, error messages will appear on the screen.

A few rules should be observed when you are handling diskettes. When you swap diskettes, be careful not to bend them or to touch the magnetic surfaces. Also, make sure that you keep your diskettes in envelopes when they are not in use, and take your time when inserting them into envelopes and disk drives. Finally, keep them away from extreme temperatures, and never expose them to magnets. If you follow these simple rules, you should not lose information stored on diskettes.

PrintGraph

The *PrintGraph* option in the Access System menu initiates the PrintGraph program for printing graph files. After this option is chosen, the PrintGraph disk must be loaded to run the program. (This topic is covered in greater detail in Chapter 10.)

As with the other programs, you can go directly to the PrintGraph program without going through the Lotus Access System. To do this, you would enter the word "graph" from the DOS operating system prompt.

Translate

The *Translate* option accessses the Translation Utility. This utility provides a link between 1-2-3 and outside programs, including VisiCalc and dBASE II. Like some of the other programs discussed above, the Translation Utility is located on the Utility disk. (The Translation Utility is discussed in detail in Chapter 7.)

Exit

Exit is the final option in the Lotus Access System menu. You must choose *Exit* (Version 1A) or *PC* DOS (Version 1) to end the Lotus Access System program. When you do so, the DOS operating system prompt A> will appear.

If you exit from the Lotus Access System prematurely, you can easily re-enter it by typing LOTUS from the system prompt A>.

User Friendliness

One of the biggest selling points of 1-2-3 is its user friendliness. Lotus Development obviously went to a great deal of trouble to ensure that the spreadsheet is easy to learn and use.

The Tutorial Disk

The most outstanding user-friendly feature of 1-2-3 is its Tutorial disk. This disk contains a series of lessons on how to use the commands and functions of 1-2-3. To our knowledge, 1-2-3 and a competitive product, Multiplan, are the only programs that offer such comprehensive and well-conceived tutorials.

The lessons include:

Lesson	Topic
A	Getting Started
B	The Loan-Analysis Worksheet I
C	The Loan-Analysis Worksheet II

D	The Loan-Analysis Worksheet III
E	Using a 1-2-3 Data base
F	1-2-3 Graphics

Although this list is not exhaustive (one notable missing topic is macros), it is more than adequate for getting you started.

Lotus designed the Tutorial to take as few hours of your time as possible, but it is too much for one sitting. We found that it was best to do a lesson or two at a time, and we often went back later to different lessons to refresh our memories.

One of the outstanding features of the Tutorial is that it covers many special techniques that just don't sink in when you read the manual the first time. It is also especially good at bringing together concepts from different areas and making connections that you might not otherwise see. For example, the Tutorial covers the use of the / Copy command in the data base lesson, hinting at its potential as a helpful tool for adding data base records.

The lessons are arranged in an increasing order of difficulty and build on one another. Lotus Development's attitude is that the Tutorial should not cover all the functions and commands, but just enough to "get a good head start." They have done a good job accomplishing this.

The Tutorial is very friendly. It leads you by the hand every step of the way. For this reason, it is very appealing to users who are unfamiliar with spreadsheets and are trying to get started.

This self-paced program first tells you what to type in, then acts on your response. If you enter the proper letters and characters (it beeps with each missed keystroke), the program will perform actual functions. Because the lessons are basically a series of 1-2-3 screens, with explanatory text mixed in, they give you good hands-on experience.

Lotus has a "speed typing" provision for experienced spreadsheet users who do not have the patience to enter all the precise keystrokes. If you hit the space bar each time a special keystroke is requested, the Tutorial will automatically enter the proper keystrokes for you, giving you the benefit of the tutorial without having to do all the work.

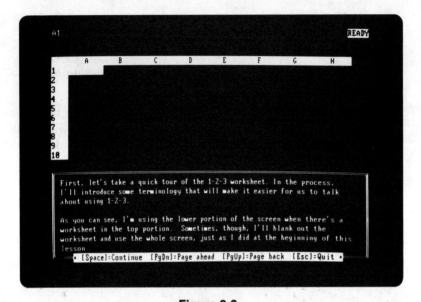

Figure 2.3

Sample Tutorial Screen

The Tutorial is an excellent way to get started with 1-2-3. If the tutorial were a little more comprehensive, however, it would be truly outstanding.

On-Screen Help

Another friendly feature of 1-2-3 is its extensive series of inter-connected help screens. By hitting the *Help* (F1) key, you can gain access to the Help Index screen. This screen has headings that can connect you to more than 200 other screens.

Each screen contains information about a single topic as well as reverse video headings positioned at the foot of the screen. These headings allow you to move to other topics or back to the Main Index screen.

To move to another topic, use the cursor-movement keys to position to a heading, then press RETURN.

/

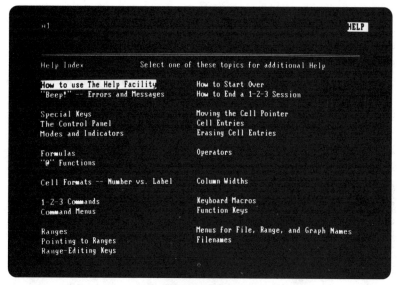

Figure 2.4
Help Index Screen

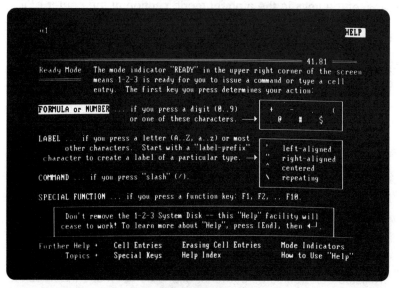

Figure 2.5
Help Screen

One of the best features of the on-screen help facility is that you can hit the F1 key at any time during a 1-2-3 session, even while issuing a command or defining a cell. Once you have the information you ESC key.

Other good features of this help facility are that many of the screens refer to pages in the 1-2-3 manual so that you can get more explanation if you need it. Also, by hitting the BACKSPACE key, you can view previous help screens again.

The 1-2-3 Keyboard

1-2-3 makes more use of the keys of the IBM PC than any of the earlier spreadsheet programs. The keyboard is divided into three sections: the alphanumeric keyboard in the center, the numeric keypad on the right, and the special-function key section on the left. This arrangement makes it easier to take a general look at how groups of keys are used in 1-2-3.

A General Look

Most of the keys in the alphanumeric section at the center of the keyboard are found on a normal typewriter and maintain their normal function in 1-2-3. Several keys, however, take on new and unique functions: ESC, TAB, SHIFT, and ALT.

The numeric keypad on the right-hand side of the keyboard is normally used for entering numbers in most programs on the IBM PC. The main purpose in 1-2-3, however, is cursor movement. Although this method works well, it limits the use of these keys for entering numbers.

The special-function keys on the left-hand side of the keyboard are designed for special situations ranging from getting help to drawing graphs.

The Alphanumeric Keyboard

Although most of the alphanumeric keys have the same functions as on a typewriter, several keys have special functions in 1-2-3, which are listed below. If some of the functions do not make much sense the first time through, don't worry. Their meaning will become clearer as you read more of this and later chapters.

Keyboard Diagram

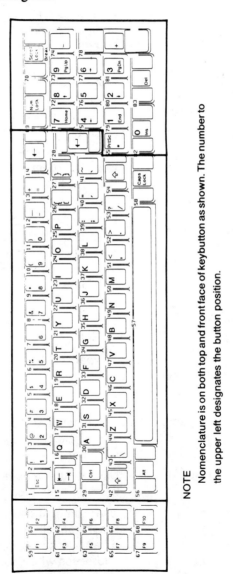

NOTE

Nomenclature is on both top and front face of keybutton as shown. The number to the upper left designates the button position.

Figure 2.6

Key	Function
Esc	Erases current entry when specifying a command line or range, erases a command menu, or returns from a help screen
⊣(Tab)	Moves cursor one screen to the right when used alone, and one screen to the left when used with the SHIFT key
Alt	Used simultaneously with other alpha keys to invoke keyboard macros. Covered in detail in Chapter 12 on Keyboard Macros.
↑ (Shift)	Changes the central section of the keyboard to upper-case letters and characters. It also allows you to key in numbers, using the numeric keypad on the right (equivalent of a temporary NUM LOCK).

The Numeric Keypad

The keys in the numeric keypad on the right-hand side of the keyboard are mainly used for cursor movement.

Keys	Function
←(Backspace)	When defining the contents of a cell, erases the previous character in the definition
/ (Slash)	Used to start a command. Also used in its normal function as a division sign.
. (Period)	Used to separate cell addresses when ranges of cells are designated and, in a different manner, to anchor cell addresses when pointing. (For more on ranges, see the Ranges section of Chapter 4.) It is also used as a decimal point.

Figure 2.7
The Alphanumeric Keyboard

HOME	Returns to cell A1 from any location in the worksheet. Also used after the END key to position the cursor at the active end of the worksheet. Also used in the edit mode to jump to the beginning of the edit line.
PgUp	Moves the cursor 20 rows up in the column where it currently resides
End	When entered prior to any of the arrow keys, positions the cursor in the direction of the arrow key to the cell on the boundary of an empty and filled space. Also used in the Edit mode to jump to the end of the edit line.

Figure 2.8

← →	Left and right arrow keys. Used to position the cursor one column left or right.
↑ ↓	Up and down arrow keys. Used to position the cursor one row up or down.
Num Lock	Activates the numeric character of the keys in the numeric keypad
Del	Used in editing command lines (covered under F2 in the next section) to delete the character above the cursor
Scroll Lock/ Break	In the Scroll Lock position, used to scroll the entire screen one row or column in any direction each time the

cell pointer is moved. In the Break position, used with CTRL as the equivalent to hitting the ESC key several times, it returns 1-2-3 to the Ready mode.

1-2-3 uses the END key in a unique way. When the END key is followed by an arrow key, the cursor will move in the direction of the arrow key to the next boundary between a blank cell and a cell that contains data. Although this process may sound complex, in practice it is very useful. We'll look at several interesting applications for the END key in the following chapters. Figure 2.9 demonstrates the movement of the cursor with the END key.

When you want to use the numeric keypad to enter numbers rather than for positioning the cursor, you can do one of two things. First, you can use the NUM LOCK key before entering the numbers, and hit it again when you are done. (This is the method used in most IBM PC software.) Of course, if you do this, the keys cannot be used to move the cursor. The second way is to hold down the SHIFT key while simultaneously pressing the number keys. Neither way is ideal, but this is one of the trade-offs that Lotus Development made when it decided to use the numeric keypad for cursor movement.

In Chapter 12, you will learn how to create a macro that will enter numbers down a column of cells without having to press the NUM LOCK key or hold down the SHIFT key. You can easily apply it to entering numbers in any direction.

The Special-Function Keys

The special-function keys, F1 through F10, are used for special situations in 1-2-3. Lotus Development provides a plastic function-key template that fits over the function keys of the IBM PC. A special version of this template is also available for Compaq™ owners when the purchase registration card is sent to Lotus Development. Unfortunately, the template does not give you enough information when you are first starting out. For this reason, we have designed a special function-key graphic (see figure 2.11) to help you in the first sessions until you have memorized the functions.

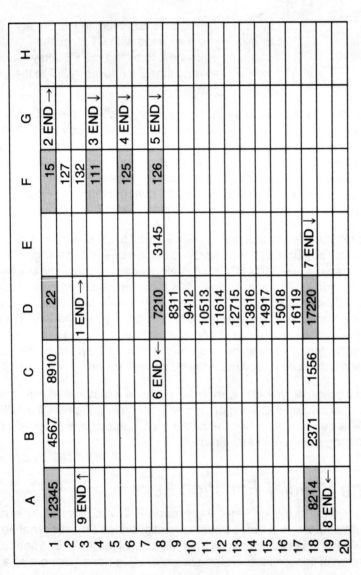

Figure 2.9
Using the End Key

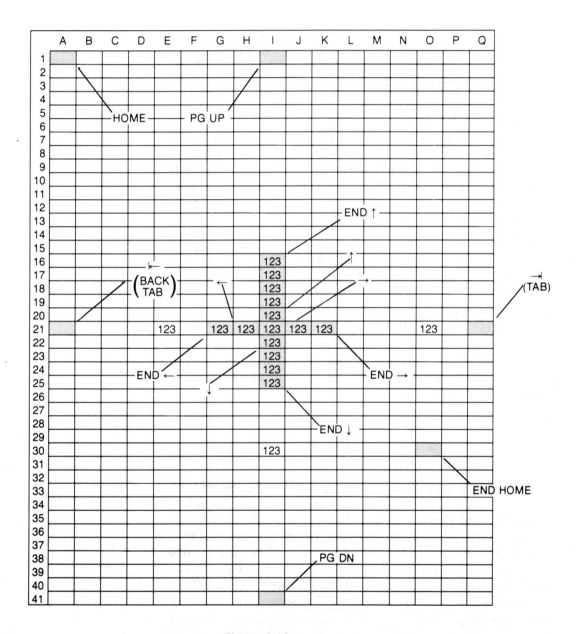

Figure 2.10
Cursor Movement Chart

The special-function key graphic refers you to different sections in this book for further explanations of the various function keys. Because all of the keys except F5 are explained sufficiently elsewhere, only F5 is discussed here.

Jumping to a Cell

The F5 (GOTO) key saves your having to position the cursor manually to a cell location. When 1-2-3 is in the Ready mode, F5 allows you to position directly to a cell. It cannot be used when you are in the middle of entering a 1-2-3 command or making a cell entry (that is, when you are not in the Ready mode). For VisiCalc users, 1-2-3's F5 is the equivalent of VisiCalc's >.

Another nice feature of the F5 key is that you can combine it with range names. When 1-2-3 asks you for the address "to go to," you can enter "Ratios" instead of A94, for example. (This is covered in the "Naming Ranges" section of Chapter 4.)

The 1-2-3 Display

The main 1-2-3 display is divided into two parts: the control panel at the top of the screen, and the worksheet area itself. A reverse video border separates the two areas. This border contains the letters and numbers that mark columns and rows.

Other important areas of the screen are the mode indicator, the "lock" key indicator, and the error messages area.

The Control Panel

The control panel is the area above the reverse video border. This area has three lines, each with a special purpose. As figure 2.12 indicates, the first line contains all the information about the *current cell*. A current cell is the cell where the pointer is currently located. The first item in the line is the address of the cell. The second item is the display format, which is always displayed in parentheses. (Display formats will be covered in detail in Chapter 5.) The last item in the first line is the actual contents of the current cell.

The second line in the control panel contains the characters that are being entered or edited. The third line contains explanations of the current command menu item. If you move the pointer from one item

F1 HELP Accesses 1-2-3's on-line help facility Chapter 2, "Help"	**F2 EDIT** Shifts 1-2-3 into EDIT MODE. Allows contents of cells to be altered without retyping the entire cell. Chapter 3, "Editing"
F3 NAME In the POINT MODE, displays a list of the range names in the current worksheet Chapter 4, "Using Range Names"	**F4 ABS** Used during cell definition to change a relative cell address into an absolute or mixed address. Chapter 4, "Relative and Absolute Addressing"
F5 GOTO Moves the cursor to the cell coordinates (or range name) provided Chapter 2, "Special Function Keys"	**F6 WINDOW** Move the cursor to the other side of a split screen. Chapter 4, "Window"
F7 QUERY Repeats the most recent Data Query operation Chapter 11, "Data Query"	**F8 TABLE** Repeats the most recent Data Table operation Chapter 11, "Data Table"
F9 CALC Recalculates the worksheet Chapter 4, "Recalculation"	**F10 GRAPH** Redraws the graph defined by the current graph settings Chapter 9, "The F10 Key"

Figure 2.11

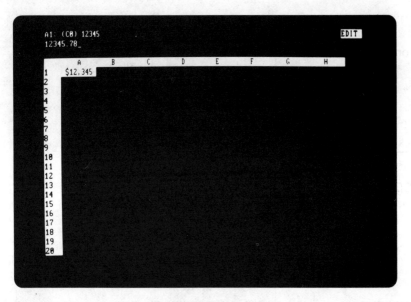

Figure 2.12
The 1-2-3 Display

to the next in a command menu, the explanation on the third line of
the control panel will change each time. If a command menu is not in
effect, this line will be blank.

The Mode Indicators

There are several modes in 1-2-3, one of which is always in effect
depending on what you are doing. The Mode Indicator is located in
the upper right-hand corner of the screen and always shows the
current mode that 1-2-3 is in. The mode indicators and related
modes include:

Indicator	Mode
READY	Waiting for you to enter a command or make a cell entry
VALUE	Number or formula is being entered
LABEL	Label is being entered
EDIT	Cell entry is being edited
POINT	Range being pointed to

MENU	Menu item being selected
HELP	Using a help screen
ERROR	Error has occurred, and 1-2-3 is waiting for you to press ESC or RETURN to acknowledge it
WAIT	1-2-3 is in the middle of a calculation and cannot respond to commands. Flashes on and off.
FIND	1-2-3 is in the middle of a /Data Query operation and cannot respond to commands.
CMD	Appears in front of the mode indicators listed above during the execution of a keyboard macro. (Keyboard macros are covered in Chapter 12.)
SST	Appears instead of CMD when in single-step execution of a keyboard macro

The Lock Key Indicators

There are three "lock" keys on the IBM PC: NUM LOCK, CAPS LOCK, and SCROLL LOCK. In the other spreadsheet programs, it is hard to tell whether these keys are on or off. But in 1-2-3, you always know their status because a special area of the screen has been set aside to show that information. Each key has its own reverse video indicator that will appear in the lower right-hand corner of the screen when its respective key is on.

Other Indicators

Other indicators in 1-2-3 appear in the lower right-hand corner of the screen. They display the status of certain keys and special situations and are listed below.

| STEP ALT | F1 was pressed, and you are currently stepping through a macro one cell at a time. (Covered in Chapter 12.) |
| END | The END key has been pressed and is now active. |

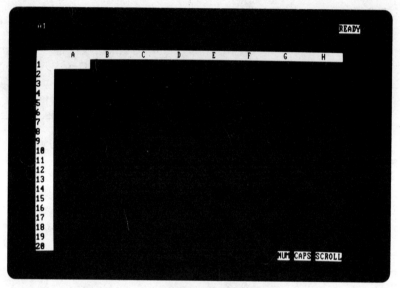

Figure 2.13
The Lock Key Indicators

CALC	*Global Recalculation* has been set to *Manual.* (Covered in the "Recalculation" section of Chapter 4.)
CIRC	A circular reference has been found in the worksheet. (Covered in the "Circular References" section of Chapter 4.)

The Error Messages Area

When an error occurs in 1-2-3, a message will appear in the lower left-hand corner of the screen. The error may occur for many reasons: the disk you are trying to save a file to is full, a cell formula is too long, there are no files on disk of the type you are looking for, etc.

To clear the error and get back to the Ready mode, you must hit ESC or ENTER. If you do not hit one of these keys, the message will not clear.

Conclusion

The initial steps to getting started with 1-2-3 have included tailoring the program to your particular computer system as well as learning how to use several basic features of the 1-2-3 program. In this chapter, you have learned how to use the Lotus Access System, the Tutorial, the keyboard, and various parts of the screen. There is only one barrier left to your actually using 1-2-3, and that is how to use the 1-2-3 spreadsheet itself.

3

The 1-2-3 Spreadsheet

If 1-2-3 were simply a spreadsheet program without graphics and data base functions, it would still be an amazing software product. The spreadsheet is the foundation of the program.

The importance of the spreadsheet as the basis for the whole product can not be overemphasized. All the commands for the related features are initiated from the same main command menu as the spreadsheet commands, and they are all in the same style.

Also, all the special features of 1-2-3 originate from the spreadsheet. For instance, in data management, the data base is composed of records that are actually cell entries in a spreadsheet. Similarly, macros are statements that are placed in adjacent cells in out-of-the-way sections of a spreadsheet. Finally, all the commands for displaying graphs refer to entries in the spreadsheet and use these entries to draw graphs on the screen.

As we have seen, the 1-2-3 worksheet contains 2,048 rows and 256 columns, or more than 500,000 cells. Each column is assigned a letter value ranging from A for the first column to IV for the last. A good way to visualize the worksheet is as one giant sheet of gridded paper that is about 21 feet wide and 42 feet high!

Like many other spreadsheets, the 1-2-3 worksheet is too large to be viewed at one time on a computer video display. If the default column width of 9 characters is used, only 20 rows and 7 columns can be seen at a time on the screen. As demonstrated in figure 3.1, the screen is like a window onto the 1-2-3 worksheet.

Size

The 1-2-3 spreadsheet is more than thirty-eight times larger than the original VisiCalc spreadsheet of 63 columns by 254 rows. Practically speaking, however, there are some limitations to using the entire sheet. If you imagine storing just one character in each of the 524,288 cells that are available, you end up with a worksheet bordering on the size of the largest hardware configuration that 1-2-3 can support—544K.

For Version 1A, the program alone requires 98K of RAM. Its large size stems primarily from the programming required for all the extra features that 1-2-3 provides beyond the standard spreadsheet function. Another important reason for the program's size is 1-2-3's extensive memory. 1-2-3 remembers cell formats, worksheet and command ranges, print options, and graph settings. Some information is saved automatically by 1-2-3, but some information must be saved by the user.

In addition to the size of the 1-2-3 program, the size of the worksheet in RAM must be considered. There is no simple way to equate the number of active cells in a worksheet to its RAM requirements because the contents of cells can vary so much. Perhaps the best way to get a realistic notion of the potential size of a worksheet is to conduct two simple tests. In the first, we'll relate the size of the worksheet to the number of standard 8.5" x 11" pages that can fit into it. For the second, we'll experiment with filling cells in the worksheet, using the / Copy command, and see when we run out of main memory. From these two tests, we can draw conclusions about realistic worksheet size.

To begin the first analogy, we will use the maximum configuration possible for 1-2-3, 544K of RAM. After subtracting the 98K for the 1-2-3 program, a maximum worksheet size of 446K remains. If we divide the remaining RAM by the number of characters on a standard 8.5" x 11" page using pica type (66 lines by 80 characters = 5,028), we get approximately 85 pages. Although this is a very rough measure, it points out the tremendous capacity of the 1-2-3 sheet.

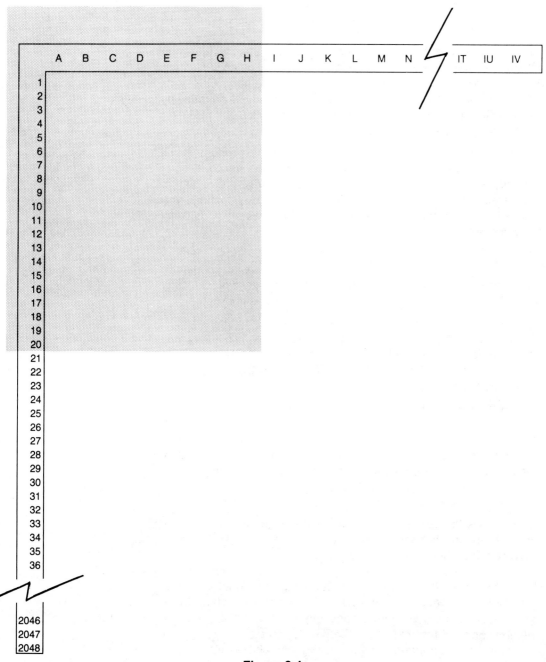

Figure 3.1

For the second analogy, we will use a more common configuration of 320K. We begin by entering the label 'ABCD' in cell A1. We then duplicate this cell until we run out of main memory. Our tests indicate that you can fill a rectangular range of nearly 50 columns by 445 rows before you run out of memory. This size is a constraint on only the very largest models.

There are very few situations in which the size of your worksheet will exceed main memory, unless your system is configured at substantially less than 320K. Looking at it another way, the minimum suggested requirement of 128K with Version 1 still offers you approximately the same capacity as the original version of VisiCalc, approximately 30K.

All other things being equal, it is better to have too much memory than too little. Because RAM is relatively inexpensive (and is getting even more so) and is so important to increasing your productivity with 1-2-3, it makes sense to buy as much RAM as you can.

No matter how much RAM you buy, you can expect that some of it will be consumed by growth in a future version of the 1-2-3 program. For example, version 1A of 1-2-3 requires 192K of RAM. Because the basic program requires approximately 140K, the maximum spreadsheet size is about 52K.

One recommendation that Lotus Development makes to help you make the maximum use of RAM is to keep your active worksheet area as close to cell A1 as possible. If you scatter your model about with no consideration for this, you may find yourself running out of memory because RAM is required to store the contents of cells between entries even though there may be nothing more than blanks in the cells.

For example, the spreadsheets in figures 3.2 and 3.3 contain the same information, but one requires nearly one and a half times more RAM than the other.

Remember that when you delete a part of a worksheet, the main memory requirements for that worksheet do not diminish until you save it to diskette, then load it back into RAM. 1-2-3's built-in optimization routines are not activated until you store a worksheet. (The commands for storing and retrieving worksheets are covered in Chapter 7.)

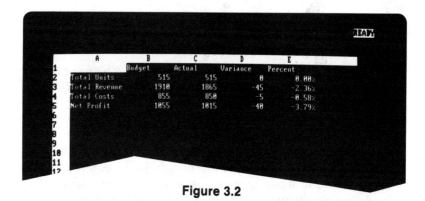

Figure 3.2

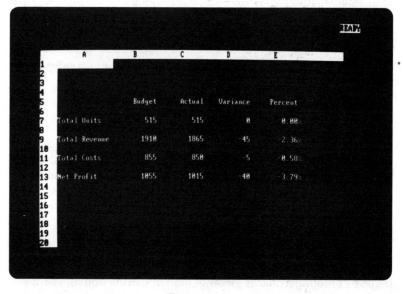

Figure 3.3

Speed

1-2-3's speed of recalculation is another of its outstanding features. In our extensive comparisons with other spreadsheet programs, no other program came close. The fact that 1-2-3 is written in 8088 Assembler has a great deal to do with its speed. Context MBA, the closest competitor to 1-2-3 in functional breadth, is written in Pascal and is nowhere near as fast. Even for the most difficult recalculations, 1-2-3 took no more than 3 seconds.

Two other points to mention with respect to 1-2-3's speed are its cursor movement and system loading time. 1-2-3's cursor movement is very fast when compared with other spreadsheet programs. When you press a cursor-movement key, the cursor reacts instantly with almost no visible delay. In contrast with several other spreadsheet programs where the screen flickers each time the cursor is moved, 1-2-3 shows almost no flickering. The screen reacts fast enough for you to move quickly to the cell you are interested in without overshooting your mark and ending up several cells beyond.

The system loading time, however, is another story. It is probably the slowest thing about 1-2-3 because of the size of the system program itself, just over 98K for Version 1A. On a per-byte basis, it is relatively fast, although this fact doesn't do you much good when you are waiting to get started. Our tests indicate that loading time takes roughly 15 seconds.

Entering Data in the Worksheet

As you will recall from earlier spreadsheet experience, or from Chapter 1, there are three different types of cell entries: numbers, formulas, and labels. Data is entered in a cell simply by positioning the cursor in the cell and typing the entry. 1-2-3 guesses the type of cell entry you are making from the first character that you enter. If you start with one of the following characters:

    0   1   2   3   4   5   6   7   8   9   +   -   .   (@   # $

1-2-3 will treat your entry as either a number or a formula. If you begin by entering a character other than one of the above, 1-2-3 will treat your entry as a label.

Numbers

The rules for entering numbers are very simple.

    1. A number cannot begin with any character except 0 through 9, a decimal point, or a dollar sign ($).

2. You can end a number with a percent sign (%), which indicates to 1-2-3 to divide the number that precedes it by 100.

3. A number cannot have more than one decimal point.

4. Although you may not use commas or spaces when you enter a number, it can be displayed with them. (See Chapter 5.)

5. You can enter a number in scientific notation—what 1-2-3 calls the *Scientific* format (e.g., 1.234E+06).

If you do not follow these rules, 1-2-3 will beep when you hit RETURN while trying to enter the numbers into the spreadsheet. 1-2-3 will also automatically shift to the Edit mode just as though you had hit F2. (The "Editing" section below explains how to respond.)

Formulas

In addition to simple numbers, you can also enter formulas into cells. Formulas are a complicated topic in 1-2-3 because they incorporate so many different concepts.

Suppose that you want to create a formula that adds a row of numbers. In figure 3.4, you would want to add the amounts in cells B1, C1, D1, and E1 and place the result in cell F1.

One formula that will perform the addition is +B1+C1+D1+E1. Notice the + sign at the beginning of the formula. For 1-2-3 to

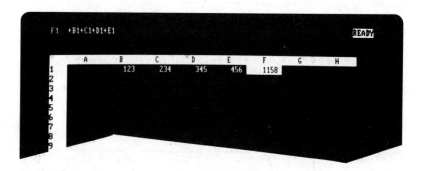

Figure 3.4

recognize the formula as a formula and not a label, the formula must begin with one of the following characters:

    0   1   2   3   4   5   6   7   8   9   .   +   -   (@   # $

Because we started with +, 1-2-3 recognizes our entry as a formula and switches to the Value mode, the appropriate mode for entering numbers and formulas.

Two methods can be used to enter cell addresses in formulas: typing them in and pointing to them. Both accomplish the same thing, and you can mix and match the two techniques within the same formula. Typing in cell addresses is self-explanatory, but pointing to cell addresses requires some explanation. The method used is the same as the one used in pointing to cell ranges (see the "Ranges" section of Chapter 4), but in this case the range is only a single cell.

In the example above, to enter the formula by pointing, you would move the cell pointer to B1 after entering the first plus sign. Notice that the address for the cell appears after the plus in the second line of the control panel—that is, +B1. The mode indicator in the upper right-hand corner of the screen shifts from Value to Point mode as you move the cell pointer to cell B1.

To continue on to the next address in the formula, you would type another plus sign. The cursor will move immediately from cell B1 back to the cell where it started from when you began entering the formula—in this case cell F1. Also, the mode indicator will shift back to Value. You continue this sequence of pointing and entering plus signs until you have the formula you want. Remember that nothing prohibits you from using a combination of pointing and typing. Use whatever works best for you.

It is usually easier to point at cells that are close to the cell you are defining and type references to far-away cells. VisiCalc users, however, will find pointing to even far-away cells easier in 1-2-3, thanks to the END, PgUp, PgDn, and TAB keys that help you move quickly around the spreadsheet.

Operators

Operators indicate arithmetic operations in formulas. They can be broken down into two types: mathematical and logical. The mathematical operators are listed below.

Operator	Meaning
^	Exponentiation
+,—	Positive, Negative
*,/	Multiplication, Division
+,—	Addition, Subtraction

An important part of understanding operators is knowing their order of precedence. The list above is arranged in order of precedence, with those operators with the highest order of precedence at the top. Operators with equal precedence are listed on the same line. In these cases, the operators are evaluated from left to right. You can always use parentheses to override the order of precedence.

Consider the order of precedence in the following formulas, where B3 = 2, C3 = 3, and D3 = 4, and see if you get the same answers. Notice particularly how parentheses affect the order of precedence, and ultimately the answer, in the first two formulas.

Formula	Answer
C3-D3/B3	1
(C3-D3)/B3	(.5)
D3*C3-B3^C3	4
D3*C3*B3/B3^C3-25/5	(2)

According to the 1-2-3 manual, it is possible to create a formula that is too complicated for 1-2-3 to understand, but this has not been our experience. The manual mentions specifically formulas with many levels of nested parentheses as the problem, in which case 1-2-3 displays ERR instead of the answer. A message may also appear in the message area in the bottom left-hand corner of the screen—for example, "Formula too long." In the unlikely event that this happens to you, Lotus suggests splitting up the formula into one or more intermediate calculations.

Functions

Like most electronic spreadsheets, 1-2-3 includes built-in functions. These functions are simply abbreviations for long or complex mathematical formulas and are considered formulas by 1-2-3. All 1-2-3 functions consist of three parts: the "@" sign, a function name, and an argument or range. The @ sign simply signals to 1-2-3 that a function is coming. The name indicates which function is being used. The argument or range is the data required by 1-2-3 to perform the function.

Before we cover functions in detail (in Chapter 6), we will need to cover several other topics, such as the concept of ranges. However, the following simple example is provided to help you begin to understand 1-2-3 functions.

In figure 3.4, we needed to refer to four cells individually to create the desired formula. We could, however, use the @SUM function to "sum" the numbers in the example. The concept of ranges is important to the @SUM function. (Ranges are also covered in detail later in this chapter and in Chapter 4.) For now, think of a range as simply a continuous group of cells.

The equivalent to the +B1+C1+D1+E1 formula, using the the @SUM function, is @SUM(B1..E1). The only difference between the two formulas is one of convenience. If we had several more entries extending down the row, the @SUM function would change only slightly to use the address of the last cell to be summed, e.g., @SUM(B1..Z1), which would sum the contents of the first row all the way from B to Z.

The following formulas perform the same function in our example; yet they all look slightly different.

@SUM(B1..E1)   @SUM(B1..E1)
@SUM($B1..$E1)   @SUM(B1..$E1)
@SUM(B$1..E$1)   @SUM(B1..E1)

Notice the dollar signs in the formulas. These signs are strategically placed to distinguish between *relative, absolute,* and *mixed addressing.* (These concepts are covered extensively in the "Copying" section of Chapter 4.)

Labels

The third type of data that can be entered in a cell is labels. Labels are commonly used for row and column headers. They can be up to 240 characters long and can contain any string of characters and numbers. If a label is too long for the width of a cell, it will continue across the cells to the right for display purposes as long as there are no other entries in the neighboring cells.

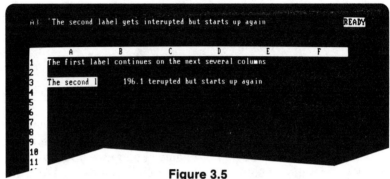

Figure 3.5
How a Label Continues Across Cells

When you enter a value into a cell and the first character is not one of the ones in the list mentioned above for entering numbers and formulas, 1-2-3 assumes that you are entering a label. As you type the first character, 1-2-3 shifts to the Label mode.

One of the advantages of 1-2-3 is that you can left-justify, center, or right-justify labels when you display them. To do this, the label must be preceded by one of the following *label-prefix* characters.

Character	Action
'	Left-justifies
^	Centers
"	Right-justifies
\	Repeats

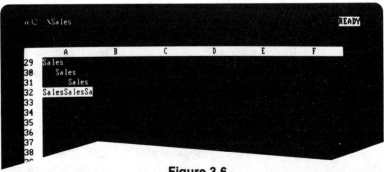

Figure 3.6
Label Alignment

The standard default for displaying labels is left-justification. You don't have to enter the label-prefix in this case because 1-2-3 will automatically supply it for you.

What You Enter	What 1-2-3 Stores
Net Income	'Net Income

The one exception, for all types of alignment, appears when the first character of the label is on the list for entering numbers and formulas mentioned above. For example, suppose you wanted to enter the number "1983" as a label. If you type 1983, 1-2-3 will assume that you are entering a value. You will need some way to signal that you intend this numeric entry to be treated as text. You can indicate this by using one of the label-prefix characters. In this case, you could enter 1983 as a centered label by typing ^1983.

The most unusual label prefix is the backslash (\), which is used for repetition. One of the most frequent uses of this prefix is to create a separator line.

The first step in creating the separator line is to enter * into the first cell (here, cell A7). This entry causes asterisks to appear across the entire cell. Once you have set up the first cell, you can use the / Copy command to replicate the cell across the page. (For more information about the / Copy command and replication in general, see Chapter 4.)

There are several ways to control label prefixes. For example, suppose that you have entered a series of labels, using the standard default of left-justification, but you decide that you would rather have the labels centered. You could go in and manually change all the label prefixes, or you could change them all at once, using the / Range Label-Prefix command.

When you select the / Range Label-Prefix command, you are given the following choices:

    Left   Right   Center

Each choice gives you the label prefix that its name indicates.

If you select Center, as in the example, 1-2-3 will ask you to designate a range of cells to change. When you specify a range and hit RETURN, the cells will be displayed as centered.

Another option for changing label prefixes is to change the default setting for text justification. The command to do this is / *Worksheet Global Label-*Prefix. This command gives you the same options as the / *Range Label-*Prefix command. One thing to keep in mind, however, is that previously entered cells will not be affected by this command. Only subsequent entries will show the change. In addition, cells that have been previously set, using / *Range Label-*Prefix, will maintain the alignment set by that command.

Editing

One of the first things you will want to do when you start using 1-2-3 is modify the contents of cells without retyping the complete entry. This is quite easy to do in 1-2-3. You begin by moving the cursor to the appropriate cell and pressing the F2 (EDIT) key. An alternative is to press F2 when you are entering cell contents. You might do this if you discover that you made a mistake earlier.

When you press F2, 1-2-3 enters the *Edit mode*. Normally 1-2-3 is in the *Ready mode*. The main difference between the two modes is that some keys take on different meanings. These keys are listed below:

Key	Action
←	Moves the cursor one position to the left
→	Moves the cursor one position to the right
⊣	Moves the cursor one screen to the right
⏐←	Moves the cursor one screen to the left. You have to hold down the SHIFT key when you press ⏐←.
HOME	Moves the cursor to the first character in the entry
END	Moves the cursor to the last character in the entry
BACKSPACE	Deletes the character just to the left of the cursor
DEL	Deletes the character above the cursor
ESC	Clears the edit line and takes you out of the Edit mode

After you press F2, the mode indicator in the upper right-hand corner of the screen will change to *Edit*. The contents of the cell will then be duplicated in the second line of the control panel (what we call the "Edit Line") and be ready for editing.

To show how the various keys described above are used, let's consider two examples. First, suppose you want to edit an entry in cell E4 that reads "Sales Comparissons." After you position the cursor to cell E4, the actions are

Keys	Edit Line	Explanation
F2	'Sales Comparisson_	The cursor always appears at the end of the edit line when you press F2.
←	'Sales Comparisson	
←	'Sales Comparisson	The cursor now appears below the errant "s."
←	'Sales Comparisson	
DEL	'Sales Comparison	The DEL key deletes the character above the cursor.
RETURN		You must hit RETURN to update the entry in the spreadsheet and return to the Ready mode.

One thing to remember about using the Edit mode is that you can also use it when you are entering a cell for the first time and you make a mistake. With this method, you can eliminate retyping.

Now suppose that you want to modify a formula in cell G6 from +D4/H3*(Y5+4000) to +C4/H3*(Y5+4000). After you move the cursor to that cell, the actions are

Keys	Edit Line	Explanation
F2	+D4/H3*(Y5+4000)_	Again, the cursor always appears at the end of the edit line when you first press F2.
HOME	+D4/H3*(Y5+4000)	The HOME key takes you to the first position in the edit line.

→	+D4/H3*(Y5+4000)	The → key moves the cursor one position to the right.
"C"	+CD4/H3*(Y5+4000)	Whenever you enter a character in the Edit mode, the character is inserted to the left of the cursor. Entering a character will never cause you to write over another. Unwanted characters can be eliminated with the DEL and BACKSPACE keys.
→
DEL	+CD4/H3*(Y5+4000)
+C4/H3*(Y5+4000)	Move right and use the DEL key to delete the character above the cursor.
RETURN		Again, you must hit RETURN to update the entry in the spreadsheet and return to the Ready mode.

The EDIT and CALC (F9) functions can be used together to convert a formula stored in a cell to a simple number. As figure 2.11 in Chapter 2 indicates, F9 is normally used for recalculating when / Worksheet Global Recalculation is set to Manual. (This is covered in detail in Chapter 4.) However, when you are in the Edit mode, pressing F9 will cause a formula to be converted to a number, its current value.

For example, suppose that you want to use F9 to convert the formula in the previous example to its current value (which we'll assume is 64,000) and store the result.

Keys	Edit Line	Explanation
F2	+C4/H3*(Y5+4000)	F2 puts 1-2-3 in the Edit mode.
F9	64000_	F9 converts the formula to its current value. We picked 64000 at random.

RETURN   Stores the entry in the
                                                current cell and shifts
                                                back to the Ready mode.

Ranges

1-2-3's commands and functions often require that you deal with a group of cells in aggregate. 1-2-3 calls this type of group a *range*. Before we go on to learn more about 1-2-3's commands, we need to learn a bit about ranges.

1-2-3's definition of a range is one or more cells in a rectangular group. With this definition, one cell is the smallest possible range, and the largest range is the size of the worksheet itself.

The advantages of using ranges are that they make your work easier and faster. They allow you to process blocks of cells in commands and formulas at the same time. This represents a significant change in philosophy from earlier spreadsheet programs because these programs allow you to process only individual cells, rows, or columns. They hardly ever allow you to group the cells, rows, or columns together in any significant fashion.

When you will actually use ranges in 1-2-3 depends to some degree on your personal preference because in many cases it is your choice whether to provide them. In many other cases, however, 1-2-3 will prompt you for ranges.

The Shape of Ranges

Ranges are rectangles, as illustrated in figure 3.7. The expanding-cursor feature allows you to see the shape of ranges in 1-2-3. When a range is designated, the cells of the range show up in reverse video. This makes pointing an easy way to designate ranges because as the cursor moves, the reverse video rectangle expands, as shown in figure 3.8.

Designating Ranges

There are three ways of designating ranges: entering cell addresses, pointing to cells, and naming ranges. These three methods allow you to communicate to 1-2-3 the diagonally opposite corners of the rectangular group of cells that the range represents.

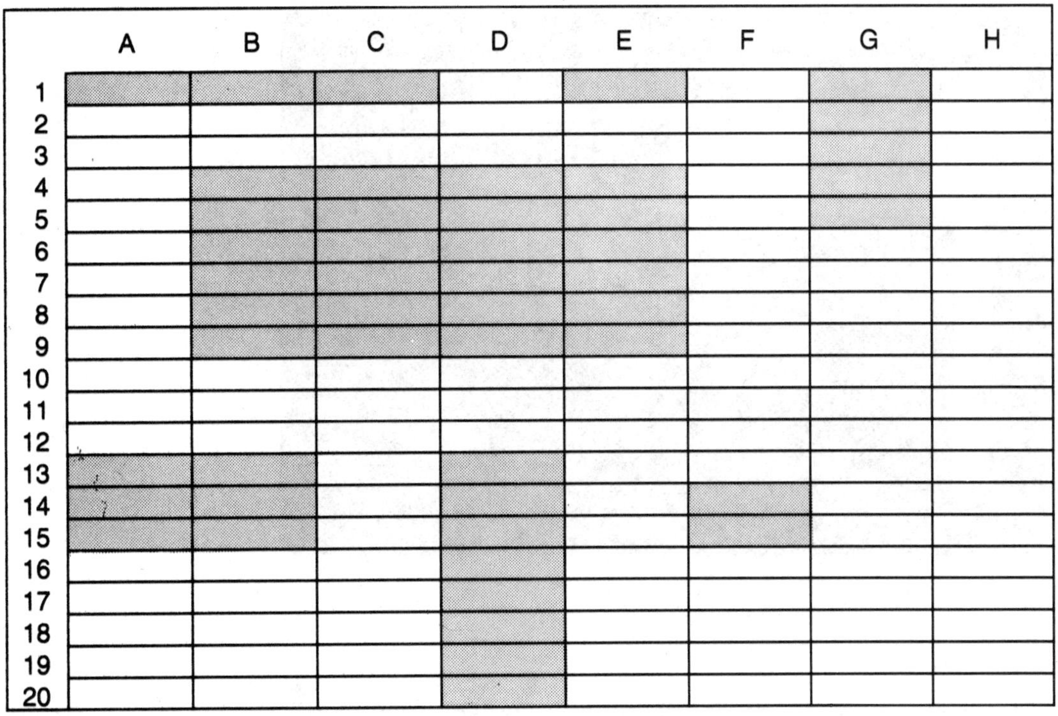

Figure 3.7
A Sample of 1-2-3 Ranges

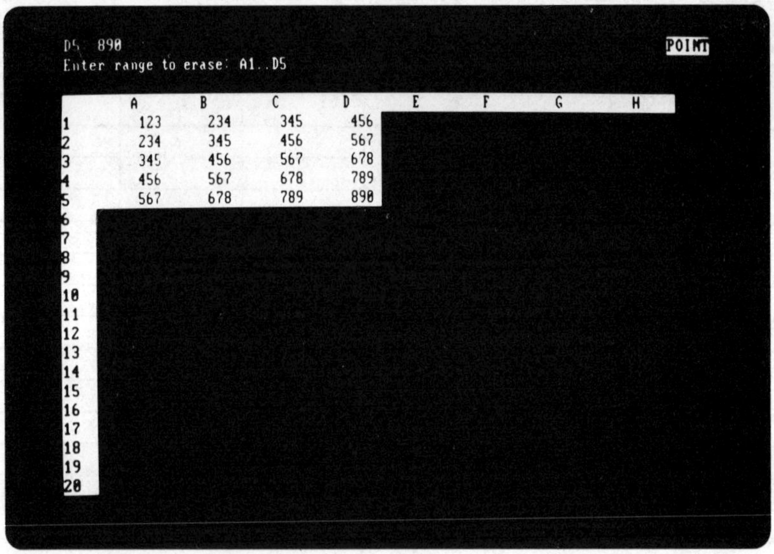

Figure 3.8

Ranges are specified by diagonally opposite corners, which usually means the upper left- and lower right-hand cells. The other set of corners, however, is perfectly permissible. For example, the range shown in figure 3.9 could be identified as A1..F16 or F1..A16.

The two cell addresses that specify the corners are usually separated by one or more periods. For example,

    A7..D10
    AA1.AB20
    J2...K4

If you choose anything other than two periods to separate the cell addresses, however, 1-2-3 will automatically change the number to two.

In the next few chapters, the concept of ranges will be used over and over again. Most of 1-2-3's functions and several of the program's commands require the use of ranges. In addition, 1-2-3 has a whole set of commands that operate on ranges. These commands, and several others, are covered in the next chapter.

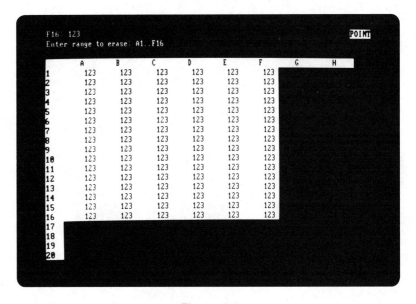

Figure 3.9

4

1-2-3's Commands

Like all electronic spreadsheets, 1-2-3 offers a number of exciting spreadsheet *commands*. Commands are the instructions you give 1-2-3 to perform a variety of different tasks, such as formatting the worksheet, saving a worksheet, creating a graph, or accessing a data base. These commands include a new kind of replication (which has a different treatment of relative versus absolute cell addressing), inserting and deleting of multiple rows and columns, and moving data.

Command Menus

Command menus are the devices used by 1-2-3 to present command alternatives to the user. The command menus are especially helpful in 1-2-3 for several reasons. First, unlike earlier spreadsheet programs, such as VisiCalc, which display single-letter commands in their menus, 1-2-3 lists the full command words. 1-2-3's main command menus is shown in figure 4.1

To display this menu you would press the slash (/) key. In fact, all commands are preceded by a slash in 1-2-3 and are presented in this manner throughout this book.

A second feature of the command menus is illustrated on the third line of the display in figure 4.1. This line contains an explanation of the *Worksheet* menu item on which the command cursor is sitting. In fact as you point to the different items in the command menu by moving the cursor across the list, a new explanation will appear in the third line for each command-menu item. This happens in every command menu.

A third friendly aspect of the command menus relates to how a command is initiated. You can either point to the option you want or enter the first letter of the command name. To point to the command-menu item, use the left and right cursor keys on the right-hand side of the keyboard. When the cursor is positioned at the proper item, hit RETURN. If you move the cursor to the last item in the list, then strike the → key again, the menu cursor will "round the horn" and reappear on the first item in the list. Similarly, if the menu cursor is on the first item in the menu, typing the left arrow will move the cursor to the last option.

Entering the first letter of the command-menu item accomplishes the same thing. For example, to select the */Worksheet Status* command, which informs you of the status of several of 1-2-3's global parameters, you would type / to select the main command menu, followed by W to select *Worksheet*. At this point, another menu appears:

Global Insert Delete Column-width Erase Titles Window Status

From this line, select *Status* by typing S. A menu similar to the figure 4.37 should appear.

If you find that you have made the wrong command selection, you can hit ESC at any time to return to the previous command menu. For instance, if you realize that you should not have entered *Insert* above but *Delete*, press ESC to return to the *Worksheet* menu. You can enter a series of escapes (for example, ESC ESC ESC) to return as far back as you want in the series of command menus, even out of the Menu mode altogether. One alternative to typing ESC repeatedly is to type the CTRL (control) and BREAK keys simultaneously. This will cancel the entire command and return you to the Ready mode.

The first letter of each word in a command name is highlighted in italics throughout this book. This emphasizes that the first letter of the command name can be used to select the command.

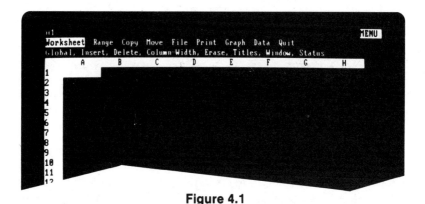

Figure 4.1

The two different methods of selecting commands are just one of the ways that 1-2-3 has successfully oriented itself to both the novice and the experienced user. The novice can point to the different commands and get a full explanation of each one, and the experienced user can enter at high speed a long series of commands using the first-letter convention, without reading the explanations.

If you look back at 1-2-3's main command menu, you will see the wide range of commands offered by 1-2-3. Instead of addressing each command in the order in which it appears in the menu, we have grouped them into several logical divisions. For example, this chapter covers most of 1-2-3's *Worksheet* and *Range* commands (except *Worksheet Format* and *Range Format*, which are discussed in Chapter 5). The graphics commands are covered in Chapter 9. Data commands are explained in Chapter 11, printing in Chapter 8, and file management in Chapter 7.

Range Commands

1-2-3 has a set of commands that operate on ranges. These commands give you the ability to name, erase, format, or protect a range. The command root for the Range commands is /*Range*. When you type /R from the Ready mode, the following menu appears:

Format Label-prefix Erase Name Justify Protect Unprotect Input

The *L*abel-prefix command is covered in Chapter 3 in the "Labels" section. The other range commands are discussed here.

Range Erase

The */R*ange *E*rase command allows you to erase sections of the worksheet. This command can operate on a range as small as a single cell or as large as the entire worksheet.

As an example of this command, suppose you created the simple sheet shown in figure 4.2. Now, suppose you want to erase the range from A1 to C3. To remove this range, issue the command */R*ange *E*rase. 1-2-3 prompts you to supply a range to delete. Either by pointing or by entering the coordinates from the keyboard, you instruct 1-2-3 to erase the range A1..C3. After you type ENTER, 1-2-3 immediately erases the range.

Be Careful! Once you have erased a range, it cannot be recovered except by re-entering all of the data in the range from the keyboard.

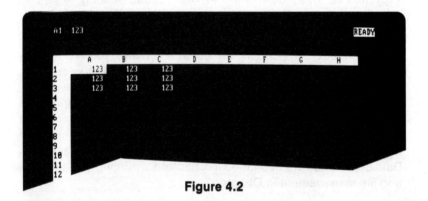

Figure 4.2

Naming Ranges

In 1-2-3, a name can be assigned to a range of cells. Range names can be up to 15 characters long and should be descriptive. The advantage to naming ranges is that range names are easier to understand than cell addresses and allow you to work more intuitively. For example, describing gross margin by the phrase Sales - COGS is more understandable than B = A17 - B10.

Range names are created with the /Range Name Create and /Range Name Label commands. Once names are established, they can be easily applied in both commands and formulas.

Creating Range Names

The /Range Name Create command allows you to specify a name for any range, even one cell. In executing the command, range names are specified by one of two methods: entering the cell addresses or pointing. /Range Name Create can also be used to respecify a range if its location has changed. If minor changes occur to the range, however, such as a column or row of numbers being deleted from the range, 1-2-3 will handle these changes internally without any respecification.

Range names can also be used in naming macros. Although macros are covered in detail in their own chapter, we should note here that macros are named with the same command as any other range.

Range Name Labels

The /Range Name Label command is very similar to /Range Name Create except that the names for ranges are taken directly from adjacent label entries. Figure 4.3 illustrates one example.

If you use the /Range Name Label command and specify that the appropriate name for cell B1 is to the left in cell A1, you can assign the name "Cash" to the range B1. Be careful not to try to do this for

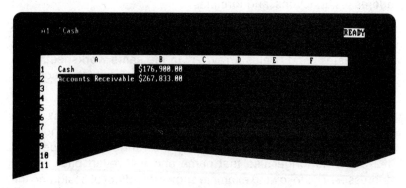

Figure 4.3

"Accounts Receivable" because the label is too long, and there is a space between the words. One alternative would be to change the label as it appears in the worksheet by shortening it and removing the space. Another alternative would be to leave the label as it is and use the /*Range Name Create* command with an appropriate label.

Deleting Range Names

Range names can be deleted individually or all at once. The /*Range Name Delete* command allows you to delete a single range name, and the /*Range Name Reset* command causes all range names to be deleted. Because of its power, the latter command should be used with caution.

Using Range Names

Once range names have been created, they can be useful tools in processing commands and generating formulas. In both cases, whenever a range must be designated, a name can be entered instead. This often eliminates the repetitive task of either entering cell addresses or pointing to cell locations each time a range specification is called for. For example, suppose you had designated a range name "Sales" for the range A5..J5 in one of your worksheets. The simplest way to compute the sum of this range would be the formula @SUM(SALES). Similarly, to determine the maximum value in the range, you could use the formula @MAX(SALES). Range names can always be used in place of cell addresses, functions, and formulas.

Notice that 1-2-3 allows you to use multiple names for the same range. For example, a cell can be given the range names "1978_Sales" and "Sales_Prev_Yr" in the same worksheet. We'll see an application for this trick in Chapter 12, which discusses keyboard macros.

Still another advantage is that once a range name has been established, 1-2-3 will automatically use that name throughout the worksheet in place of cell addresses. If a range name is deleted, 1-2-3 will no longer use that name and will revert back to cell addresses. The following example shows the effect of assigning the name "Revenues" to the range A5..J5.

Prior to Creating Range Name	After Creating Range Name
@SUM(A5..J5)	@SUM(REVENUES)

Examples Using Range Names

The first example, illustrated in figure 4.4, is a simple case of adding two rows of numbers together.

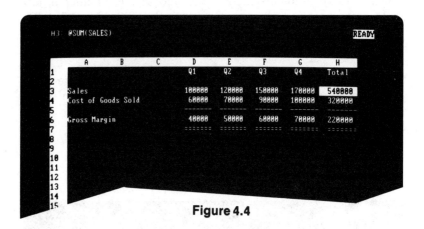

Figure 4.4

If the range name "SALES" is assigned to the range D3..G3 and the name "CGS" to range D4..G4, cell H3 can be defined with the formula

@SUM(SALES)

Similarly, cell H4 can be assigned the formula

@SUM(CGS)

Finally, cell H6 can contain the formula

@SUM(SALES)-@SUM(CGS)

Another example uses names to designate the ranges of cells to be printed or saved. Suppose that you set up special names corresponding to different areas and wanted to print, or save to another worksheet, the corresponding portions of the current worksheet.

When 1-2-3 prompts you for a range, a predefined name can be entered rather than actual cell addresses. For example, in response to the print range prompt, you could enter the range name "Page_1" or the name "Page_5."

A third example using range names involves the F5 (GOTO) key. You will recall that the F5 key allows you to move the cell pointer directly to a cell when you specify the cell's address. Another alternative is to provide a range name instead of a cell address. For example, you could enter "Instruct" in response to "Enter address to go to." If "Instruct" was the range name for a set of cells that included a set of instructions, you might get the results shown in figure 4.5.

Using our example again, suppose that you had assigned the name "CGS" to the range D4..G4. You could erase this portion of the worksheet by typing /Range Erase and entering the range name CGS instead of the cell coordinates D4..G4.

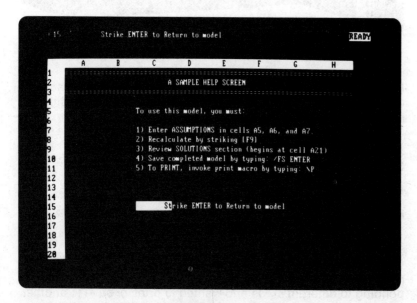

Figure 4.5

To see how this function works, look at the example in figure 4.4. Suppose that after you typed the /Range Erase command, you could not remember the name of the range you wanted to erase. You could type the F3 key to produce a list of the range names in the current worksheet. Figure 4.6 shows the screen at that point. After the list appears, you can use the cursor to point to the first alternative, CGS, and select it by typing ENTER.

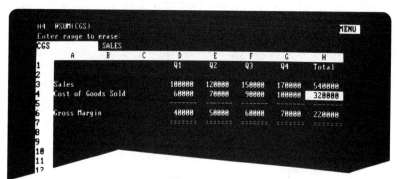

Figure 4.6

Protecting Ranges

1-2-3 has special features that *protect* areas of a worksheet from possible destruction. With a series of commands, you can set up ranges of cells that cannot be changed without special effort. In fact, rows and columns containing protected cells cannot be deleted from the worksheet. These commands are particularly beneficial when you are setting up worksheets in which data will be entered by people who are not familiar with 1-2-3.

When a worksheet is first created, every cell is "protected." However, the global protection command is disabled. This means that each cell has the potential of being protected, but is not at the moment. Lotus uses the analogy that a series of electric fences are set up around all the cells in the worksheet. The "juice" to these fences is turned off when the sheet is first loaded. This means that all the cells in the worksheet can be modified, which is appropriate because you will want to have access to everything in the worksheet at this time. Once you have finished creating the worksheet, however, there may be areas that you do not want modified, or you may want to set up special form-entry areas and not allow cursor movement anywhere else.

To accomplish either of these tasks, you must first enable global protection. This is accomplished with the /Worksheet Global Protection Enable command. Once this command is issued, all of the cells in the worksheet are protected. To continue the analogy, this command is like the switch that activates all of the electric fences in the worksheet. Now you can selectively unprotect certain ranges with the /Range Unprotect command. To use Lotus Development's analogy once again, you tear down the fences that surround these cells. You can, of course, reprotect these cells at any time by issuing the /Range Protect command.

Suppose that you created a worksheet which included a number of long and important formulas. You might want to protect these formulas against accidental deletion by using 1-2-3's protection capability. But what if you need to make a change in several of these formulas? You could move around the sheet, Unprotecting cells, changing the formulas, then Protecting the cells again. You could also, however, simply use the Global Protection Disable command to "lower the fences" around all of the cells. After you made the necessary changes, the Protection Enable command would restore the protection to all the cells.

For even more protection, you can limit the movement of the cursor by using the /Range Input command. This command will allow movement to only /Range Unprotected cells and must be used when you set up the special form-entry areas mentioned above.

For example, suppose you created the simple worksheet in figure 4.7. Notice that most of the cells in the sheet are displayed in half-intensity, which indicates that they are protected. In fact, every cell in the sheet is protected except cells E4, E6, and E8.

Now suppose that you issue the /Range Input command. 1-2-3 will prompt you to supply a data input range. In our example, this could be the range A1..F20, or the range E1..E8. The exact size of the range doesn't matter, as long as the range includes all of the unprotected

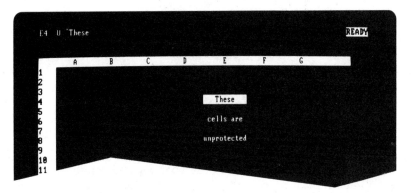

Figure 4.7

cells. After the range is specified, the cursor will immediately jump to cell E4 and wait for you to enter a number or label. Don't use ENTER to terminate the input; use one of the arrow keys. In the example, you might use the down arrow. Notice that the cursor jumps to cell E6. Once again, you will want to make a cell entry and use an arrow key to move on.

The /RI command will remain in effect until you strike either the ENTER key or the ESC key. When you do, the cursor will return to the upper left corner of the input range.

The / Range Input command can be used to automate the process of entering data in the worksheet. This command can be included in a keyboard macro that will automatically execute when a model is loaded into the worksheet. Such a macro would allow a 1-2-3 novice to enter information into the sheet with no risk of erasing or overwriting important information.

Cutting and Pasting

In the days of manual spreadsheets, the process of moving data around on the page was called *cutting and pasting* because it was accomplished with scissors and glue. 1-2-3 contains several commands that accomplish the same thing automatically.

1-2-3 gives you almost complete control over the appearance of worksheets by allowing you to rearrange items in almost any manner. There are three cut-and-paste commands: one that enters blank rows and columns in the worksheet, one that deletes rows and columns, and one that moves the contents of cells. We will show you how to cut and paste a worksheet using these techniques.

Moving Cell Contents

The command used to move cell contents is / Move. It allows you to move ranges of cells from one part of the worksheet to another.

For example, suppose that you created the sample sheet shown in figure 4.8. Suppose further that you want to move the contents of range C1..D3 to the range E1..F3. After you enter / Move, 1-2-3 will respond with the message "Enter range to move FROM." You will notice that a range is already specified after this message. If the cursor was at cell D7 when you started, the range specified is D7..D7. 1-2-3 always tries to stay one step ahead in helping you designate ranges. To enter the appropriate range, start typing. The D7..D7 will immediately disappear. As you type, the characters will appear where the D7..D7 was. To designate the proper FROM range for our example, enter C1..D3, followed by ENTER.

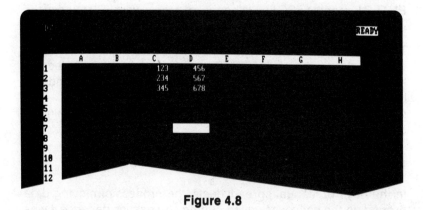

Figure 4.8

1-2-3 will then ask you to "Enter the range to move TO." Again, a range is already specified for you, and just as before, it corresponds to the address of the cell where the pointer was when you initiated the command.

Just as before, D7..D7 will appear. To enter your own range, start typing again. For the TO range, you can specify just the single cell E1. 1-2-3 is smart enough to know that E1..F3 is implied and will use that range. As soon as you finish designating the TO range and hit ENTER, the pointer will return immediately to where it was when you initiated the command. Figure 4.9 shows the results of the / Move operation.

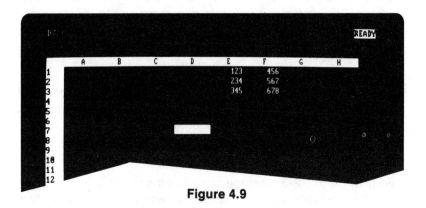

Figure 4.9

One of the points of this example is that you don't have to have the cursor at the beginning of the TO or FROM ranges when you initiate a command. You can designate a range while the cursor is positioned anywhere on the sheet.

Points to Remember

As with the / Worksheet Insert and / Worksheet Delete commands, all the formulas involved in a Move operation are updated automatically. For example, suppose that you defined a simple three-cell worksheet that contained the following data:

    A1 = +D1*100
    C1 = 15
    D1 = +C1

Now, suppose that you / Move the contents of cell D1 to cell E1. The formulas would be altered to the following:

```
A1 = +E1*100
C1 = 15
E1 = +C1
```

As with the / Copy command, you must be careful about the finality of the / Move command. When you move a range of cells, the TO range is completely overwritten by the FROM range, and the previous contents of those cells are lost forever. If there are other cells whose formulas depend on the cell addresses of the lost cells, the other cells will be given the value ERR instead of the cell address. For example, if you add one more cell to the example above:

```
E2 = +E1
```

and repeat the move operation (/ Move D1 E1) the value of cell E2 will change from 0 to ERR, and the contents of that cell will become +ERR. The cell E2 once referred to, E1, has been removed and replaced as a result of the Move operation.

To VisiCalc Users

Two features of 1-2-3's method of moving the contents of cells differ from the methods used in earlier spreadsheet programs like VisiCalc. First, in VisiCalc you can move only one column or row of cells at a time. VisiCalc cannot operate on rectangular ranges. 1-2-3's ability to move rectangular blocks is a major improvement over VisiCalc.

On the other hand, when you do move rows or columns in VisiCalc, the contents of the target area are automatically shifted to make room for the incoming lines or columns. 1-2-3 overwrites the target area. To duplicate VisiCalc's / M command in 1-2-3, you would have to insert blank rows or columns in the target range before moving a range of cells. If you are an experienced VisiCalc user, be sure to remember this difference between the programs.

Pointing to Cells - The Expanding Cursor

The unique pointing capabilities of 1-2-3 can also be used to specify a range, as mentioned above. This method is somewhat similar to menu pointing, but you will find that it has a character all its own.

Suppose that you want to shift the contents of the range C1..D3 to E1..F3, but this time you don't want to enter the cell addresses from the keyboard. We will assume that the cursor was positioned in cell D7 before you initiated the command. When 1-2-3 asks for the FROM range, press ESC.

ESC is used because cell D7 has been automatically "anchored" for you by 1-2-3. This means that 1-2-3 has automatically designated D7 as one corner of the FROM range. If you do not press ESC and move the cursor, you will see the reverse video field begin to expand starting at cell D7. Because you do not want to have cell D7 as one corner of the range, press ESC.

You can also anchor cells yourself by entering a period (.) when you are entering a range. Because you *do* want C1 to be one corner of the FROM range, move the cursor up to this cell. As you move the cursor upward from cell to cell, you will see the address designation in the command field change. When you arrive at cell C1, press (.) to anchor it.

From this point on, cell C1 is referred to as the *anchor* cell, and the cell diagonally opposite the anchored cell as the *free* cell. The free cell has the blinking underscore character in the middle of it. At this point, cell C1 is both the anchor and the free cell. As you move the cursor down to cell E3 to point to the other corner of the range, however, you will see the reverse video field expand as you shift the free cell. You will also see the second part of the range designation change as you move from cell to cell. For example, C1..D1 will appear when the cursor is at cell D1.

When you reach cell E1 from cell C1, start moving over to cell E3. Now you will see the cursor expand in a columnar fashion. When you reach cell E3, lock in the range by hitting ENTER. The designation of the FROM range will appear, as though you entered it from the keyboard.

The process is very similar for designating the TO range. Once you have specified the FROM range, the cursor will automatically return to cell D7. Again, you press ESC so that you are no longer anchored to cell D7. You then move the cursor over to E1 and hit RETURN. You can designate the TO range by pointing to the entire range, but remember that 1-2-3 knows what you are implying when you enter just E1.

The ESC key can also be used when you are in a command, but a cell has not been anchored. Pressing this key will return you to the previous command step. If you are in the middle of a formula, pressing the ESC key will erase the cell address from the end of the formula and return the cursor to the current cell.

The BACKSPACE key can also be used in pointing to ranges. Pressing BACKSPACE will cancel the range specification, whether or not a cell has been anchored, and return the cell pointer to where you began the command or formula. The BACKSPACE key is slightly more powerful than the ESC key in returning you to where you started from when you began entering a command or formula.

Using the END Key to Point

1-2-3's implementation of the END key makes the job of pointing to large ranges much simpler than in older spreadsheets. For example, suppose that you want to move the contents of the range A1..C5 to the range that begins at cell A7. By now, the /Move command should be familiar enough. But the use of the END key to point to the range is not. When the range prompt A1..A1 appears, type the END key followed by →. The cursor will jump to cell A5, and the prompt will read A1..A5. Now, move the cursor by typing END ↓. The prompt will now read A1..C5.

The END key can really speed up the process of pointing out ranges. Using the END key, we were able to define the range in our example with only four keystrokes. If we had used the two arrow keys instead of the END key, the process would have taken seven keystrokes. The difference becomes even more dramatic when you work with larger ranges.

The END key can even be used in some situations where it appears to be of little value. For example, figure 4.10 shows a worksheet consisting of two rows of information: one continuous and one broken. Suppose you want to erase the contents of the broken row. To do this, issue the /Range Erase command. 1-2-3 then prompts you for a range to delete. You can, at this point, enter the range by either typing the coordinates or pointing with the cursor. If you point, you may want to try using the END key; but because the range is not continuous, the END key will not easily move you from

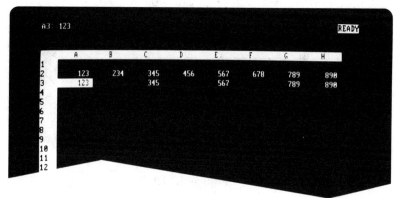

Figure 4.10

one end of the range to the other. Try this trick. When you specify the range, first move the cursor *up* one row to cell A2; use END→ to move the cursor to the end of the range; then move the cursor down one row. Presto! The correct range has been specified. Figure 4.11 shows this process. Although this technique appears to waste keystrokes, it is actually *much* more convenient that simply using the → to point. You should use this technique as often as possible when you define ranges.

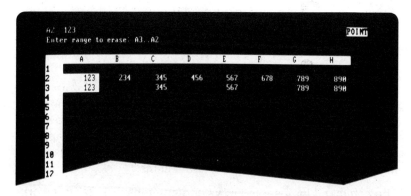

Figure 4.11A

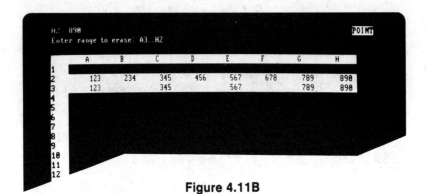

Figure 4.11B

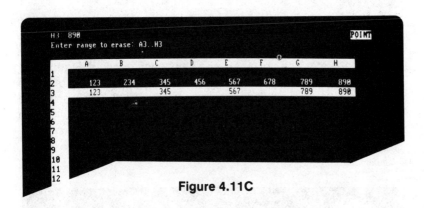

Figure 4.11C

Inserting Blank Rows and Columns

Suppose that you have finished building a model in a worksheet, but want to dress up its general appearance before you show it to anyone. One of the techniques for improving a worksheet's appearance is to insert blank rows and columns in strategic places to highlight headings and other important items.

The command for inserting rows and columns in 1-2-3 is / Work-sheet Insert. You can insert multiple rows and columns each time you invoke this command. After you enter / Worksheet Insert, you are asked for the method of insertion, Row or Column. After you have selected one or the other, you are asked for an Insert Range. Depending on how you set up this range, you will get one or more columns or rows inserted.

Inserted columns appear to the left of the specified range, and inserted rows appear above the specified range. For example, suppose you created the worksheet shown in figure 4.12. If you issue the / Worksheet Insert Column command and specify an insert range of A10..A10, you will get a single blank column inserted to the

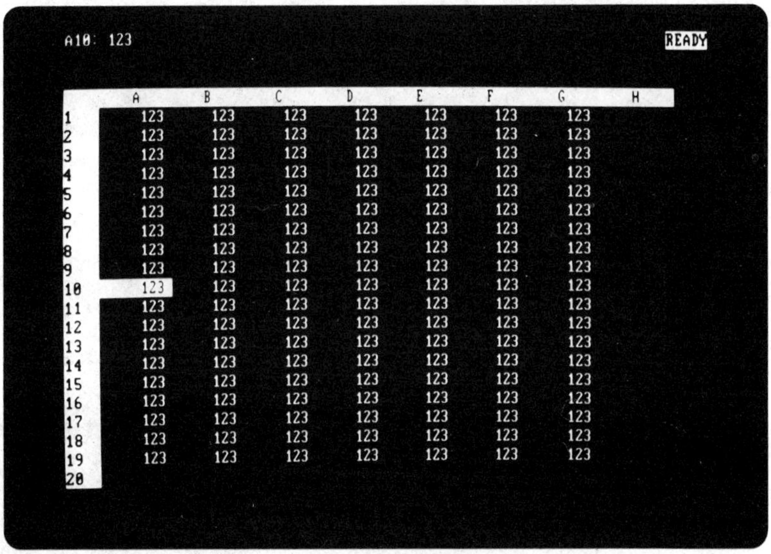

Figure 4.12

left of the values in column A, as shown in figure 4.13. 1-2-3 automatically shifts everything over one column and modifies all the cell formulas for the change. If you then repeat the command, but specify the Row option and a range of A10..A10, 1-2-3 will insert one blank row below row 9. Figure 4.14 illustrates the results of that operation.

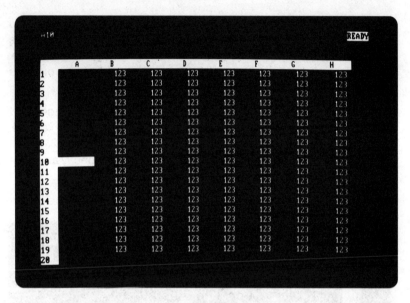

Figure 4.13

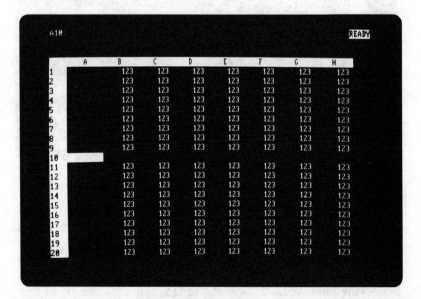

Figure 4.14

Earlier spreadsheet programs, such as VisiCalc, allow you to insert only one column or row at a time. This can be very time consuming, especially when you want to rearrange a spreadsheet completely. With 1-2-3, it is possible to insert more than one row or column.

On the other hand, 1-2-3 does not have one feature that is available in its competitor Multiplan: the ability to delete partial rows and columns and have the worksheet automatically readjust itself. This feature can be very helpful in cutting and pasting.

Deleting Rows and Columns

Deleting rows and columns is the opposite of inserting them. 1-2-3 allows you to delete multiple rows or columns at the same time with the / Worksheet Delete command. After you choose this command, you then choose Columns or Rows from the submenu that appears on the screen. If you choose Rows, 1-2-3 asks you to specify a range of cells to be deleted. Just as for the / Worksheet Insert command, the range you specify includes one cell from a given row.

For example, to delete rows 2 and 3 in the worksheet in figure 4.15, you should specify A2..A3. Other acceptable range designations are B2..B3, C2..C3, C2..G3, etc. The results of the deletion are shown in figure 4.16.

The easiest way to designate the range to be deleted is by pointing to the appropriate cells. You can also enter the cell addresses from the keyboard. However, pointing to cells helps you avoid inadvertently choosing the wrong range. Remember that when you use the / Worksheet Delete command, the rows or columns you delete are gone for good. This includes all the cells in the rows or columns, not just the range of cells you specify. You may be able to get the values back if you have previously saved a copy of the model on disk. If this is not the case, however, the rows and columns are lost.

Notice that the worksheet in figure 4.16 is automatically readjusted so that all the contents below row 3 are shifted up. In addition, all the formulas, command ranges, and named ranges are adjusted for the deletion. Formulas that contain references to the deleted cells are given the value ERR.

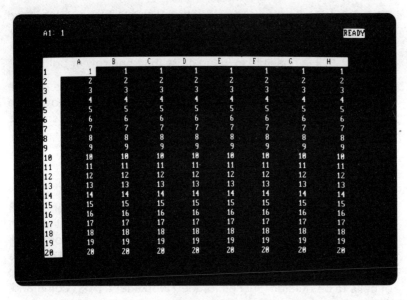

Figure 4.15

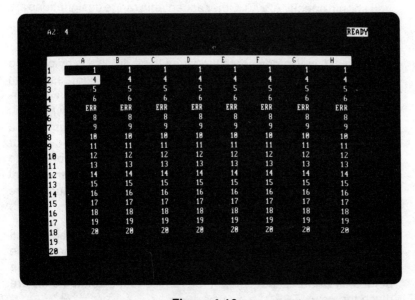

Figure 4.16

The process to delete one or more columns is very similar to that discussed above for rows. After you select the *Columns* option from the */WD* submenu, specify a range that corresponds to one or more cells in each column to be deleted. For example, suppose you wanted to delete column B in figure 4.17. A suitable range to designate for the */WD* command is B1..B1. Again, pointing is the best way to designate the range so that you avoid selecting the wrong column. Figure 4.18 shows the worksheet after column B is deleted.

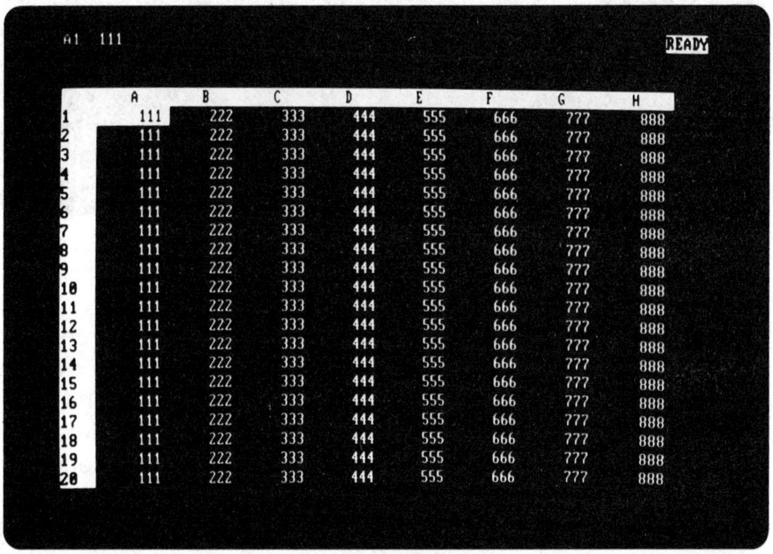

Figure 4.17

The / *Worksheet Delete* command is very different from the / *Range Erase* command. This difference is best explained by using the analogy of a paper spreadsheet. The manual equivalent of the / *Worksheet Delete* command is to use scissors to cut the columnar sheet apart and remove the unwanted columns and/or rows. Then the sheet is pasted back together again. The / *Range Erase* command, on the other hand, is like using an eraser to erase ranges of cells in the sheet. Don't forget the difference between these powerful commands.

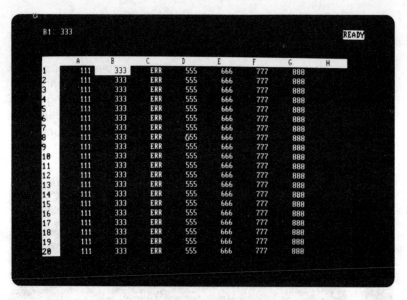

Figure 4.18

In native 1-2-3 terms, there are two differences between deleting cells using /Worksheet Delete and erasing cells using /Range Erase. First, /Worksheet Delete deletes entire columns and rows within a worksheet, whereas /Range Erase erases particular ranges of cells, which may be as small or large as you wish. Second, the worksheet is automatically readjusted to fill in the gaps created by the deleted columns or rows when you use the /WD command. This is not he case, however, for the /Range Erase command. The cells in the range that has been erased are merely blanked.

Copying

There will be many times when you will want to copy the contents of cells to other locations in a worksheet. These times can be broken down into four different categories.

First, you may want to copy from one cell to another. For example, in the worksheet shown in figure 4.19, you might want to copy the contents of cell A1 to cell A2. To do this, you would issue the command /Copy. 1-2-3 would then prompt you to supply a FROM range with the message "Enter range to copy FROM:" Because you want to copy from cell A1, enter A1 in response to this message. (If the cursor were on cell A1, you could also strike ENTER). Next, 1-2-3 will prompt for a TO range with the message "Enter range to copy TO:" Because you want to copy the contents of cell A1 to cell A2, enter A2 as the TO range. Figure 4.20 shows the results of this operation.

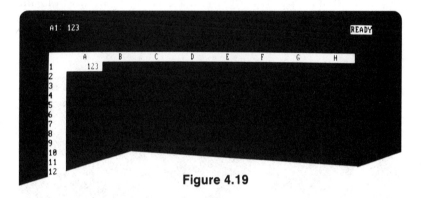

Figure 4.19

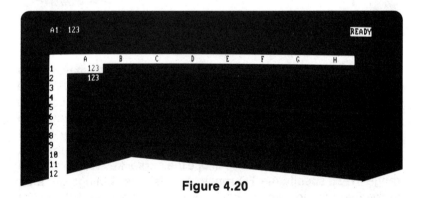

Figure 4.20

The steps required for all copy operations are basically like this simple example: first, issue the / Copy command; second, specify the FROM range; third, specify the TO range. The only things that will change from time to time are the size, shape, and locations of the TO and FROM ranges.

A second type of copy operation would be to copy from one cell to a range of cells. Using the same worksheet shown in figure 4.19, suppose that you want to copy the contents of cell A1 into the range A1..H1. To do this, issue the /Copy command, specify A1 as the FROM range, then specify A1..H1 as the TO range. Remember that you can either type the coordinates of the TO range from the keyboard or point to the range using 1-2-3 Point mode. The results of this copy are shown in figure 4.21.

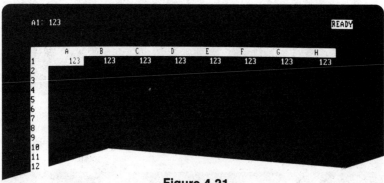

Figure 4.21

The third type of copy is a little more complicated. You may want to copy a range of cells to another place in the worksheet. Using the results of our copy in figure 4.21 as an example, suppose you wanted to copy the range A1..H1 to the range A2..H2. As always, you would begin by issuing the /Copy command. Next, you would specify the FROM range—in this case, A1..H1. Remember that you can either type the coordinates or use the cursor keys to point to the range. Next, specify the TO range. This is where things get a bit tricky. Even though we are copying into the range A2..H2, the TO range in this example would be the single cell A2. The result of this command is shown in figure 4.22.

Although this TO range does not seem to make sense, it really is perfectly logical. Think about it this way. You want to Copy the

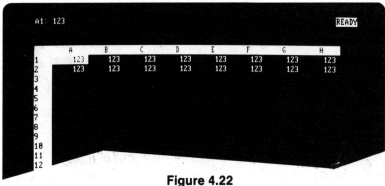

Figure 4.22

eight-cell partial row A2..H2. Because the FROM range is an eight-cell partial row, the TO range must also be an eight-cell partial row. Since the TO range must be an eight-cell partial row, the first cell in that partial row is sufficient to define the range. Given a starting point of A2, the only possible destination for the copy is the range A2..H2. Similarly, specifying the single cell H3 as the TO range would imply a destination of H3..O3. In other words, 1-2-3 is smart enough to deduce the rest of the destination from the single cell provided as the TO range.

The same principle applies to copies of partial columns. For example, looking back at figure 4.20, which shows the results of our first copy example, suppose you wanted to copy the range A1..A2 to the range B1..B2. The first two steps should be familiar by now: issue the /Copy command and specify the FROM range A1..A2. What would the TO range be? Because we want to copy the two-cell partial column A1..A2 into the two-cell partial column B1..B2, we need supply only the starting point of the target—B1—for the TO range to create figure 4.23.

Finally, you may want to copy a range of cells to an even larger range of cells somewhere else in the worksheet. Using figure 4.21 once again as an example, suppose you wanted to copy the range A1..H1 into the rectangular block A2..H20. As before, you would issue the command /Copy and define the FROM range as A1..H1. The TO range would be A2..A20. Figure 4.24 shows the results of this copy.

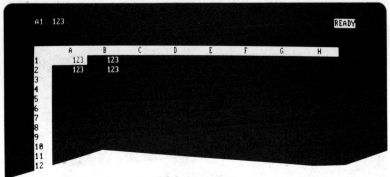

Figure 4.23

You can think of this type of copy as an extension of the previous type. In essence, the copy we made in figure 4.24 could also have been created by repeating the copy command 19 times and specifying 19 different single-row TO ranges. That is, the first TO range would be A2, the second would be A3, the third A4, and so on.

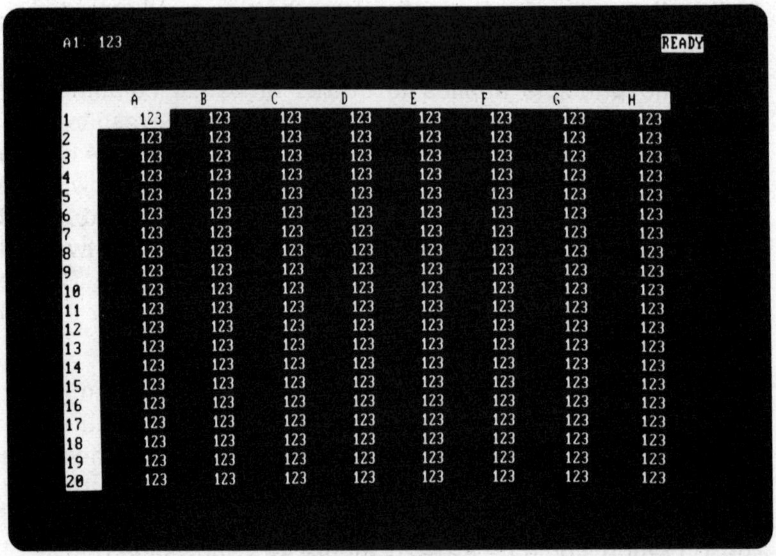

Figure 4.24

The result would be the same using either method, but you can save a lot of time by using the A2..A20 range shown above.

The concept of TO ranges is tricky. The best way to learn about the affects of different TO and FROM ranges is to experiment on your own. After awhile, the rules of copying will be old hat.

Relative vs. Absolute Addressing

Two different methods of addressing cells can be used in replication: *relative* and *absolute*. As mentioned earlier, these two methods are also important in building formulas. In fact, it is very difficult to talk about the two methods of addressing without treating both topics at once.

Relative Addressing

As an example of relative cell addressing, suppose that you want to sum the contents of several columns of cells, but you don't want to enter the @SUM function over and over again. Figure 4.25 shows a sample worksheet with five columns of numbers. Only column C has been summed, using the formula @SUM(C3..C7) in cell C8.

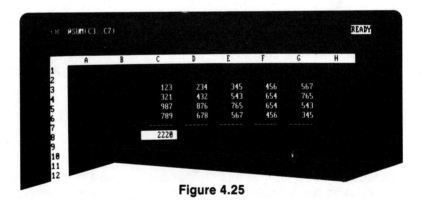

Figure 4.25

We want to add the contents of the cells in columns D, E, F, and G in the same manner that the contents of the cells in column C were added. To do this, we use the /Copy command, which is the command for replicating cells in 1-2-3.

To initiate the command, Copy is chosen from the main command menu. 1-2-3 then asks for a range of cells to copy FROM, and we enter C8 for the range, followed by RETURN. Next, 1-2-3 asks for a range of cells to copy TO. Here we enter D8..G8 by either pointing or entering the cell addresses. When we hit RETURN, 1-2-3 will replicate the @SUM formula in cell C8 to the other cells, as shown in figure 4.26.

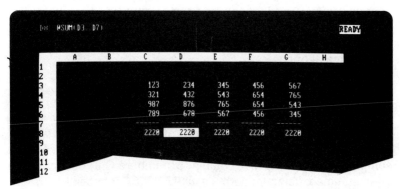

Figure 4.26

If you look at the formula in the first line of the control panel, you will see that the formula contains the proper cell addresses for adding the cells in column D and not column C, just as it should. 1-2-3 was smart enough to know that we actually meant the *relative* addresses of the cells in column B and not their *absolute* addresses.

Absolute and Mixed Addressing

In some cases, a formula has an important address that can't be changed as the formula is copied. In 1-2-3, you can create an address that will not change at all as it is copied. This is called an absolute address. You can also create an address that will some-times change, depending on the direction of the copy. This is called a *mixed* address. The following examples will help to make the concepts of absolute and mixed addresses clear.

Mixed Cell Addressing

Mixed cell addressing refers to a combination of relative and absolute addressing. Because a cell address has two components—a row and a column—it is possible to fix (make absolute) either portion while leaving the other unfixed (relative). The best way to convey its meaning is to use an example.

Suppose that you want to do a projection of monthly sales in dollars of Product 1. In the first pass, you want to use a specific retail price, average discount rate, and unit volume for the projection, but later you will want to change these parameters to see what happens. Figure 4.27 shows how you might set up the projection.

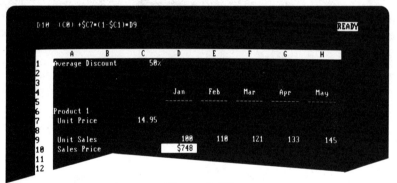

Figure 4.27

Notice the dollar signs in the formula for cell D10 in the first line of the control panel. The dollar signs signal 1-2-3 to use absolute addressing on the column portion of the addresses. Because there are no dollar signs in front of the row portion of the addresses, 1-2-3 will use relative addressing there.

To see the importance of this type of referencing, let's / Copy the contents of cell D10 into the range E10..H10. As before, we first issue the / Copy command and designate the FROM range (D10) and the TO range (E10..H10). Figure 4.28 shows the results of the command.

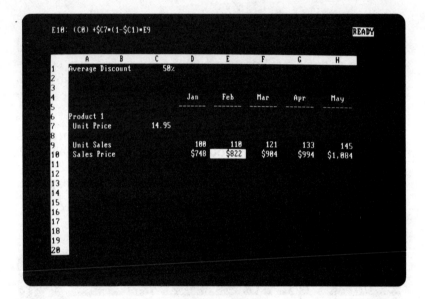

Figure 4.28

Compare the formula in cell E10 with the original formula in cell D10:

    E10 = +$C7*(1-$C1)*E9
    D10 = +$C7*(1-$C1)*D9

Notice that the formulas are identical except for the last term. 1-2-3 has held the addresses for C7 and C1 constant. Only the reference to cell D9 has been altered. In essence, this formula says, Using a constant price (C7) and a constant discount (C1), compute the dollar sales for Product 1 at each month's sales volume (D9..H9).

Now suppose that you wanted to create a projection for a second product. You would duplicate the labels in column A and change the product name to Product 2. Finally, you would copy the contents of the range C7..H10 to the range C14..H17. Figure 4.29 shows the results of the copy operation.

Notice that the numbers in row 17 are not correct. Despite assigning the same price and unit sales volumes to Product 2, that product is

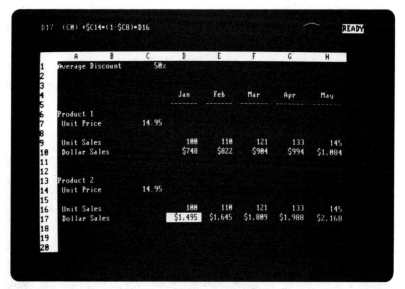

Figure 4.29

showing monthly dollar sales double those for Product 1. To figure out why, look at the formula in cell D17:

+$C14*(1-$C8)*D16

The references to cell C14 and cell D16 are correct—these cells contain the unit price and unit sales for Product 2. But notice that the reference to cell C1 has changed so that it refers to cell C8. This occurred because the row designation in that address—8—was relative and not absolute. When you copied the formulas containing the address $C1 down the worksheet, 1-2-3 assumed you wanted to adjust the row component of the address.

Absolute Addressing

We can correct the problem by changing the reference to cell C1 from a mixed reference to an absolute reference. Going back to the model in figure 4.28, edit cell D10 and change the formula to:

+$C7*(1-$C$1)*D9

The only difference between this formula and its predecessor is the addition of a $ in front of the 1 in the address C1. The added $ changes this address from mixed to absolute.

Now, you must copy the new formula in cell D10 TO the range E10..H10 so that all of the formulas in the row are the same. You can then recopy the area D9..H10 into the range D16..H17. Figure 4.30 illustrates the adjusted worksheet.

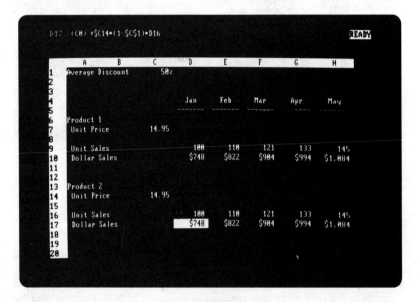

Figure 4.30

Notice that the numbers in cells D17..H17 are now correct. If you look at the formula in cell D17:

   +$C14*(1-$C$1)*D16

you will see that the reference to cell C1 has remained fixed as it was copied.

Notes for VisiCalc Users

To copy cells in 1-2-3 using absolute addressing, you must prepare the cell to be copied prior to initiating the command. That is, you must enter dollar signs in strategic places when the cell is defined. This is one of the ways that 1-2-3's method of replication differs from earlier spreadsheet programs, such as VisiCalc. In VisiCalc, you normally designate the method of addressing, relative or absolute, at the time of the *Replicate* (/R) command.

Earlier spreadsheet programs, such as VisiCalc, do not have mixed cell addressing. To accomplish the replication in figure 4.28 in VisiCalc, you would have to use a hodgepodge of relative and absolute addressing indicators on the end of the replication command and issue the command several times.

Setting Absolute and Relative References

There are two ways that dollar signs can be entered in the formula for cell D10 in the example above. You can type them in as you enter the formula, or you can use the F4 (ABS) key to have 1-2-3 automatically enter the dollar signs for you. One of the limitations of the F4 key is that you must be in the Point mode to use it. As you will recall from the "Formulas" section of Chapter 3, in Point mode you must use the cell pointer to enter addresses.

After typing, pointing, or a combination of the two, suppose that you have the first portion of the formula shown in the control panel of figure 4.27 above, C7. To change this to an absolute address, you would strike the F4 key. The formula in the control panel would change to C7. Striking the F4 key again would shift the address to C$7. A third press of F4 would change the address to $C7, which is the result we want.

Finally, you use the F4 key to make 1-2-3 automatically enter dollar signs into formulas for absolute cell addressing. In the latest version of 1-2-3 (Version 1A), you can use F4 to have 1-2-3 help you enter mixed cell addresses. Here is what happens to a cell address when you press F4 in the Point mode.

First time	C7
Second	$C7
Third	C$7
Fourth	C7

More Examples

A second example of mixed cell addressing appears in figure 4.31. Here we have created a table to explore the effect of different interest rates and years-to-maturity on the present value of an annuity that pays $1,000 a year. (See the @PV built-in function in the Appendix at the back of this book if you don't know what a present value is.) The general format of the function is

@PV(payment,interest,term)

The object of this example is to use a single formula for the entire model and copy it using mixed cell addressing, as shown in figure 4.31.

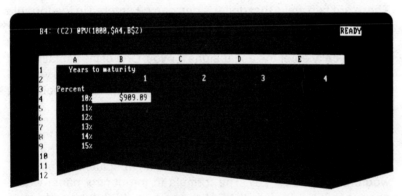

Figure 4.31

Once again, if you look at the command line, you will see the special places where the dollar signs appear. The idea in this example is to use absolute addressing on the column portion of the interest rate address and relative addressing on the row portion ($A4). Conversely, we want to use relative addressing on the column portion of the years-to-maturity address and absolute addressing on the row portion (B$2).

Compare the formula for cell B4 in the control panel in figure 4.31 with the one for cell D8 in figure 4.32. Notice that column A for the interest rate and row 2 for the years-to-maturity have not changed, but the other portions of the addresses have.

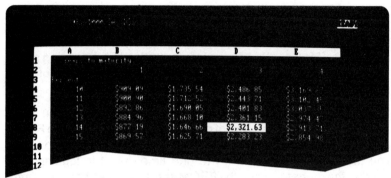

Figure 4.32

A third way mixed cell addressing can be used is to accumulate a running total across a row of numbers. In this example, we will use the formula @SUM(A1..B1) in cell A2 and copy it across cells B2 through F2. In figure 4.33, notice the formula in the first line of the control panel for cell B2 and how the relative address in the formula changes as we copy it.

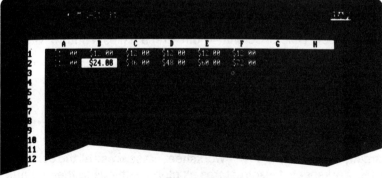

Figure 4.33

The best way to become comfortable with mixed cell addressing is to experiment with it. Try several different examples and see what you come up with.

Miscellaneous Comments on Copying

When you copy a cell, 1-2-3 automatically copies the format of the cell with it. (See Chapter 5 for more information.) This copying saves you from having to preset the format for an entire range of cells before copying to them.

Sometimes the TO and FROM ranges will overlap when you copy. The general rule is if you do not overlap the end points for the FROM and TO ranges, you will be okay. If you do overlap them, however, you may get mixed results. The one time that it is legitimate to overlap the ranges is when the FROM and TO ranges have the same upper-left boundary.

You should also note particularly the finality of the */ Copy* command. If you copy over the contents of a cell, there is no way to retrieve them. Make sure that you have your ranges designated properly before you hit RETURN.

Worksheet Commands

1-2-3 offers a group of commands that are similar to the range commands but affect the entire worksheet. The command root of all these commands is the */ Worksheet* command. After this command is issued, the following menu appears:

Global Insert Delete Column-width Erase Titles Window Status

We've already looked at two of these commands: */ Worksheet Delete* and */ Worksheet Insert*. The rest are explained below.

Worksheet Erase

The */ Worksheet Erase* command is used to clear the entire spreadsheet. Not only does */ Worksheet Erase* erase all the contents of the worksheet, it also restores all global settings to their default condition, destroys any range names or graph names in the worksheet, and clears any title lock or window split in the sheet.

Be sure that you understand the difference between the */ Worksheet Erase* command and the */ Range Erase A1..IV2048* command. The *Range* command will remove the contents of every cell in the sheet, except those that are protected. It will not, however, alter any of the global settings, including column widths or print settings. / Worksheet *Erase*, however, literally restores the 1-2-3 worksheet to its default configuration. After the /WE command is issued, the worksheet is exactly as it was when loaded.

Obviously, the / Worksheet *Erase* command is a very powerful and, potentially, destructive command. For this reason, 1-2-3 will always force you to type a Y, for "Yes, I want to erase the entire worksheet," before it will execute this command. *Be careful!* Once a sheet has been erased in this way, it cannot be recovered. Always save your worksheets before you erase them.

The Global Command

The largest subgroup of commands under the *Worksheet* command is the *Global* command. The / Worksheet *Global* command menu looks like this:

Format Label Prefix Column-width Recalculation Protection Default

We have already covered the *Protection* command in this chapter, and the *Format* command will be considered in the next chapter. Label-prefixes were covered in Chapter 3. The *Default* command controls the default settings used by 1-2-3 for printing and file management. This command is discussed in Chapters 7 and 8. The other *Global* commands are *Column Width* and *Recalculation*.

Recalculation

One of the primary functions of a spreadsheet program is to recalculate all the cells in a worksheet when a value or a formula in one of the cells changes. How this recalculation is actually done says a lot about where a program fits in the evolution of spreadsheet software. 1-2-3 is among the most advanced spreadsheet programs to date in its method of recalculation, as you can see from the following discussion of VisiCalc.

VisiCalc's Recalculation Method

VisiCalc, like most first-generation spreadsheets, gives the option of Column-wise or Row-wise recalculation. In Column-wise recalculation, VisiCalc starts recalculating at the entry in cell A1 and proceeds down column A, then continues at cell B1 and moves down column B, etc. In contrast, Row-wise recalculation starts at cell A1 and proceeds across row 1, then moves down to cell A2 and across row 2, etc. In VisiCalc, you can specify one method or the other.

The problem with these methods of recalculation is that they can often lead to the wrong answer, unless you are very careful about how you set up the worksheet. Among the recalculative errors that can occur with VisiCalc are forward and circular references.

A *forward reference* occurs when a cell refers to another cell that is lower in the worksheet. For example, imagine that you created a sheet with four cells: A1, C1, C2, and C3. Suppose that those cells had the following contents:

    A1 = +C3
    C1 = 100
    C2 = 200
    C3 = +C1+C2

A1 and C3 would both have the value 300. Now, suppose that the number in cell C2 is changed to 100. Let's step through the recalculative process. Because VisiCalc begins recalculating at the upper left corner of the worksheet, cell A1 would be evaluated first. Since the prior value of C3, 300, has not changed, A1 would retain the value 300. VisiCalc would then proceed either column by column or row by row across the sheet until it came to cell C3. Because the value of cell C2 has changed, the value in C3 would change to 200.

Clearly, it does not make sense to have A1 and C3 contain different values when cell A1 is defined to be equal to C3. Although recalculating the sheet again would eliminate the inequality, it would not remove the basic problem. In large and complex models, it is possible to have undetected forward references.

1-2-3's Natural Recalculation

As you might expect, 1-2-3 can recalculate in a linear fashion just like VisiCalc. To do this, you override the *Natural* default setting using /Worksheet Global Recalculation <Column-wise or Row-wise>. In fact, this method is recommended if you import a VisiCalc file that is built around either method of recalculation.

But 1-2-3 normally recalculates in what Lotus Development calls a *natural order*. This means that all the active cells in a worksheet are interrelated, and that 1-2-3 does not recalculate any given cell until the cells that it depends on have been recalculated first. Because the relationship between cells is rarely linear, the method of recalculation is not linear. Rather, recalculation occurs in a *topological* fashion, starting at the lowest level and working up.

```
                 C3
          B1   B3   B4
       A1   A2   A4   A7   A9
```

With *Natural* recalculation, you no longer have to worry about the order of recalculation and the problem of forward references. If we recreated our forward reference example in 1-2-3 and used natural recalculation, cell C3—the most fundamental cell in the sheet—would be evaluated before cell A1, eliminating the forward reference.

Iteration

In most cases, it takes only one pass to recalculate a worksheet. When a worksheet contains a circular reference, however, this is not possible.

A classic example of a circular reference is when you try to determine the amount of borrowing required by a firm. The thought process involved is

1. Borrowings =Assets - (Total Liabilities + Equity). Borrowings represent the difference between projected asset requirements and the sum of total projected liabilities and equity.

2. But the level of equity is a function of net income and dividends.

3. And net income is a function of gross margin and interest expense.

4. Finally, interest expense and gross margin are a function of borrowings.

You can see the circular pattern. When this kind of circular reference occurs, 1-2-3 displays a CIRC indicator in the lower right-hand corner of the screen. When you recalculate this type of sheet using regular natural calculation, 1-2-3 will not accurately recompute all of the values. Because each value in the circular set depends, directly or indirectly, on all of the others, 1-2-3 cannot find a "toe hold;" that is, it cannot find the most fundamental cell in the worksheet because there is no such cell.

Iterative recalculation allows 1-2-3 to overcome this problem. When 1-2-3 is in the Iterative mode, the sheet will recalculate a specified number of times for each time you strike the CALC (F9) key. Normally, the sheet will only recalculate once for each time the F9 key is struck. The default number of iterations under the Iteration mode is 20, but you can alter this number as you see fit. If you have circular references in your sheet, however, we suggest that you keep the number of recalculation passes high.

Iterative recalculation overcomes a circular reference because each recalculative pass through the sheet causes the actual values of the cells to approach more closely their correct values. For example, suppose you built a sheet with the following set of relationships:

A3 = .05*A5
A4 = 100
A5 = A3+A4

When you first enter this formula, A3 has a value of 0, A4 equals 100, and A5 equals 100. Assume that the number of iterations is set to 5. Table 4.1 shows the values of each cell after each recalculative pass.

Table 4.1

	A3	A4	A5
1	5	100	105
2	5.25	100	105.25
3	5.263	100	105.263
4	5.2632	100	105.2632
5	5.26316	100	105.26316

Notice that on each pass, the difference between the prior and the current value of cells A3 and A4 becomes smaller. After only five passes, the difference is so small as to be insignificant. After 20 passes, the difference would probably be too small for 1-2-3 to recognize. At that point, the problem with the circular reference is eliminated.

Two things should be noted about iterative recalculation. First, it is possible to create a set of circular references that is too complicated for 1-2-3 to sort out in twenty passes. If this happens with one of your models, simply recalculate it *twice*, using twenty iterations each time. This process is identical to setting the iteration count to 40 (if that were possible). Second, remember that 20 calculations of a large sheet take a long time. Be patient; control over 1-2-3 will be returned to you soon enough.

Automatic vs. Manual Recalculation

When you are working on a large worksheet that involves many formulas, it may take some time for the worksheet to recalculate. This occurs each time a new entry is made or a value is changed. One way to get around this problem is to change from the standard *Automatic* to *Manual* recalculation.

With *Manual* recalculation, you can control 1-2-3 so that it recalculates only when you press the F9 (CALC) key. This is an advantage only with large worksheets where you are changing a lot of values. Otherwise, 1-2-3 is fast enough that recalculation occurs almost instantly.

Column Width Control

One of the problems in earlier spreadsheet programs was that the widths of worksheet columns could be controlled only as a group. If you were setting up a projection of expenses for the next five years and wanted to display the full descriptions of the expense items (some of them 20 characters), you would have to set all the columns to a width of 20 characters. To avoid that situation, you would have to abbreviate or truncate the labels.

In 1-2-3, you don't have this problem. You can control separately the width of each column. You can set the first column of your projection of expenses to be 20 characters wide and the rest to whatever you wish.

The command used to set individual column widths is / *Worksheet Column-width Set.* You can set one column width at a time by either entering a number or using the ← and → cursor keys followed by ENTER. The advantage of the ← and → cursor keys is that the column width actually expands and contracts each time you press them. To get a good idea of what the width requirements are, experiment when you enter the command.

There are two things to remember about this command. First, you must locate the pointer in the proper column before you initiate the command. Otherwise, you will have to start over. Second, to reset the column width to the standard setting, you must use the / *Worksheet Column-width Reset* command.

As in earlier spreadsheet programs, you can control all of the column widths at once. The command to do this is / *Worksheet Global Column-width.* The standard setting for column widths is 9, but you can change this to whatever width you want for the current worksheet.

Any column width set previously by the / *Worksheet Column-width Set* command will not be affected by a change in the global setting. For example, if you set the width of column A to 12 using the / *Worksheet Column-width Set* command, then change all the columns in the worksheet to a width of 5 using the / *Worksheet Global Column-width* command, every column except A will change to 5. A will remain at a width of 12 and will have to be reset to 5 with the / *Worksheet Column-width Set* command.

Splitting the Screen

One of the features of 1-2-3 is that you can split the screen into two parts, either horizontally or vertically. Suppose that you are working on a very large model which spans several columns and are having trouble keeping track of the effect the changes you are making in one area of the worksheet are having on another. By splitting the screen, you can make the changes in one area and immediately see their effect in the other.

The command for splitting the screen is / Worksheet Window. When you enter this command, the following menu choices appear:

Horizontal   Vertical   Sync   Unsync   Clear

Horizontal and Vertical split the screen in the manner their names indicate. Depending on where you have the cursor positioned when you enter Horizontal or Vertical, the screen will split at that point. In other words, you don't have to split the screen exactly in half. Remember that the dividing line will require either one row or one column, depending on how you split the screen.

After you split the screen using Horizontal, the cursor appears in the top window. When a Vertical division is created, the cursor appears in the left window. To jump the division between the windows, use the F6 (Window) key.

The Sync and Unsync options work as a pair. In Synchronized screens, when you scroll one screen, the other one scrolls automatically along with it. When screens are Synchronized, horizontal split screens always keep the same columns in view, and vertical split screens always keep the same rows. This is the standard default for 1-2-3.

Unsynchronized screens allow you to control one screen independently of the other in all directions. In fact, you can even show the same cells in the two different windows.

With Unsynchronized screens, you can also independently control the formats of cells in the screens. For example, you can use Unsync to display numbers on one screen and the formulas behind the numbers on another.

The Clear option removes the split window option and reverts the screen back to a single window. When you use this option, the single window takes on the settings of the top or left-hand window, depending on how the screen was split.

Titles

The / Worksheet Titles command is similar to the / Worksheet Window command. Like the / Worksheet Window command, the / Worksheet Titles command allows you to see one area of a worksheet while working on another. However, the unique function of this command is that it freezes all the cells to the left and/or above the current cell pointer position so that they cannot move off the screen.

A classic example of the advantage of this option is when you are entering the items on a pro forma Balance Sheet and Income Statement. Suppose that you are trying to set up a budget to project the level of the financial statement items month by month for the next year. Because the normal screen, without any special column widths, shows 20 rows by 7 columns, you will undoubtedly have to shift the screen so that cell A1 is no longer in the upper left-hand corner. In fact, if you enter the month headings across row 1 and the Balance Sheet and Income Statement headings down column A, as shown in figure 4.34, you have to scroll the screen several different times in order to enter all the items.

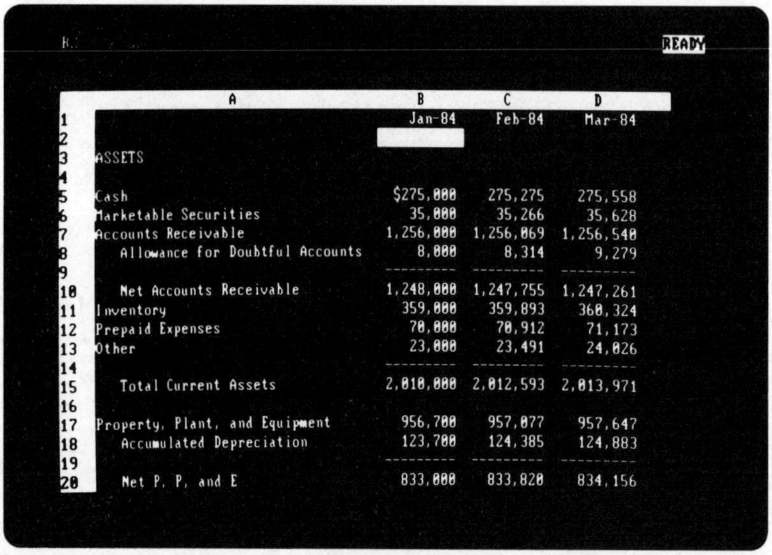

READY

	A	B	C	D
1		Jan-84	Feb-84	Mar-84
2				
3	ASSETS			
4				
5	Cash	$275,000	275,275	275,558
6	Marketable Securities	35,000	35,266	35,628
7	Accounts Receivable	1,256,000	1,256,069	1,256,540
8	Allowance for Doubtful Accounts	8,000	8,314	9,279
9		---------	---------	---------
10	Net Accounts Receivable	1,248,000	1,247,755	1,247,261
11	Inventory	359,000	359,893	360,324
12	Prepaid Expenses	70,000	70,912	71,173
13	Other	23,000	23,491	24,026
14		---------	---------	---------
15	Total Current Assets	2,010,000	2,012,593	2,013,971
16				
17	Property, Plant, and Equipment	956,700	957,077	957,647
18	Accumulated Depreciation	123,700	124,385	124,883
19		---------	---------	---------
20	Net P, P, and E	833,000	833,820	834,156

Figure 4.34

To keep the headings in view on the screen, even when you scroll the screen, enter */WT* when the cursor is in cell B2. When you enter the */WT* command, the following menu items appear:

Horizontal   Vertical   Both   Clear

If you select *Horizontal*, the rows on the screen above the cell pointer become frozen. That is, they don't move off the screen when you scroll up and down. If you select *Vertical*, the columns to the left of the cell pointer are frozen and move only when you scroll up and down (but not when you move left and right). *Both* freezes the rows above and the columns to the left of the cell pointer. *Clear* unlocks the previously set Worksheet Titles.

In our pro forma example, we have selected the *Both* option. In this case, when you scroll right and left as well as up and down, the headings always remain in view. Figure 4.35 shows two examples of how this works.

When you freeze rows or columns, you cannot move the cursor into the frozen area. In our example, if you tried to move the cursor into cell A2 from cell B2, 1-2-3 would beep and not allow the cursor to move into the protected area. Similarly, using the HOME key will move the cursor to the upper cell in the unlocked area. In our example, this would be cell B2. Normally the HOME function moves the cursor to cell A1.

One exception to this restriction occurs when you use the F5 (GOTO) key. If you use the GOTO function to jump to cell A1, you will see two copies of the title rows and/or columns. Figure 4.36 shows our example when you use the F5 key to go to cell A1. This can be very confusing.

The frozen areas are also accessible when you are in the Point mode. In our example, suppose you wanted to define cell B6 as equal to A1. You would move the cursor to cell B6, type + to begin the formula, then use the cursor keys to point at cell A1. In this case, the cursor is allowed to move into the protected area, and 1-2-3 will not beep.

A Note to VisiCalc Users

VisiCalc's method of creating worksheet titles is slightly different from 1-2-3's. Although the two programs use almost identical command logic for the *Title* command, in VisiCalc, the locked range will include the row and/or column in which the cursor currently resides. In our example, issuing the / *Title Both* command with the cursor in cell B2 would lock both rows 1 and 2 and columns A and B.

H2   READY

A	F	G	H
	May-84	Jun-84	Jul-84
ASSETS			
Cash	276,900	277,828	277,876
Marketable Securities	36,571	36,662	37,069
Accounts Receivable	1,258,317	1,258,475	1,259,361
Allowance for Doubtful Accounts	9,725	10,501	10,941
Net Accounts Receivable	1,248,593	1,247,974	1,248,419
Inventory	360,937	360,962	361,241
Prepaid Expenses	72,677	72,905	73,566
Other	25,215	25,964	26,959
Total Current Assets	2,020,892	2,022,294	2,025,131
Property, Plant, and Equipment	959,505	960,452	960,868
Accumulated Depreciation	125,846	126,171	126,438
Net P. P. and E	834,658	834,782	835,065

Figure 4.35A

B21: (,0) 396000   READY

A	B	C	D
	Jan-84	Feb-84	Mar-84
Investment-Long-term	396,000	396,186	397,107
Total Noncurrent Assets	1,229,000	1,230,006	1,231,263
Total Assets	$3,239,000	$3,242,599	$3,245,234
LIABILITIES			
Notes Payable	$276,000	276,694	277,036
Accounts Payable	378,000	378,616	378,973
Accrued Expenses	98,000	98,822	98,862
Other Liabilities	25,000	25,914	26,119
Total Current Liabilities	777,000	777,778	778,233
Long-Term Debt	333,000	333,009	333,660
STOCKHOLDERS' EQUITY			

Figure 4.35B

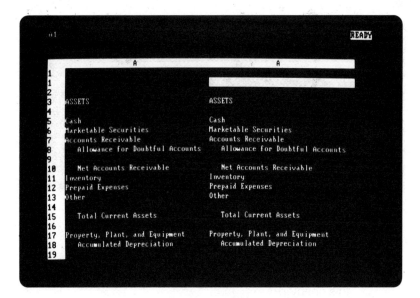

Figure 4.36

If you are a former VisiCalc user, you should practice locking titles with 1-2-3.

The Status of Global Settings

The final option on 1-2-3's main command menu, *Worksheet Status*, checks the status of various spreadsheet options. These options are called *global settings*. Figure 4.37 shows an example of what is displayed.

The information in figure 4.37 indicates that the following */Work-sheet Global* settings are active:

1. *Recalculation* is *Automatic*. This is the normal default setting (covered in the "Recalculation" section of this chapter).

2. The *Global Format* is *General*. Again, this is the default setting (covered in the next chapter).

3. The *Global Label-Prefix* is (') for left-justification. (Label prefixes were covered in Chapter 3.)

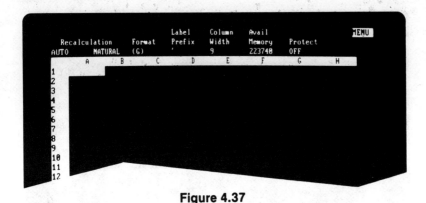

Figure 4.37

4. The *Global Column*-width is 9 characters (covered in this chapter).

5. *Global Protection* is off. (This is covered in the "Ranges" section of this chapter.)

This command gives you an easy way to check the settings without having to experiment to find out what they are.

Conclusion

This chapter showed you the basic 1-2-3 commands. You learned about several of 1-2-3's most important commands, including those that deal with ranges and worksheets. Now that you have acquired the fundamentals, you are ready to go on to more 1-2-3 commands. The next chapter extends the discussion by presenting 1-2-3's formatting commands.

5
Formats

One of the ways that 1-2-3 surpasses earlier spreadsheet programs like VisiCalc is by offering you more cell *formats* to choose from. Formats control how cell contents are displayed on the screen. 1-2-3 offers some cell formats that earlier spreadsheet programs do not:

> *Fixed*
> *, (comma)*
> *Percent*
> *Text*
> *Date*

Many of these formats will seem familiar to those who have used other spreadsheet programs. However, you will find several subtle variations.

Command Roots for Controlling Formats

The command roots for controlling formats are */Worksheet Global Format* and */Range Format*. The former controls the format of all the cells in the worksheet, and the latter controls specific ranges within the worksheet.

Generally, you will use the */Worksheet Global Format* command when you are just starting to enter a worksheet. You will want to choose what format the majority of cells will take. Once you have set all the cells to that format, you can use the /Range Format command to override the global format setting for specific cell ranges.

The /Range Format command has precedence over the /Worksheet Global Format command. This means that whenever you change the Global Format, all the numbers and formulas affected will change automatically unless they were previously formatted with the /Range Format command.

In addition, only labels entered after a format change, either Global- or Range-specific, will be affected by that change. As you may recall, the way labels are displayed is determined by label prefixes. When a format is changed, previously entered label prefixes do not change unless you use the /Range Label-Prefix command. Labels are, therefore, slightly different from numbers and formulas when you change their format.

When a command root is entered, a common menu appearswith the following entries:

Fixed Scientific Currency , General +/- Percent Date Text

General

The General format is the only format that is common to 1-2-3 and earlier programs in a very pure sense. Other formats have attributes that make them unique to 1-2-3.

When numbers are displayed in the General format, insignificant zeros to the right of the decimal point are suppressed. If numbers are too large or too small to be displayed normally, scientific notation is used. Some examples of this format for numbers are shown below:

    123.456
    5.63E+14
    -22.1
    1.9E-09

Labels are displayed as left-justified in the General format. They are preceded by a single quotation mark that signals 1-2-3 to left-justify. As mentioned earlier, you can use the /Worksheet Global Label-Prefix or the /Range Label-Prefix command to change the default of left-justification.

General is the default setting for *Global Format*. You can check the default setting by entering */Worksheet Status*. (This command is explained in Chapter 4.)

Currency

The *Currency* format may look familiar to spreadsheet users, but it has changed significantly in the transition from earlier programs to 1-2-3.

The differences between the 1-2-3 *Currency* format and those of other programs are that in 1-2-3 a dollar sign appears in the same cell before each entry and commas separate hundreds from thousands, thousands from millions, etc. Another major change is that negative values appear in parentheses (). This format also gives you the option of controlling the number of places to the right of the decimal point. This feature is helpful if you are having trouble getting values displayed because they are a little too large for the column width. One solution is to override the default of two places to the right of the decimal point.

If the value you want to display in the *Currency* format is too large for the column width, a series of asterisks will appear across the cell instead of the value. In fact, this is true for all formats. The problem of space is particularly acute with this format because the dollar sign and commas take up quite a bit of space. The best way to handle this situation is to experiment with the formatting parameters and the column width until you get the appearance you want.

You will recall that column width is controlled through either the */Worksheet Column-width* or */Worksheet Global Column-width* command. The former controls specific columns in the worksheet, and the latter controls all the columns at the same time.

When numbers appear in the command line after they are entered, they are preceded by the format indicator for *Currency*. In fact, all number formats other then *General* display format indicators in the command line. You do not have to enter them yourself; 1-2-3 automatically provides them based on the number of decimal places you have specified.

The format indicator for *Currency* is "C," followed by an integer to indicate the number of decimal places you have chosen, all in parentheses. Below are some examples of how numbers appear in the command line after you have entered them, and how they are displayed in the worksheet with the *Currency* format.

In the Command Line	In the Worksheet
(C2) 45	$45.00
(C2) 1612.3	$1,612.30
(C3) 22.805	$22.805
(C1) 105.56	$105.6
(C2) -210.99	($210.99)

Cell formats are controlled with the */Worksheet Global Format* or the */Range Format* command, depending on how cell-specific you want the control to be, followed by *Currency* in this case.

Fixed

1-2-3's *Fixed* format is not offered in earlier spreadsheet programs. In some ways, this format is similar to the *General* format in that it does not display commas or dollar signs. The difference is that the *Fixed* format lets you control the number of places to the right of the decimal point. When you select the *Fixed* format, 1-2-3 prompts you for the number of decimal places you want displayed. After you have chosen a number, 1-2-3 will pad the cells you have selected with zeros to the right of the decimal to the number of places you indicated. Conversely, if you decide to display fewer than the number of decimal places you have entered, the number will be rounded to the specified number of places.

Some examples of how numbers appear in the *Fixed* format appear below.

In the Command Line	In the Worksheet
(F0) 15.1	15
(F2) 1000.2145	1000.21
(F3) -21.405	-21.405

You do not have to enter the format indicator (for example, F0) in the command line because 1-2-3 automatically does it for you.

This format can be useful when you want to control specifically the number of places to the right of the decimal point without the automatic removal of insignificant digits that occurs in the *General* format. The *Fixed* format is particularly appealing when you have columns of numbers and want all the numbers to show the same number of decimal places.

Scientific

The *Scientific* format causes 1-2-3 to display numbers in exponential scientific notation. You will recall that this notation is used in the *General* format when numbers are too large or too small to be displayed any other way. One small difference between the way the *General* format defaults and the way the *Scientific* format controls scientific notation is their treatment of precision. You control the number of decimal places in the latter, whereas 1-2-3 controls them in the former. Some examples follow:

In the Command Line	In the Worksheet
(S2) 27.1	2.71E+01
(S4) 453.235	4.5324E+02
(S1) -21	2.1E-01
(S0) -1	-1E+00

Comma

The , (comma) format is another new 1-2-3 format. It is like the *Currency* format, except that no dollar signs appear when the numbers are displayed, and commas separate hundreds from thousands, thousands from millions, etc.

This format can be particularly useful in financial statements to display all the numbers, except those on the very top and bottom of the statement, with commas but without dollar signs. For example, a portion of a balance sheet is shown below.

Cash	$1,750
Receivables	3,735
Inventories	9,200
Current Assets	$8,685

The numbers corresponding to Receivables and Inventories are displayed with the ,(comma) format, and those corresponding to Cash and Current Assets are displayed with the *Currency* format.

The +/- Format

The +/- format creates a horizontal bar graph of plus or minus signs depending on the value of the number you enter in the cell. Asterisks are displayed if the size of the bar graph exceeds the column width. If zero is entered in a cell, a "." will be displayed on the graph.

In the Command Line	In the Worksheet
(+) 6	++++++
(+) -4	----
(+) 0	

Unless you develop some unusual applications, you will probably not find much use for this format. Because 1-2-3's graphics capability is available, it is almost as easy to create a high-quality bar graph as a simple graph like the ones above.

Percent

The *Percent* format is another new 1-2-3 format that is used to display percentages with the number of decimal places controlled by you. The values displayed in the worksheet are the result of what you enter multiplied by 100, and followed by a percent sign.

In the Command Line	In the Worksheet
(P0) .12	12%
(P4) 12.134	1213.4000%
(P2) .5675	56.75%

One of the difficulties with this format is that it seems natural to want to enter integers instead of decimals (for example, 12 instead of .12 in the first example above). 1-2-3, however, persists in its method of storing cell contents in only one way and allowing you to control only the display of the output.

For VisiCalc Users

One thing to watch out for when you use the Translation Utility to transfer files from VisiCalc to 1-2-3 is cell entries where you used the Currency format to enter percentages. You may have used the Currency format in VisiCalc to display percentages, thereby avoiding the removal of insignificant digits that occurs when you use the General format. If you specified the Currency format in VisiCalc, when you translate the spreadsheet to 1-2-3, you will get 1-2-3's Currency format and not the percentages you expect.

Text

The *Text* format displays formulas as they are entered in the command line, not the computed values that 1-2-3 normally displays. Numbers entered using this format are displayed in the same manner used in the General format.

One of the most important applications of this format is setting up Table Ranges for / *Data* Table commands.

Another important application of this format is debugging. Because you can display all the formulas on the screen with the *Text* format, it is easier to find problems and correct them.

Some examples of the *Text* format follow:

In the Command Line	In the Worksheet
(T) +C4/B12	+C4/B12
(T) (A21*B4)	(A21*B4)
(T) 567.6	567.6

Date

The / *Range* Format *Date* command causes numbers in the worksheet to be displayed as dates. This command is explained in detail in the "Date Arithmetic" section of Chapter 6.

1-2-3 and VisiCalc Format Comparisons

The table in figure 5.1 shows a comparison of the 1-2-3 and VisiCalc formats for displaying the number 1234567.890.

Figure 5.1

1-2-3 vs. VisiCalc Display Formats for the Number 1234567.89

Format	1-2-3's Display	VisiCalc's Display
General	1234567.89	1234567.89
Currency (2 decimals)	$1,234,567.89	1234567.89
Fixed (3 decimals)	1234567.890	N/A
Scientific (5 decimals)	1.23457E+06	N/A
Comma (3 decimals)	1,234,567.890	N/A
+/-	*	*
Percent (2 decimals)	123456789.00%	N/A
Text (formula)	+A9+G20	N/A

*Neither 1-2-3 nor VisiCalc can display values in this format when the number is greater than the width of the cell.

General Problems with 1-2-3 Formats

Despite the variety of 1-2-3's formats, you may encounter some problems in using them. First, there is no provision to left-justify or center numbers. Unlike labels, numbers can only be right-justified.

This can create an unsightly appearance when you have different size numbers displayed in the same column. This problem eliminates some of the convenience of using the /Data Fill command for numbers used as column headers. An example of this problem is shown in figure 5.2.

The only way around this particular problem is to make the Quarter numbers labels; then you can control the alignment.

Another appearance problem occurs when you center labels that are an odd number of characters long and those that are an even number of characters in the same column. The result appears to be slightly off kilter because the extra character from odd-length labels

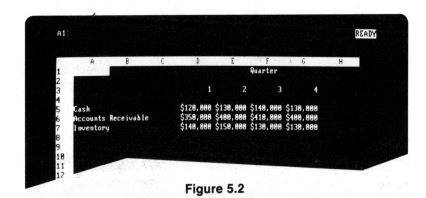

Figure 5.2

is always used on the left. The example below illustrates this problem.

> RALPHS
> SOFT
> SHOES

This problem is not unique to 1-2-3, and there is really no way around it except to try different alignments by inserting blanks or extra characters wherever possible. Because 1-2-3 can only right-justify numbers, it might be better if it used the extra character from odd-length labels on the right instead of the left. In any case, this problem of alignment is one that you will have to learn to live with and do your best to work around.

The /Range Justify Command

1-2-3's /Range Justify command is something of an orphan. This command provides 1-2-3 with the first hint of word-processing capabilites, but it is completely unsupported by other text processing tools. Lotus Development has indicated that more comprehensive word-processing capability will be available in Version 2.0 of 1-2-3. But for now, the word-processing capabilities of 1-2-3 are very limited. For this reason, we think of the /Range Justify command as an advanced formatting tool, rather than a simple word processor.

As we have seen, 1-2-3 allows text entries to be wider than the width of the column in which they are entered. The labels will overwrite adjoining cells, unless they encounter a cell that already contains text. Once the text is entered, a justify command will block the text into the space you indicate. For example, suppose you typed the line of text shown on the 1-2-3 worksheet in figure 5.3.

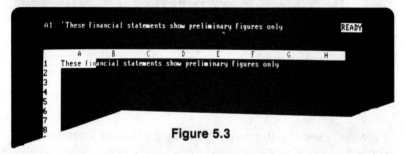

Figure 5.3

Notice that this label, which was entered in cell A1, extends across the cells from A1 to F1. Using the /Range Justify command, you can ask 1-2-3 to justify this text into columns A and B; A, B, and C; or A, B, C, and D. For example, you could specify that the text be blocked into three 9-character width columns (A, B, and C) by issuing the command /RJA1..C1. The results are shown in figure 5.4.

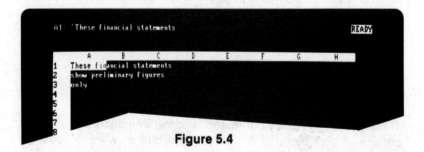

Figure 5.4

This function can be used to fine tune the captions and notes that are commonly attached to financial documents. But it has some limitations. The worst of these is that the /Range Justify command pushes down any entries in cells below the cell being justified. Normally this is not a problem, but in some cases it can mess up a carefully constructed worksheet. For example, figure 5.5 shows a sample worksheet. Figure 5.6 shows the same sheet after the */RJ* command has been used on cell A1. Notice how the labels that were aligned in the first figure are no longer aligned in the second. Be careful when you use */RJ*—its results are sometimes hard to predict.

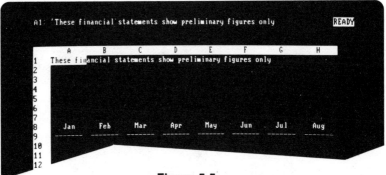

Figure 5.5

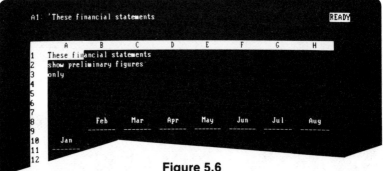

Figure 5.6

Conclusion

1-2-3's wide range of formats set it apart from other spreadsheet programs. In this chapter you learned about 1-2-3's formatting options, saw examples of the various formats, and were exposed to some of the problems you may encounter with them. You also learned about the */Range Justify* command and how it works as a formatting tool.

6
Functions

1-2-3 contains a number of built-in mathematical formulas called *functions*. Functions are abbreviations of formulas and are quick ways of performing a task that would take much longer (or could not be done at all) with mathematical symbols alone, such as +, /, *, or -. Functions are divided into several categories according to their purpose and are announced to the computer in 1-2-3 by typing @ before the function's name. The @ distinguishes the formula from a normal label entry.

Most functions refer to an argument to obtain their value. The argument specifies the cell or cells that the function will evaluate. In 1-2-3, these arguments are always written in parentheses. For example, the following function (which we'll assume lies in cell B21) computes the total of a range of 8 cells:

@SUM(B12...B19)

In this function, @ signals that the entry is a function; SUM is the name of the function being used; and the statement (B12...B19) is the argument. This function tells 1-2-3 to compute the sum of the numbers located in cells B12, B13, B14, B15, B16, B17, B18, and B19, and display the result in cell B21.

A few functions, like @ERR and @NA, do not take an argument. These functions are discussed in detail later.

Table 6.1

@SUM(A2..H14)	Computes the sum of the numbers in the rectangular range A2 to H14
@COUNT(A1..A7)	Returns the number of nonblank cells in the range A1 to A7
@MAX(C15..H32)	Returns maximum value in the rectangular range C15 to H32
@SUM(A2..H14,A15..J16)	Computes the sum of the numbers in the ranges A2 to H14 and A15 to J16
@YEAR(@TODAY)	Returns the year component of the current date
@NPV(.15/12,A1..A17)	Computes the net present value of the 18-months range A1 to A17 at the monthly rate of 1.25 percent
@ATAN(1)	Returns the measure in radians of the angle whose tangent is 1

Like mathematical formulas, functions can be much more complex than those shown above. For example, several functions can be mixed in a singe cell. Functions can even use other functions as their argument. When a function is used by another function in the same cell, it is called *nesting* the function. Like formulas, functions are also limited to a maximum of 256 characters per cell.

New Built-in Functions

1-2-3 has several built-in functions that are not found in earlier spreadsheet programs. (The feature list in the back of this book has a complete list of all the 1-2-3 built-in functions. The new functions are highlighted with asterisks [*].)

1-2-3's new built-in functions are designed for statistical, financial, mathematical, logical, and calendar applications. The new functions were created to fill the gap not satisfied by earlier spreadsheet programs and to take advantage of the special features of the IBM PC, specifically its date capability. In each of the sections below, we have identified the new functions. If you are already an experienced spreadsheeter, you will probably want to concentrate on these new functions.

Mathematical Functions

1-2-3 contains several functions that are used to perform mathematical operations. These functions include:

@ABS(number or cell reference):
> Computes the absolute value of a number or cell reference. For example, the function @ABS(-4) returns the value 4, and the function @ABS(-556) returns the value 556. The function @ABS(3) returns 3.

@EXP(number or cell reference)
> Computes the value of the constant e (approximately 2.7182818) to the power specified by the number or cell reference. For example, the function @EXP(5) returns 148.41316. If cell A1 contains the value 2.75, the function @EXP(A1) returns 15.642632. If the number or cell reference is greater than 230, the function returns the message @ERR.

@INT(number or cell reference)
> Computes the integer portion of the number or cell reference. For example, the function @INT(4.356) returns the value 4. IF cell A1 contains the value 55.666, the function @INT(A1) returns the value 55. Notice that, unlike the @ROUND function (explained below), the @INT function simply truncates all digits to the right of the decimal.

@LN(number or cell reference)
>   Computes the natural logarithm (base e) of the number or
>   cell reference. For example, the function @LN(17.634)
>   returns the value 2.8698289. The number or cell ref-
>   erence must be a postive number; otherwise, the function
>   will return the value @ERR.

Notice that the @LN function is the reciprocal of the @EXP function.
That is, the function @LN(148.41316) returns the value 5. As we have
seen, the function @EXP(5) has a value of 148.41316.

@LOG(number or cell reference)
>   Computes the logarithm (base 10) of the number or cell
>   reference. For example, the function @LOG(4.56) returns
>   the value 0.658964. If cell A1 contains the value 3.555, the
>   function @LOG(A1) returns the value 0.550839.

@SQRT(number or cell reference)
>   Computes the square root of the number or cell ref-
>   erence. For example, the function @SQRT(5) returns the
>   value 2.236067. If cell A1 contains the value 16, the
>   function @SQRT(A1) returns the value 4.

Trigonometric Functions

1-2-3 also has a complete set of trigonometric functions. Many
1-2-3 users will never use these functions, because they have little
application in the world of finance. But those who use 1-2-3 to solve
engineering problems will find that these functions are invaluable.
1-2-3's trigonometric functions include:

@PI
>   This function, which requires no argument, returns the
>   value of the constant pi, accurate to 15 decimal places, or
>   3.141592653589794.

@SIN(number or cell reference), @COS(number or cell reference), @TAN(number or cell reference)
>   These functions compute the common trigonometric
>   functions. The value of the number or cell reference is
>   interpreted by 1-2-3 in radians as an angle.

@ASIN(number or cell reference), @ACOS(number or cell reference), @ATAN(number or cell reference)

These functions compute the arc sine, arc cosine, and arc tangent of the number or cell reference. The arc functions are the reciprocals of the @SIN, @COS, and @TAN functions. The "A" at the beginning of each function is interpreted as "The angle whose." Therefore, the function @ASIN(1) returns "the angle whose" sine is 1, or 1.570796 in radians. The function @ATAN(.567) returns the value 0.515801. The number or cell reference must have a value of between 1 and -1, or the function will return the @ERR message.

New Mathematical Functions

The new mathematical built-in functions offered by 1-2-3 are

@RAND	Used for random number generation
@ROUND	Rounds numbers to a given precision
@MOD	Returns the remainder (the modulus) from division

Random Number Generation

The @RAND built-in function generates random numbers between 0 and 1 with up to eight decimal places. If you enter the function @RAND in a cell, that cell will display a different value between 0 and 1 each time the worksheet is recalculated. For example, the following two examples show a sheet filled with @RAND functions. Notice that in the second sheet, each cell has a different value from that in the first. The reason is that the sheet was recalculated between the two photographs.

One important use of random number generation is in scenario generation, especially risk analysis. One popular type of scenario generation is Monte Carlo simulation, where simulated values are substituted into probabilistic models in a systematic way, and results are tabulated. A Monte Carlo simulation model can be set up using 1-2-3, but Monte Carlo simulation is a complicated subject well beyond the scope of this book. If you want more information on Monte Carlo simulation, see "Risk Analysis in Capital Investment,"

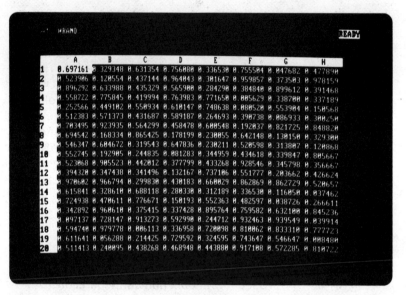

Figure 6.1

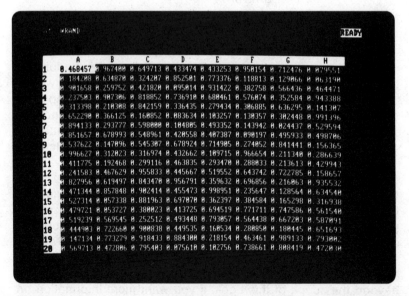

Figure 6.2

by David B. Hertz, *Harvard Business Review*, January-February 1964 and November-December 1979.

Rounding Numbers

The @ROUND built-in function is used to round numbers to a specified precision. The general format of the function is

@ROUND(x,numb_digs)

where x is the number to be rounded, and numb_digs is a number between 15 and -15 representing the number of digits to the right of the decimal. Some examples of this function are show below:

@ROUND(123.456,3) = 123.456
@ROUND(123.456,2) = 123.46
@ROUND(123.456,1) = 123.5
@ROUND(123.456,0) = 123
@ROUND(123.456,-1) = 120
@ROUND(123.456,-2) = 100

The advantage of the @ROUND function over / *Range* *Format* *Fixed* is that you avoid the errors inherent with adding rounded currency amounts. If you add the following two sets of numbers, the numbers in the right column will appear to have the wrong total.

Value Stored	Value Displayed in Currency Format to Nearest Cent
123.025	$123.03
123.025	$123.03
246.05	$246.05

The @ROUND built-in function gets around this problem by making the columns total properly.

Value Stored	Value Displayed in Currency Format to Nearest Cent
123.025	$123.03
123.025	$123.03
246.05	$246.06

The total on the right has the format @ROUND(@SUM(A1..A2),2).

Returning a Remainder

The @MOD function returns the remainder (modulus) from a division. Its general format is

@MOD(number,divisor)

The following examples illustrate how @MOD is used:

@MOD(7,3) = 1
@MOD(71.3,21) = 8.3
@MOD(31,0) = ERR

If you specify 0 for the divisor, 1-2-3 will issue an ERR message.

The @MOD function is helpful in determining the number of parts that will be left over if you run equal size batches of 33 items and total demand for a product is expected to be 500 items during the course of a year. The result would be five items.

@MOD(500,33) = 5

Statistical Functions

1-2-3 has functions that perform simple statistical analyses. These functions require an argument consisting of a *range* of cells. A range is a series of contiguous cells, either by row, or column. 1-2-3's statistical functions include: @SUM, @MAX, @MIN, @STD, and @VAR.

The @SUM(range) computes the sum of a range of entries. The range is typically a partial row or column, but it can also be a named area or a block defined by cell coordinates. For example, if the simple sheet in figure 6.3 were created, the function @SUM(A1..A2) would return the value 1110, or 345+765. The function @SUM (A1..C1) would return the value 1368, or 345+456+567. The function @SUM(A1..C2) would return the value 3330, the total of all of the numbers in the six-cell range. Notice that the range in this case consists of two partial rows.

You could even define the range of the @SUM function as a discontinuous set of cells. For example, the function @SUM (A1,B2,C1) returns the value 1566. This function is equivalent to the formula +A1+B2+C1. A more useful hybrid is the function @SUM

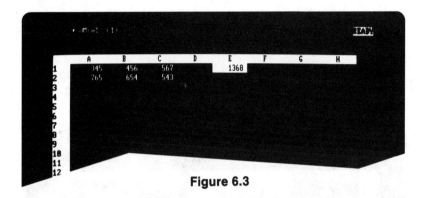

Figure 6.3

(A1..B2,C1), which computes the total of the range A1 to B2 plus the value in C1, or 2787.

In the above example, using @SUM would be only slightly faster than using the long-hand arithmetic +A1+A2+B1+B2+C1+C2. But in cases where the range is very long, this function can save time.

Another advantage of the @SUM function (and other range functions as well) is that it is more adaptable than a formula to changes made in the sheet with cut-and-paste commands. For example, in the sheet above, the function @SUM(A1..C1) is equivalent to the formula +A1+B1+C1. But if we use the /WDC (for Worksheet Delete Column command) to delete column B from the sheet, it would look like figure 6.4.

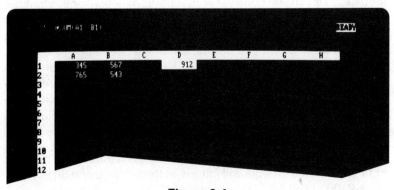

Figure 6.4

The formula has changed to +A1+ERR+B1, which returns the message ERR. The function, on the other hand, has changed to @SUM(A1..B1) and returns the correct answer, 912.

If we had gone the other way and inserted a column using /WIC, what would have happened? The sheet would look like figure 6.5.

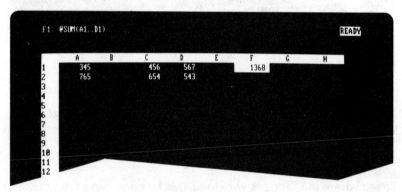

Figure 6.5

The formula would be +A1+C1+D1 and would still have the value 1368. The function would now be @SUM(A1..D1). If we inserted a number in the new cell B1, the function would include that number in the new total; but the formula would not.

Modeling Tip: There is one very practical application for this feature. Whenever possible, we define a sum range to include one extra cell at the end of the function. Frequently this can be done by including the cell that contains the underline to mark the addition in the range. For example, in the sheet shown in figure 6.6, we could enter the formula @SUM(A1..A4) in cell A5. Because the label in cell A4 has a mathematical value of 0, it does not affect our sum. But because we include it in the formula, we can add an extra item in the list simply by inserting a row at row 5. The sheet will then look like figure 6.7.

The formula in cell A6 is now @SUM(A1..A5). If we insert the number 111 in cell A4, the formula will immediately pick it up and display the value 2100 in cell A6.

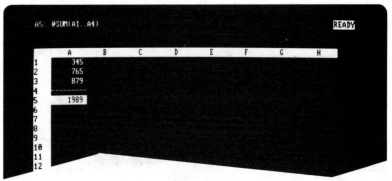

Figure 6.6

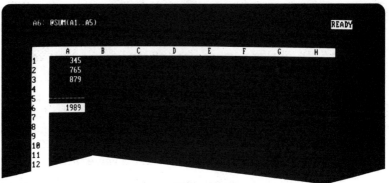

Figure 6.7

Other statistical functions include @MAX, @MIN, @COUNT, and @AVG. The @MAX and @MIN functions return the maximum and minimum values in a range. As with the @SUM function, the range can be a partial row or column, a block or several partial rows and columns, a named area, or a discontinuous group of cells joined by commas. Both of these functions assign a value of 0 to labels, but completely ignore empty cells. For example, in the simple sheet in figure 6.8, the function @MAX(A1..A5) returns the value 777. The function @MIN(A1..A5) returns the value 134, and the function @MIN(A1..A6) also returns 134 because cell A6 is blank. But if the label "abcd" had been entered in cell A6, the function @MIN(A1..A6) would return the value 0.

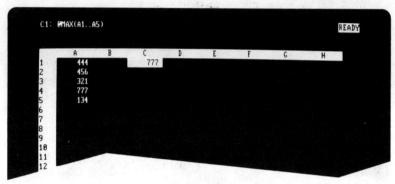

Figure 6.8

The @COUNT function is similiar to the @MIN, @MAX, and @SUM functions. It returns the count of the number of nonblank entries in a range. In the example above, the function @COUNT(A1..A6) returns the value 5. If a label or number was entered in cell A6, the value of the function would be 6.

One interesting feature of the @COUNT function is the way it reacts to a single blank cell. Assuming that cell A1 is blank, the function @COUNT(A1) would return the value 1. However, the function @COUNT(A1..A2) returns the value 0. In fact, every @COUNT function that refers to a single cell will have a value of 1.

The final function in this group is @AVG. This function computes the mean, or average, of all the cells in the range. In essence, the @AVG function is similar to the @SUM function divided by the @COUNT function. Because blank cells are ignored by the function, an @AVG function that refers to a range with all blank cells will return the value ERR.

A Quick Review of Statistics

The *mean*, often called the arithmetic average, is commonly used to mark the midpoint of a group of data items. It is calculated by adding up the items in a group and dividing the total by the number of items. The mean is not to be confused with the *median* or the *mode*, which are also measures of central tendency. The median is the value midway between the highest and lowest value in the group, in terms of probability. Half of the values in the group are above it, and half are below. The mode is the most likely value in a group of items (that is, the value you see most often).

Variance and *standard deviation* are related dispersion statistics. To calculate the variance, you subtract the mean of the numbers from each number in the group and square each result. You then add the squares and divide the total by the number of items in the group. To compute the standard deviation, you take the square root of the variance. 1-2-3's new built-in statistical functions automatically do these things for you.

What does the standard deviation tell you? As a general rule, about 68% of the items in a normally distributed population will fall within a range plus or minus one standard deviation of the mean. About 95% of the items fall within plus or minus two standard deviations of the mean.

To understand 1-2-3's new built-in statistical functions, you should know the difference between *population* and *sample* stastistics. Population statistics are used when you know the values of all the items in a population. However, when the number of items is very large and you don't know them all (which is usually the case), you are unable to compute the population statistics. Instead, you must rely on sample statistics as estimates of the population statistics.

For more information on statistics, see *Statistics for Management Decisions,* by Donald R. Plane and Edward B. Oppermann, © 1977, Business Publications, Inc., Dallas, Texas.

New Built-in Statistics Functions

The new statistics functions offered by 1-2-3 are

@VAR(list)	Computes the *population* variance
@STD(list)	Computes the *standard* deviation of a population

A very simple example that uses both functions is shown in figure 6.9. This example shows a list of salesmen and the number of items they sold during a given period. The list of the number of items sold is the population in this example. The population is used as the range for all the statistical functions.

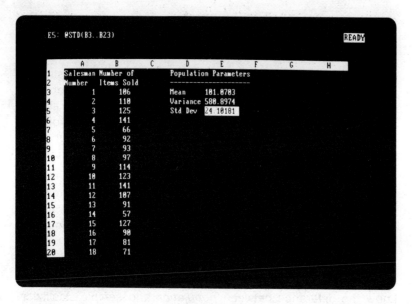

Figure 6.9

The mean of the population (about 101) is computed using the @AVG function. The standard deviation is about 24, which means that roughly 68% of the salesmen sold between 77 and 125 items.

If we take a more realistic approach and assume that we did not have the entire population of sales figures, but only a small portion of it, we can compute the *sample* statistics. This is a more realistic assumption if we are told that the actual population is all the monthly sales for the year, and we were given only one month's worth of sales. When we move into the realm of sample statistics, we start dealing with much more sophisticated statistical concepts.

To calculate the sample variance for the sales data used above, you multiply the population variance by n/n-1 (degrees of freedom), where n equals the number of items in the sample. The degrees of freedom tell you how much freedom you have in calculating a variance. The results of this calculation are shown in figure 6.10.

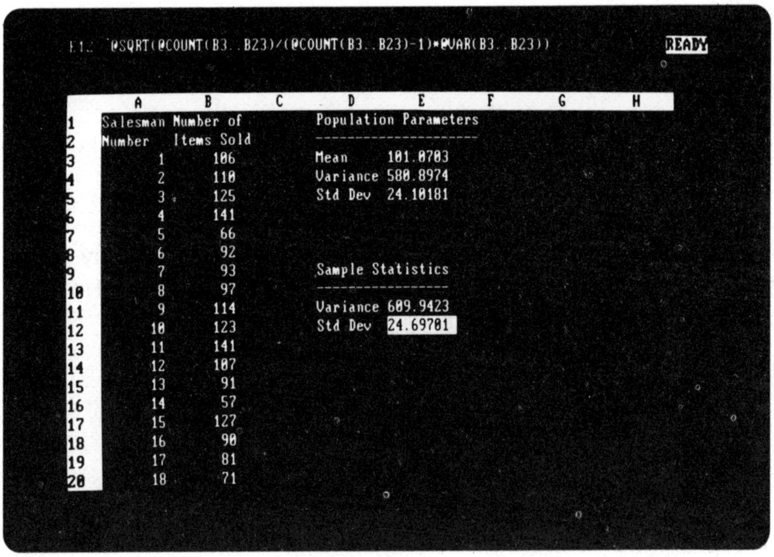

Figure 6.10

To compute the sample variance in figure 6.10, we used the built-in @COUNT function to determine the degrees of freedom.

Sample Variance = @COUNT(list)/(@COUNT(list)-1) * @VAR(list)

To compute the standard deviation of the sample, we took the square root of the sample variance. A convenient way to do this is to use the built-in @SQRT function.

Sample Standard Deviation = @SQRT(Sample Variance) = @SQRT(@COUNT(list)/(@COUNT(list)-1) * @VAR(list))

Financial Functions

1-2-3 also has several built-in financial functions. Like VisiCalc, 1-2-3 has a @NPV function that computes the net present value of a stream of flows. The form of this function is

@NPV(Discount Rate,Range)

The *discount rate* is the interest rate that 1-2-3 will use to compute the net present value. The *range* is the stream of flows to be discounted. The interval between the flows must be constant. It is determined by the specified rate. For example, if the flows occur one year apart, an annual discount rate should be used. If the flows occur every month, a monthly rate should be used.

The @NPV function can be used to evaluate a variety of investment opportunities. For example, suppose you had an opportunity to buy a piece of property that would create the following stream of income in each of the next five years:

Year 1	100,000
Year 2	120,000
Year 3	130,000
Year 4	140,000
Year 5	50,000

We could create a simple worksheet to evaluate this problem, as illustrated in figure 6.11. The function @NPV(A3,A1..E1) would return the value 368075.1, the net present value of that stream at a discount rate of 15 percent. If this rate accurately represents the rate we want to earn on the investment and the price of the property is equal to or less than $368,075, then we would say that the property was a good investment.

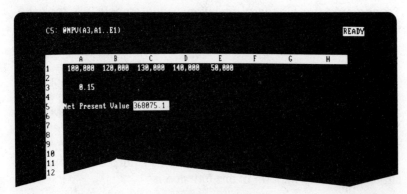

Figure 6.11

Notice that we use a cell reference, A3, to enter the discount rate into the function. Because it would be just as easy to enter the formula @NPV(.15,A1..E1), it is worth asking why we took the approach we did. In fact, there is no advantage to using either method *until you want to make a change in the rate*.

For example, assume that in our example you wanted to evaluate this investment using a rate of 14 percent. With the method we used, all you need to do is enter the number .14 in cell A3 and recalculate the sheet. If we had embedded the rate in the formula, we would have to edit the cell, replace the .15 with .14, close the cell, then recalculate. If several changes were required, this operation would consume a lot of time unnecessarily.

This technique can be used in a variety of situations to facilitate changing a worksheet.

New Financial Built-in Functions

The new financial built-in functions offered by 1-2-3 are

@PV   Computes the present value of an ordinary annuity.

@FV   Computes the future value of an ordinary annuity.

@IRR   Calculates the internal rate of return of a series of cash flows.

@PMT   Calculates the payment per period for a mortgage.

Present Value of an Annuity

The @PV built-in function is used the calculate the present value of an ordinary annuity given a payment per period, an interest rate, and the number of periods. An *ordinary annuity* is a series of payments made at equally spaced intervals, and *present value* is the value today of the payments to be made or received later, discounted at a given interest or discount rate. Calculating the present value of an ordinary annuity gives you a way to compare different investment opportunities or potential obligations while taking into account the time value of money.

The general form of the @PV function is

    @PV(payment,interest,term)

The actual equation for calculating the present value of an ordinary annuity is

$$PV = payment * \frac{1-(1+interest)^{-n}}{interest}$$

Figure 6.12 shows an example of how the @PV built-in function is used.

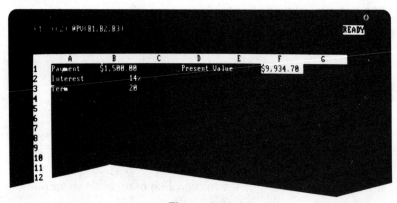

Figure 6.12

The most realistic way to compute the present value of an ordinary annuity for an earlier spreadsheet program like VisiCalc is to enter the actual equation into a cell. The disadvantages of this method are that entering the equation is a long process, and that the equation is hard to interpret. The following is an equivalent VisiCalc cell formula for calculating the present value of an annuity (with parentheses to improve processing time):

    B35*((1-((1+B36) ^ -B31))/B36)

The difference between @NPV, the built-in function for net present value, and @PV stems from the difference in cash flows and the way they are laid out in the worksheet. @NPV calculates the net present value of a series of flows that may or may not be equal, but which are all contained in a range of cells in the worksheet. The cash flows in the @PV function must all be equal, and the amount of the flows must be contained in a single cell or entered as a value in the @PV function.

Future Value of an Annuity

The @FV built-in function is similar in form to the @PV function, but is used to calculate the future value of an ordinary annuity. *Future value* is the value at a given day in the future of a series of payments or receipts, discounted at a given interest or discount rate. Calculating the future value of an annuity allows you to compare different investment alternatives or potential obligations.

@FV(payment,interest,term)

The equation for calculating the future value of an ordinary annuity is

$$FV = payment * \frac{(1+interest)^{-n}-1}{interest}$$

An example using the @FV built-in function is shown in figure 6.13.

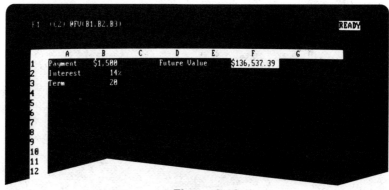

Figure 6.13

1-2-3's method of computing the future value of an annuity is similar to its method of computing the present value, except that the future value equation is used.

Internal Rate of Return

Internal rate of return (IRR) is the discount rate that equates the present value of the expected cash outflows with the present value of the expected inflows. In simpler terms, IRR is the rate of return, or profit, that an investment is expected to earn. Like the other financial calculations, IRR determines the attractiveness of an investment opportunity.

The internal rate of return function is built around an iterative process whereby you provide an initial ballpark guess for a discount rate (actually anything between 0 and 1 will do), and 1-2-3 calculates the actual discount rate that equates the present value of a series of cash outflows with the present value of a series of inflows. 1-2-3's method may seem awkward, but it is actually very logical. The same method is used to calculate IRR manually.

Given the format of the equation, all the inflows and outflows must be in the same range. The general form of the @IRR function is

@IRR(guess,range)

1-2-3 should reach convergence on a discount rate within .0000001 after a maximum of 20 iterations, or ERR is returned. Figure 6.14 shows an example of how the @IRR built-in function is used.

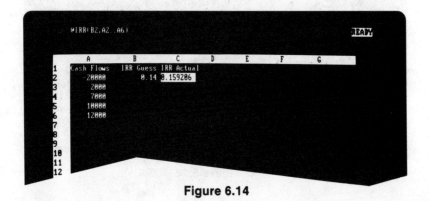

Figure 6.14

The internal rate of return, or profit, for the project illustrated in figure 6.14 is about 16 percent.

Payment per Period

The final new financial built-in function provided by 1-2-3 calculates the mortgage payment required for a given principal, interest rate, and number of periods. The format of this function is

@PMT(principal,interest,n)

where n = the number of periods.

Again, the formula behind the function calculates the present value of an ordinary annuity, but is rearranged to yield the period payment as the result.

$$PMT = principal * \frac{interest}{1-(1+interest)^n}$$

This built-in function is a slight variation of the @PV built-in function discussed earlier.

You can use this function to build a table of mortgage rate payments similar to those in the SAMPLES.BAS program supplied with DOS. Such a table is very easy to construct, using the /Data Table command discussed in Chapter 11, but the longer method of replicating existing cell formulas is shown here for clarity.

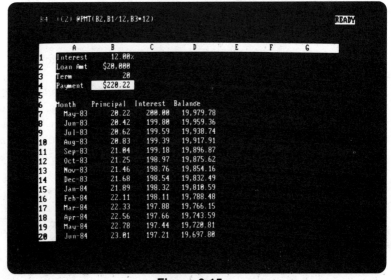

Figure 6.15

Data Management Functions

1-2-3 has three simple data management functions: @CHOOSE, @VLOOKUP, and @HLOOKUP. These functions are called "special" functions by Lotus, but we prefer the term data management functions, because the functions retrieve data from lists and tables. These functions should not be confused with 1-2-3's data base statistical functions, which operate only on data bases. Those functions are explained in Chapter 11.

CHOOSE

The @CHOOSE function uses a key value provided by the user to select a number from a list. This function has the following form:

> @CHOOSE(Key,Argument,Argument,...,Argument)

@CHOOSE displays the argument whose position in the list matches the key. For example, the function:

> @CHOOSE(2,3,4,5)

returns the number 4 because 4 is in the second position in the list. If the key is changed to 1, as in:

> @CHOOSE(1,3,4,5)

the function will return the value 3.

Like other functions, the arguments in the @CHOOSE function can be numbers, formulas, or functions. The @CHOOSE function can also be used to select formulas that will vary in different situations. For example, the percentage rate used to compute depreciation under the ACRS depreciation system varies with the useful life of the asset. Thus, an asset with a three-year life would be depreciated at a different rate in the first year of its life from that of an asset with a five-year life. A function like:

> @CHOOSE(Year of Life, Rate for 3 year asset, Rate for 5 year asset...)

dramatically simplifies the computation.

LOOKUP

@VLOOKUP and @HLOOKUP are two variations on the basic @LOOKUP function pioneered by VisiCalc. As their names suggest, these functions "look up" a value from a table based on the value of a test variable. The forms of these functions are

@VLOOKUP(a number or cell reference,beginning of range...end of range,column offset)

@HLOOKUP(a number or cell reference,beginning of range...end of range,row offset)

The first number or cell reference is called the *test variable*. The range is a block that includes at least two partial rows or columns. The first coordinate is the top of the comparison column. The second coordinate defines the bottom of the last data column. A range name can also be used instead of the coordinates.

The offset determines which data column should supply the data to the function. In every case, the comparison column has an offset of zero, the first data column has an offset of 1, and so on. The offset must be positive and not exceed the actual number of rows or columns in the table. If either of these conditions is not met, the function will return the value ERR.

To use these functions, a table, called a lookup table, must exist in the worksheet. This table must consist of two or more adjacent partial rows or columns. An example of a columnar lookup table is shown in figure 6.16.

The first column (B) is called the comparison column. It contains the comparison values that will be used to look up the data shown in the second and third columns (C and D). To access this columnar table, you would use the @VLOOKUP or *vertical* lookup function.

In this table, the function @VLOOKUP(5,B1..D10,1) will return the value 54999. To return that result, 1-2-3 searches the comparison column for the largest value that is not greater than the key and returns the value in the data column with an offset of 1 (in this case, column C). Remember that the comparison column has an offset of 0. Column C, therefore, has an offset of 1. Column D has an offset of two.

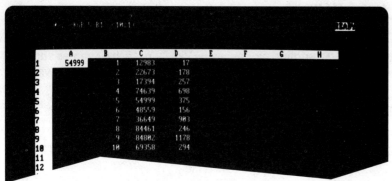

Figure 6.16

Because the lookup table does not search for a specific match, but for the largest key in the table that is not greater than the search variable, the function @VLOOKUP(5.5,B1..D10,1) also returns 54999. A key of 100 returns 69358, the number that corresponds to the largest key in the list. If 0 is used as the key, an ERR message would appear because no key in the table is less than or equal to 0.

The data in column D can also be "looked up" using @VLOOKUP. For example, the function @VLOOKUP(10,B1..D10,2) returns the value 294.

Lookup tables must follow specific rules. The key values must be arranged in ascending order, and the data items in column two cannot appear in another column. (In other words, a key cannot be repeated.) For example, the lookup table in figure 6.17 does not work because the comparison values in column B are not in ascending order. The table in figure 6.18 is also not allowed because the key 5 is repeated twice.

In addition, lookup tables in 1-2-3 can be used only to look up numeric entries. Comparison values must also be numbers: no text entries can be used. For example, in the table shown in figure 6.19, the function @VLOOKUP(5,B1..C10,1) would return a 0 because a text entry has a value of 0.

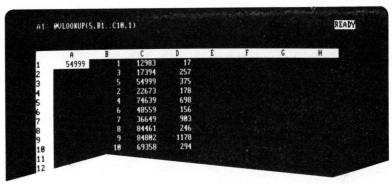

Figure 6.17

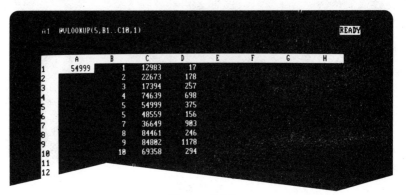

Figure 6.18

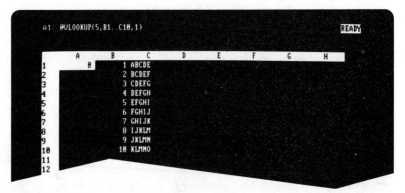

Figure 6.19

Some spreadsheet programs have the ability to use text as data in a lookup table and as a comparison value.

The @HLOOKUP function is essentially the same as @VLOOKUP, except that it operates on tables arranged across rows instead of columns. All of the same rules apply to these tables that apply to the vertical tables. Let's look at an example of how the @HLOOKUP function works. If you built the table in figure 6.20, the function @HLOOKUP(5,A3..H5,1) would return the value 567. The function @HLOOKUP(8,A3..H5,1) would return the value 890, and the function @HLOOKUP(3,A3..H5,2) would return the value 765.

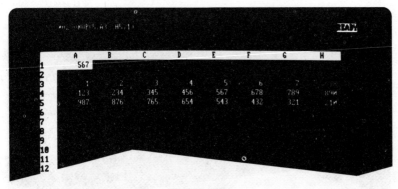

Figure 6.20

Despite their limitations, the @VLOOKUP and @HLOOKUP functions are very powerful and useful tools. They can be used in models to create tax tables that automatically retrieve the appropriate rate based on income. In fact, this is the application for which the function was originally developed. These functions can also be used for simple data management, such as handling inventory and employee lists, although in 1-2-3 these functions can be performed far better with the data base commands.

Date Arithmetic

One of 1-2-3's most advanced features is its ability to manipulate dates. This can be used for such things as mortgage analysis, bond amortization, and aging of accounts receivable. Earlier programs, such as VisiCalc, have no method for dealing with dates in a special way.

New Built-in Calendar Functions

1-2-3's date arithmetic capabilites are contained in five new built-in calendar functions:

@DATE	Returns the number of days between a given date and December 31, 1899
@TODAY	Returns an integer representing the number of days between a given date and December 31, 1899
@DAY	Extracts the day of the month from an integer representing the number of days from December 31, 1899, to a given date
@MONTH	Extracts the month number from the same integer representation as @DAY
@YEAR	Extracts the year number from the same integer representation as @DAY

How 1-2-3 Remembers Dates

All aspects of 1-2-3's date-handling capability are based on its ability to represent any given Gregorian date as an integer equal to the number of days from December 31, 1899, to that date. The @DATE function allows 1-2-3 to convert a date you enter into an integer that 1-2-3 can interpret. The form of the @DATE function is

   @DATE(year,month,day)

Some examples of how the @DATE built-in function is used appear below:

@DATE(55,12,30) =	20289
@DATE(12,1,1) =	1212
@DATE(C7,C8,D10) =	integer equivalent of the date represented by these cells. If the cells contained the values 83, 12, and 25, respectively, the function would have the value 30675.

Today's Date as an Integer

The @TODAY function returns today's date as an integer that represents the number of days since December 31, 1899. This built-in function is particularly useful for taking advantage of the IBM PC's timekeeping capability. If you have a clock that automatically supplies the date, or if you simply enter the date when you are prompted by DOS, the @TODAY function will give you access to the date in the current worksheet. For example, if you entered the date 12-31-83 in response to the PC DOS Date command, the @TODAY function would have the value

@TODAY = 30681

Because the @TODAY function is dependent on the PC DOS or MS-DOS system date for its value, it is very important that you always remember to enter the date in response to the operating system prompt before you enter 1-2-3.

Extracting the Day, Month, or Year

The @DATE, @MONTH, and @YEAR built-in functions allow you to extract parts of a date in integer form. For example,

@DAY(30284) = 29
@MONTH(30284) = 11
@YEAR(30284) = 82

These three functions, taken together, are the reverse of the @DATE built-in function because they allow you to convert from the integer format back into Gregorian format. You can use these functions for various time-related chores, such as aging accounts receivable and setting up a table for amortizing a loan.

Displaying Dates

The five calendar functions are extremely useful for entering dates in the worksheet in a form that 1-2-3 can understand. But there is a problem. The results of these functions are integers that don't look like dates and are very hard to comprehend. For example, do you know the dates represented by the numbers 30124 and 32988?

The / *Range Format Date* command allows you to display dates in three different forms. As we have seen, dates are represented as integers that equal the number of days that have elapsed since December 31, 1899. The *Date* format takes these integers and displays them in one of the following three arrangements, depending on which one you select:

1: Day-Month-Year
2: Day-Month
3: Month-Year

The following examples show a single date in the three different formats as they appear in the command line and in the worksheet.

In the Command Line	In the Worksheet
(D1) 30524	27-Jul-83
(D2) 30524	27-Jul
(D3) 30524	Jul-83

Notice that the first option (D1) creates a string that is 9 characters long—too long to be displayed in a column with the default width of 9. In general, you will need to expand any column containing dates formatted in the DD-MM-YY format to be 10 or more characters wide. Because the other date formats can be displayed in normal width columns, we frequently use them in place of the more detailed, but wider, DD-MM-YY format.

General Comments on Date Arithmetic

Notice that 1-2-3's date arithmetic capabilities actually incorporate both a set of functions and a set of formats. Don't be confused by this mix. The functions, like @DATE, enter dates in the worksheet; the formats display these functions in an understandable form. Although the format can be used without the function, and the function without the format, the two tools are not very meaningful when used alone.

In most cases, date arithmetic calculations will simply involve subtracting one date from another. By subtracting, you can easily determine the number of days between dates. For example, subtracting the function @DATE(83,7,31) from the date @DATE(83,8,15) results in the value 15. To 1-2-3, this problem is as simple as subtracting the integer value for @DATE(83,7,31) (30528) from the value of the function @DATE(83,8,15) (30543).

Taking it one step further, you can even determine the number of weeks, months, and years between two dates by dividing the difference by an appropriate number. If you need only a rough idea, you can use the banker's conventions of 7 days in a week, 30 days in a month and 360 days in a year. If you want to be more exact, you can build in such things as odd-numbered months and leap years.

The selection of December 31, 1899, as the starting date for date arithmetic may seem arbitrary, but when you actually use 1-2-3's date formats and built-in functions, you will find that this choice is a good one. The selection of the ending date is more important. In Version 1, the ending date is December 31, 1999. For later versions, it is December 31, 2099.

In one sense, the starting and ending dates for date arithmetic do not really matter. You are interested more in the relative difference between dates than in the absolute integers the dates represent. There are cases, however, where dates are used in absolute terms, as in the mortgage example below. In these cases you may run into a problem with the original December 31, 1999, ending date.

To illustrate this, if you look at the example of a thirty-year loan, it will be well after the year 2000 before the loan is paid off. To set up a table showing principal and interest amortization month by month or year by year, you have to go beyond 1-2-3's original ending date of December 31, 1999, for the date function. This explains why Lotus Development changed the ending date. If your copy of 1-2-3 does not reflect this change, you should get your copy upgraded.

As mentioned earlier, besides using date functions in arithmetic calculations, you can use them in logical expressions. For example, you can use the statement @IF(@DATE(83,15,05)>B2,C3,D4). In simple English, this statement says, If the integer equivalent of May 15, 1983, is greater than the value in cell B2, then assign the value in cell C3 to the current cell; otherwise, use the value in cell D4. This kind of date test can be used to help track investment portfolios or to help manage accounts receivable.

Using Date Arithmetic

To show 1-2-3's date arithmetic capability, we have developed a simple mortgage amortization worksheet that illustrates the interest and principal payments for the first months of a loan (shown in figure 6.15). This should remind you of the mortgage amortization routine in the SAMPLES.BAS program provided with DOS.

1-2-3's ability to show the actual months in this example is based on its ability to represent any given date as an integer equal to the number of days elapsed since December 31, 1899. In our case, the date is May 14, 1983, which is represented by the integer value 30450.

To enter the dates in the example, we begin by setting the format of the cells in column A where the dates should go. Formats control how 1-2-3 actually displays on the screen the contents of cells. You begin formatting the cells by selecting the */Range Format Date* command. When you select this command, 1-2-3 gives you a choice of three different ways of displaying a Gregorian date on the screen:

    1: Day-Month-Year   14-May-83
    2: Day-Month   14-May
    3: Month-Year   May-83

For our example we chose option *3*. The range of cells to be formatted is A7..A60. If you do not choose one of these formats, 1-2-3 will display the date as its integer value (for example, 30450). 1-2-3 stores dates in their integer formats (as shown in figure 6.15). Our choice of format affects only the displaying of the date.

Once the range of cells is properly formatted, we use the built-in @DATE function in cell A7 to convert the Gregorian date of May 14, 1983, to an integer. The function has the following format:

    @DATE(year,month,day) = @DATE(83,5,14)

We use this function so that 1-2-3 will understand the date we give it, and to display the integer in the example to show how 1-2-3's date arithmetic works.

The next step is to define the second cell in the date range. This cell will show the date of the next payment in the mortgage. We know that this payment will occur on June 14. We could enter this date, using the function @DATE(83,6,14). But there is an easier way. Because June 14, 1983, is 31 days after May 14, 1983, we can define the second cell in range (A8) as

    A7+31

This formula will result in a value that 1-2-3 will interpret as the date June 14, 1983.

You can now use 1-2-3's /Copy command to copy the same formula into the entire range A9..A60. Because the source cell, A8, contains a relative formula, when the copy is completed, each cell in the range will be equal to the value in the cell above plus 31. Thanks to the date format, each cell will contain the dates shown in figure 6.15.

Modeling Note: Because not all months have 31 days, you will generally be better off incrementing dates in a problem like this one by 30.7 instead of 31. Try it both ways to see what we mean.

Logical Functions

Like most electronic spreadsheets, 1-2-3 includes conditional, or logical, functions. These functions allow you to build conditional tests into cells. These tests return different values depending on the truth or falsity of the test. 1-2-3's primary conditional function is @IF.

Logical Operators

Conditional functions require logical operators. These operators help to determine the realtionship between different numbers. The following is a list of *simple* logical operators and their meanings:

Operator	Meaning
=	Equal
<	Less than
<=	Less than or equal to
>	Greater than
>=	Greater than or equal to
<>	Not equal

Simple logical operators have lower precedence than any mathematical operator, but they all have equal precedence within their group.

All statements that contain a logical operator are either true or false. For example, the statement 5<3 is clearly false, whereas the statement 16<27 is true. 1-2-3's @IF function can determine whether mathematical statements like these are true or false.

Let's create a logical statement using the @IF built-in function. This function has the general format:

@IF(a,vtrue,vfalse)

where the first argument *a* is tested for true or false. If the result of the test is true, the function will take the value of the second argument *vtrue*. However, if the value of the first argument is false, the function will take the value of the third argument *vfalse*. The following are examples of logical statements that use the @IF function, followed by their English-language equivalents.

@IF(B4>=450,B5,C7)
>   If the value in cell B4 is greater than or equal to 450, then use the value in cell B5. Otherwise, use the value in cell C7.

@IF(A3<A2,5,6)
>   If the value in cell A3 is less than the value in cell A2, then assign the number 5. Otherwise, assign the number 6.

@IF(G9<>B7,G5/9,G7)
>   If the value in cell G9 is not equal to the value in cell B7, then use the value in cell G5 divided by 9. Otherwise, use the value in cell G7.

Complex Operators

Things get more complicated when another set of logical operators is introduced: the *complex* operators.

Operator	Meaning
#NOT#	Not (logical)
#AND#	And (logical)
#OR#	Or (logical)

The complex logical operators have lower precedence than the simple logical operators, and the #AND# and #OR# have equal precedence in this group.

Now that we have a complete set of logical operators, we can combine simple and complex operators to create the following @IF functions.

@IF(A1<>1#AND#G5<3,E7,E6)
>If the value in cell A1 is not equal to 1 and the value in cell G5 is less than 3, use the value in cell E7. Otherwise, use the value in cell E6.

@IF(#NOT#(Cost=50)#AND#A1=1,L10,K10)
>If the amount stored in the cell named "Cost" is not $50 and the value in cell A1 is equal to one, then use the value in cell L10. Otherwise, use the value in cell K10.

1-2-3's conditional functions are quite sophisticated and can be very complicated. The @IF statement can be used in a wide variety of situations to allow 1-2-3 to make decisions. The following is a simple example of how the @IF function can be used.

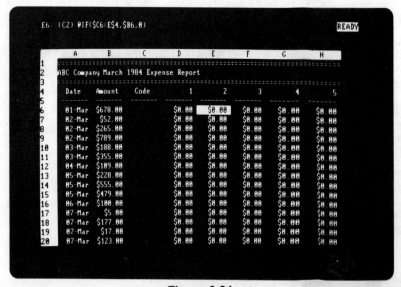

Figure 6.21

Figure 6.21 shows a simple worksheet that summarizes a company's expenditures for the month of June, 1983. Column A contains the date of each expenditure, and column B contains the amounts of the disbursements. Notice that column C has been labeled "Code" and that row 4 contains a sequence of numbers, beginning with 1 in column D and ending with 3 in column H. We'll call these numbers Accounts. Now suppose that the following formula was entered in cell E6:

@IF($C6=E$4,$B6,0)

Similarly, suppose the formula:

@IF($C6=F$4,$B6,0)

was entered in cell F6. These formulas can be translated as, If the number in cell C6 (the code) equals the number in cell E4 (or cell F4) (the account), then enter the value in cell B6 here. Otherwise, enter 0 here.

Suppose that similar formulas existed in all of the cells in range D6..H20. Now suppose that we enter a code for each check recorded in column A. The code for each disbursement should be a number less than six. Now, imagine that you recalculated the worksheet. The result would look like figure 6.22. Notice that in each cell 1-2-3 has compared each code to the accounts located above in row 3. In the cells where the code and account match, 1-2-3 has recorded the amount of the disbursement. In all the other cells, 1-2-3 has entered a zero. This is exactly what we would expect from the conditional tests we used in the these cells.

Like so many other things in 1-2-3, the best way to understand logical operators is to experiment with them. If you want more information on logical functions and more examples on how they are used, look for Que's book *1-2-3 for Business*. This book contains a number of practical business models that demonstrate a variety of interesting 1-2-3 techniques.

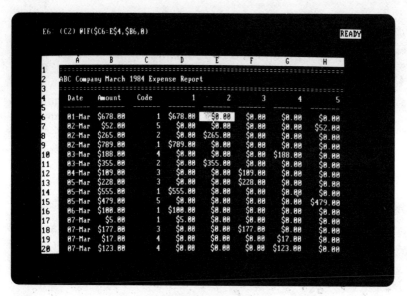

Figure 6.22

Error Trapping Functions

@NA and @ERR

If you run across a situation where you just don't know what number to put for a value, but you don't want to leave the cell blank, you can use *NA* instead (for "Not Available"). To do this, enter @NA in the cell. 1-2-3 will then display "NA" in that cell and in any other cell that depends on it.

Another situation that you may run across, particularly when you are setting up templates for other people to use, is unacceptable values for cells. For example, suppose that you are developing a check-book balancing macro, and checks with values less than or equal to zero are unacceptable. One way to indicate your dislike for these kinds of checks is to use *ERR* to signal that fact. You might use the following version of the @IF built-in function.

    @IF(B9<=0,@ERR,B9)

In simple English, this statement says, If the amount in cell B9 is less than or equal to zero, then issue ERR on the screen; otherwise, use the amount. Notice that we have used the @ERR function to control the display in almost the same way that we used @NA above.

1-2-3 also uses ERR as a signal when it finds unacceptable numbers—for example, a division by zero or mistakenly deleted cells. ERR will often show up temporarily when you are reorganizing the cells in a worksheet. If it persists, however, you may have to do some careful analysis to figure out why.

As it does for NA, 1-2-3 displays ERR in any cells that depend on a cell with an ERR value. Sometimes many cells will display ERR after only one or two small changes have been made to a worksheet. To correct this problem, you must trace back down the chain of references to find the root of the problem.

@ISERR and @ISNA

@ISERR and @ISNA relate closely to the @ERR and @NA functions. @ISERR and @ISNA, which are usually used with the @IF function, allow you to test the value in a cell for the value ERR or NA.

The @ISERR and @ISNA functions are like the logical operators we discussed earlier; they are always either true or false. The function @ISERR(A1) is false if cell A1 does not contain the value ERR, and is true if cell A1 is equal to ERR. Similarly, the @ISNA function is true if the cell it refers to contains the value NA, and is false if the cell does not.

The @ISERR function is frequently used to keep ERR messages that result from division by 0 from appearing in the worksheet. For example, at one time or another as you use 1-2-3, you will create a formula that divides a number by a cell reference, as in the formula:

23/A4

If A4 contains a value, the function will simply return the value of the division. But if A4 contains a label, a 0, or is blank, the function will return the value @ERR. The @ERR will be passed along to other cells in the sheet, creating an unnecessary mess.

Using the formula

> @IF(@ISERR(23/A4),0,23/A4)

will eliminate the ERR result. This function says, If the value of 23/A4 is ERR, then enter a 0 in this cell; otherwise, enter the value of the division 23/A4. The function essentially traps the ERR message and keeps it off the worksheet.

@ISNA works in much the same way. For example, the formula

> @IF(@ISNA(A4,0,A4)

tests cell A4 for the value NA. If the value of A4 is NA, the formula returns a 0. Otherwise, the formula returns the value in A4. This type of formula can be used to keep an NA message from spreading throughout a worksheet.

Conclusion

In this chapter, you have seen examples of all of 1-2-3's spreadsheet functions at work. You have also learned about the mathematical, statistical, financial, data management, logical, and date functions that are built into 1-2-3.

In the next chapter, we'll examine 1-2-3's file handling commands. You will learn how to save and retrieve worksheet files and how to use the the program's other, more sophisticated, file management tools.

7

File Operations

The ability to store, retrieve, and delete files to and from diskettes is common to all spreadsheet programs. But one of the things that is unique about 1-2-3 is its scale in performing these functions. The disk requirements for the program are listed by Lotus Development as either "two double-sided disk drives or one double-sided disk drive and a hard disk." Clearly, the program can function with less than these requirements (one double-sided disk drive is enough to squeak by), but this is not what Lotus had in mind. 1-2-3 was written for users who intend to have many large files that are frequently moved in and out of storage and also plan to mix and match these files often.

A General Description of 1-2-3 Files

1-2-3 file names can be up to eight characters long with a three-character extension. The two basic rules for file names are

1. File names may not include blank spaces or characters other than A through Z and 0 through 9.
2. Lower-case letters are automatically converted to upper-case in file names.

Although the eight-character name is determined by you, the extension is controlled automatically by 1-2-3 and will vary with the type of file you are dealing with. The three possible file extensions are

.WKS   For worksheet files

.PRN   For print files

.PIC   For graph files

Note that there is only one worksheet to a file, and that you work on a worksheet only when it is in main memory.

Simple Storage and Retrieval

The basic file functions of storing and retrieving entire files are very easy to perform in 1-2-3. The /File Save command allows you to save an entire worksheet in a file on diskette.

When you enter this command, 1-2-3 will try to help you by supplying a list of the current worksheet files in the diskette. You can either point to one of the entries or enter a new file name. To enter a new file name, you must use the rules detailed above. 1-2-3 will automatically supply a .WKS extension, as shown in figure 7.1.

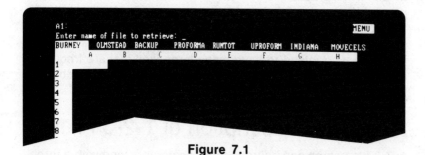

Figure 7.1

This command makes an exact copy of the current worksheet, including all of the formats, range names, settings, etc., that you have specified.

To call a file back into main memory from diskette, use the /File Retrieve command. Again, 1-2-3 will try to help you with a list of all the file names currently on diskette. Often, the list will extend beyond the single line on the first page. To see the entire list of file names, move the cursor to the right beyond the last file name in the current line. The HOME and END keys are useful tools in locating a file name. HOME will return you to the first file name on the list, and END will send you to the last one. The list of names also has wrap-around capability—that is, if you move the cursor beyond the last entry on the list, the cursor will return to the first item on the list.

For both saving and retrieving files, you can override the default disk by specifying a drive indicator in front of the file name. For example, if you decide you want to retrieve a file that has been stored on drive A and the default is drive B, you can enter A: in front of the file name when 1-2-3 asks you for the name of the file to be retrieved. For example, the name A:SALESREP would retrieve the file SALESREP from disk A.

Partial Loads and Saves

There will be times when you want to store only part of a worksheet (a range of cells, for instance) in a separate file on diskette. For example, you may want to extract outlays from an expense report or revenues from an income statement. One of the best uses for partial storage is breaking up worksheet files that are too large to be stored on a single diskette.

The / File Xtract command allows you to save a part of a worksheet file. It saves either the formulas that exist in a range of cells or the current values of the formulas in the range, depending on which you select. Both options create a worksheet file that can be reloaded into 1-2-3 with the / F Retrieve command. If you decide to save only the current values, however, the resulting worksheet file will contain numbers, but no formulas. Selecting the formula option creates a file with all of the formulas intact.

The / File Xtract command also requires that you specify the portion of the worksheet you want to save. As is generally the case with 1-2-3, the range to be saved can be as small as a cell or as large as the entire worksheet.

When the Values option is used with the / File Xtract command, you can "lock" the current values in a worksheet. To do this, issue the command and select the *Values* option. Next, specify the entire worksheet as the range to extract. This will save the current values stored in the worksheet. You can think of this as taking a snapshot of the current worksheet. The new values-only file can be re-loaded into the worksheet and printed or graphed.

Another function that you will want to perform is to make copies of certain ranges of cells from other worksheets and place them into strategic spots in the current worksheet. For example, if you work for a large firm, you may want to combine, in one all-encompassing worksheet, the balance sheets and income statements from different divisions.

A very simple technique for accomplishing this kind of consolidation is to start with and keep a copy of an "empty master." When it is time to perform a consolidation, you will always have an empty master to work from. In addition, when you start with an empty master, you can copy the first divisional worksheet onto the master and leave untouched the original copy of the divisional worksheet.

Another situation where copying a range of cells can be helpful is when you want to combine quarterly data into a yearly statement. Again, the formats must be compatible, and you will benefit by keeping an empty master.

The command used to combine data in the examples above is */ File Combine*. This command gives you the following options:

Copy	To pull in an entire worksheet or a named range of cells as is into a worksheet and have them write over the existing cells
Add	To pull in an entire worksheet or a named range of cells and add their contents to existing cell contents. (This is the option we would use for combining worksheets in both of the examples above.)
Subtract	To pull in an entire worksheet or a named range of cells and subtract their contents from the existing cell contents

Figures 7.2, 7.3, 7.4, and 7.5 show examples of the *Copy* and *Add* options. Figure 7.3 shows a worksheet that we created and stored

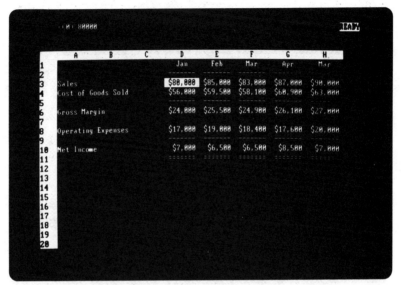

Figure 7.2

on diskette. Figure 7.2 shows another, similar worksheet that is stored in 1-2-3's memory. Figure 7.4 shows the results of Combining these two sheets using the *Copy* option; and figure 7.5 shows the

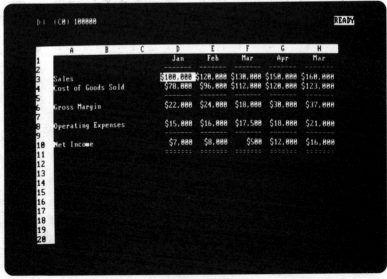

Figure 7.3

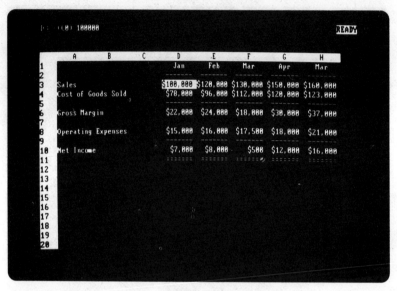

Figure 7.4

results of the *Add* option. The *Subtract* option is so much like the
Add option that we did not include it here.

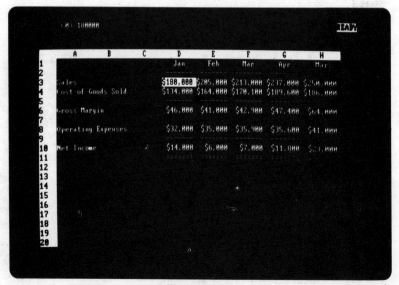

Figure 7.5

These three options are very useful in combining worksheets. The / File Combine Add command is especially helpful because it can be used to consolidate one worksheet with another. For example, the /FCA command could be used by a business with several divisions to consolidate the income statements for each division into a company-wide statement.

Deleting Files

When you save files to disk, you may sometimes find that the disk is full. 1-2-3 will inform you of this condition by flashing the message "Disk full" in the lower left-hand corner of the screen. There are two things you can do when this occurs. First, you can swap disks. Second, you can delete one or more of the current files that occupy space on the disk.

There are two ways to delete stored files in 1-2-3. The first way, as mentioned earlier, is the Erase command in the File Manager function of the Lotus Access System. The other way, which has the advantage of allowing you to remain in 1-2-3, is the / File Erase command. When you invoke the / File Erase command and enter the name of the file to be deleted, the file will be erased from the diskette. There is a confirmation step involved with this command to help you avoid mistakes.

Certain wild-card characters can also be used with this command to delete all the files of a certain type. They are the same wild-card characters used for DOS and other commands throughout 1-2-3, so they should look familiar.

* Matches the remaining characters of a file name. B* matches BOB, BARNEY, BOQUIST, etc.

? Matches all characters in a single position in a file name. B?RD matches BARD, BIRD, and BYRD, but not BURT.

A word of warning: Be careful when you use the /FE command. Once a file is deleted, it cannot be recovered by conventional means. Always check and double check before you delete a file to be sure that you really want to delete it.

A Note to SuperCalc Users

As you recall, the command to format a single cell in SuperCalc is /FE. Because this same command in 1-2-3 begins the process of erasing a file, think twice before you try using it to format a cell. Again, there is no confirmation step to the /FE command in 1-2-3, so be careful.

Specifying a Drive

The / Worksheet Global Default setting for Disk is normally drive B. This means that B is the active disk drive for storing and retrieving files. There may be times, however, when you will want to override this temporarily (for example, when drive B temporarily malfunctions and you still want to continue using 1-2-3). 1-2-3 lets you specify another drive for the duration of the current session with the / File Disk command.

Listing the Different Files on a Diskette

1-2-3 can list all the names of a certain type of file on the active drive with the / File List command. The choices for file types are

Worksheet   Print   Graph

Which drive is the active drive depends on the / Worksheet Global Default Disk (or Directory, depending on the program version) setting and whether that setting has been overridden by the / File Disk or Directory command. Normally, the active drive is drive B. A list of Worksheet files might look like figure 7.6.

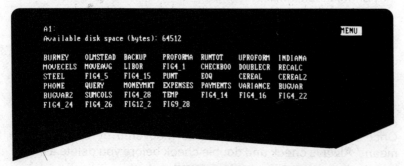

Figure 7.6

Notice that this command also indicates the amount of available room on the diskette.

Transferring Files

One thing to be applauded is Lotus Development's creation of different methods of interfacing 1-2-3 with outside programs, specifically the */File Import* and */Print File Options Other Un-*formatted commands and the Translation Utility. Although the kinds of files that can be transferred with these techniques are limited, this is only a minor setback because most files can be converted to the proper format one way or another. The following methods work well, and, with a few small exceptions, are very easy to use.

Transferring Files with /File Import

The */File Import* command is used to copy standard ASCII files to specific locations in the current worksheet. .PRN (print) files are one example of standard ASCII text files created to print after the current 1-2-3 session. (.PRN files and their uses are covered in detail in the next chapter.) Other standard ASCII files include those produced by different word-processing and BASIC programs.

In the early versions of 1-2-3, the */File Import* command was used to import records from dBASE II to 1-2-3. In version 1A, dBASE files can be translated with the Translation Utility.

Transferring Standard ASCII Files

A standard ASCII text file must have a .PRN extension before it can be transferred. If it doesn't have one, you must rename the file using either the *Rename* command in File Manager (one of the Lotus Access System functions mentioned earlier) or the DOS RE-NAME program.

Once you have a file properly named, return to the worksheet and position the cursor to the cell where you want the upper left-hand corner of the imported file to be located. You then invoke the */File Import Command* with either *Text* or *Numbers*. These two options have quite different effects on the worksheet.

The *Text* designation causes 1-2-3 to create a separate left-justified label in the first cell of a new row for each line of imported text. In other words, everything in a line gets placed in just one worksheet cell that Lotus calls a "long label." By using the */Range Justify* command on the newly created list of long labels, you can rearrange the list down a series of consecutive rows. (For more information on */Range Justify*, see the "Text Processing" section of Chapter 5.)

In contrast to the *Text* option, where numbers are treated as text, the *Numbers* option treats numbers as numbers. The rules here are that only text enclosed in double quotation marks is valid, and that each valid item in a line must be placed in its own cell within a row.

One thing you should be aware of, regardless of which option is chosen for */File Import—Text* or *Numbers*—when the file items are imported into the worksheet, everything in the space they will occupy will be written over. Be sure that there isn't anything important in the affected range of cells.

Transferring Files with the Translation Utility

The Translation Utility is used to import files from VisiCalc (in either VC or DIF format) and dBASE II into 1-2-3. This utility also enables you to export 1-2-3 files in DIF. This feature provides good communication with VisiCalc and other compatible products, which should please experienced VisiCalc users who are thinking about upgrading. Lotus Development had the good sense not to ignore the more than 400,000 VisiCalc users who might want to upgrade to 1-2-3. Lotus made it very easy to transfer VisiCalc files to 1-2-3 and provided the capability to maintain VisiCalc's mode of operation.

You can use the Translation Utility to import your VisiCalc files. From our experience, the transfer works well, with only a few minor hitches. If you are an advanced user, you may also want to export your 1-2-3 worksheet files in DIF format for use with VisiTrend/Plot or other advanced graphics programs. This allows you to take advantage of the more advanced statistical and plotting capabilities of these products.

Importing VisiCalc Files

We had only two minor problems when we tried to import VisiCalc files. The first problem did not stem from the 1-2-3 Translation Utility, but from the fundamental difference between 1-2-3 and VisiCalc.

The problem was VisiCalc's inability to control sufficiently the format of numbers for our leasing model. Because VisiCalc does not have a percentage format and its general format eliminates unnecessary zeros to the right of the decimal point, we chose to display tax rates in Currency format. This may seem strange, but it was the only way VisiCalc would display two decimal places every time (for example, .50 instead of .5).

When we imported the model into 1-2-3, using the Translation Utility, we unexpectedly got dollar signs in front of our percentages. This occurred because 1-2-3 interpreted VisiCalc's /F$ format as 1-2-3's Currency format. What you see in VisiCalc is not always what you get in 1-2-3. What you can count on, however, is a very literal translation.

The second problem was cryptic error messages that occurred during translation. The Translation Utility seemed to work properly despite these messages. The source of the problem was some formatted cells that had been left blank. Using our sample model once again, we formatted some cells for right-adjusted labels and currency but ended up leaving them blank by the time the worksheet was completed. This left some skeletons around that 1-2-3 had some difficulty recognizing, but handled properly anyway.

Here are the details of what happened. During the translation, 1-2-3 issued several error messages: "Formula Error at J38." The error for this particular cell was the result of our using the VisiCalc command /FR (or Format Right) and leaving the cell blank. 1-2-3 issued double quotation marks, which is the proper label prefix, but the error message seemed unnecessary. Another warning to users—if you leave formatted cells blank, expect error messages when you transfer files.

Aside from these problems, the transfer worked beautifully. We had no problems using our sample model once we changed the range of tax rates from the Currency to Percentage format.

Another problem you may encounter in transferring VisiCalc files occurs in translating VisiCalc's @CHOOSE, @NOT, @OR, and @AND built-in functions. 1-2-3 does not use these functions and has no equivalent functions to translate them into. If these functions are encountered, the Translation Utility issues a translation error message and converts them to labels.

Despite these few problems, those upgrading from VisiCalc to 1-2-3 should have no fear of using their models in 1-2-3.

Transferring Records between dBASE II and 1-2-3

Aside from the obvious advantage of 1-2-3's spreadsheet capability, the primary reason to transfer dBASE II records to 1-2-3 is that 1-2-3 has much faster and more easily implemented data sorting and querying capabilities. If a data base is large, only a portion of it can be imported because of 1-2-3's limitation on worksheet size. For small to medium-sized files that will be sorted and accessed frequently (such as address lists, telephone numbers, personnel files, etc.), however, there is a real advantage to using 1-2-3 over dBASE II.

Two different methods can be used to transfer records from dBASE II to 1-2-3, depending on which version of 1-2-3 you have. If you are still using Version 1, you will have a harder time transferring files between dBASE II and 1-2-3. In Version 1A, the task has been simplified considerably.

1-2-3 Version 1

Lotus was not able to complete the dBASE-to-1-2-3 conversion utility in time for Version 1 of 1-2-3. Instead, they designed an indirect method of loading dBASE files into 1-2-3. This method required the user to create a new, intermediate file using the dBASE II COPY command with the DELIMITED WITH " option. (Note that the double quotation mark is the delimiting character here.) This step created a text file that could be read by 1-2-3's / File /Import Numbers command.

This method was not particularly easy to use and suffered from some severe limitations. One problem was that any blank field in a record in the dBASE II file being transferred would be omitted from the 1-2-3 file, causing the 1-2-3 data base to be misaligned. This made it nearly impossible to transfer files of any size unless you were sure that the dBASE file contained no blanks.

It was also difficult to transfer 1-2-3 data bases into dBASE II with Version 1. 1-2-3 files could be transferred only by using the / Print File Options Other Unformatted command. This command suppresses page breaks, headers, and footers and is used to create text devoid of any special characters not recognized by dBASE II. (For a more detailed description of this command, see the next chapter.)

The steps involved in picking up 1-2-3's output with dBASE II include setting up the appropriate fields for reading the data, then appending the data onto the end of a dBASE II file. First, the dBASE II CREATE command is used to set up the fields. Then, the APPEND FROM <file.PRN> SDF command is used to append the records to the new dBASE II file. The APPEND command, in this form, will take the records from file .PRN and add them to the end of the file. The SDF designation stands for *system data format.* It tells dBASE II to accept the data in its columnar text format. (For more information on these dBASE II commands, see your *dBASE II System Manual.*)

1-2-3 Version 1A

If you have Version 1A of 1-2-3, the task of transferring dBASE II files is much simpler. Version 1A includes a completed transfer utility for dBASE that is similar to the VisiCalc transfer utility. Version 1A also has a utility that can create a dBASE II file directly from a 1-2-3 data base. Like the VisiCalc transfer utility, the dBASE II utilities are a part of the Transfer group of programs stored on the Utility disk.

Conclusion

1-2-3's file commands allow you to perform the basic operations of saving, retrieving, and deleting entire files. These are the same operations that all other spreadsheet programs perform, but 1-2-3 does not stop there. It also allows you to store and retrieve parts of files, get a list of all the files currently on a disk, and even transfer files from other programs such as VisiCalc and dBASE II. All the file operations are well polished and easy to use.

8

Printing Reports

1-2-3 gives you far more control over printing reports than earlier spreadsheet programs, such as VisiCalc. With 1-2-3 you can set options to write directly to the printer from within the program, create a print file to be printed outside of the program, print headers and footers that include the date and page numbers, print column or row headings on every page of a report, etc. There are many different print options to choose from, if you are willing to take the time to set them up. An alternative is to use the system defaults, which in most cases are more than sufficient.

The best way to describe the print options and functions is by showing how two different kinds of reports might be printed. The first report requires nothing fancy. We are more interested in the figures on the nationwide consumption of meatloaf for the next twelve months than in the format of the printed page. We will call this report the "Meatloaf Consumption Report." The only thing special that we will do when printing this report is to print all twelve months on one standard 8.5" x 11" page. Figure 8.1 shows a portion of this report.

The second report is very fancy and multifaceted. It has several pages of different financial schedules with notes to the schedules placed intermittently throughout. In addition, it goes to the Loan Officer at the bank, so it must look good and have headers, footers,

etc. We'll call this report the "Bank Loan Report." Figure 8.2 shows a
portion of this report.

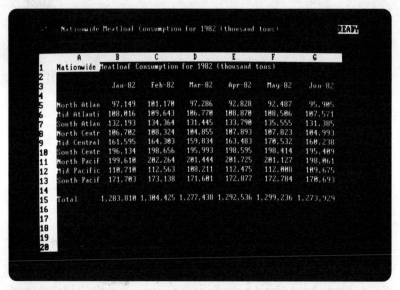

Figure 8.1

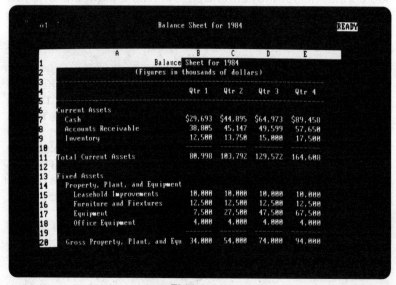

Figure 8.2

When and How to Print

The first choice you make in printing a file is whether to print it now or later. If the system you are working on doesn't have a printer, you don't know how to control the print size, or you don't want to print now, you can set up a file to be printed when the 1-2-3 session is over. The /Print Printer command is used if you want to go directly to the printer in the current 1-2-3 session, and the /Print File command is used to store output in a file to be printed later with the DOS TYPE command or a special printing routine. The /Print Printer and /Print File commands are at the root of all print commands.

Files created with the /Print File command root have a .PRN file name extension. Portions of .PRN files can be called back into 1-2-3 from disk and entered into specific locations in a worksheet with the /File Import command. Importing .PRN files is not as straightforward as it sounds, however. (Chapter 7 provides more information on importing .PRN files.)

Suppose that you want to print immediately the Meatloaf Consumption Report on your dot-matrix printer, which is currently attatched to the system; but with the Bank Loan Report, you want to wait until all of the related financial schedules are collected, then print the report on a letter-quality printer. In either case, before going any further, you must access the /Print menu.

The /Print Menu

The /Print menu is another of 1-2-3's "sticky" menus. The only way to exit from it is to specify the Quit option. This menu appears after you choose /Print Printer or /Print File and gives you the following choices:

Range   Line   Page   Options   Clear   Align   Go   Quit

Whenever you perform one of these functions, the menu returns to exactly where you were before. Be careful not to hit the RETURN key again at this point, unless you want the same function to be executed twice. It is particularly disconcerting to return from printing the worksheet using the Go function only to hit RETURN again accidentally and have the file printed a second time. If this occurs, type CTRL BREAK to stop the print.

Designating a Print Range

One of the first steps in printing any report is designating a range of cells to be printed. The command used to designate a range is / Print Range. If there are multiple ranges (as in the Bank Loan Report) corresponding to the different schedules and notes, they must be designated and printed one at a time.

Because we chose the / Print File command root for the Bank Loan Report, the ranges will be appended one after the other in the file. 1-2-3 lets you control the format of each range that is written. This is a helpful feature when you want to control the printing of each schedule. Each time a range is designated and print options are changed, you must enter Go from the / Print menu to send the range to the print file. Go is also required to send a range to the printer.

If, on the other hand, you are printing a large range, as we are in the Meatloaf Consumption Report, you will want to use the special-function keys—PgUp, PgDn, END, etc. One particularly useful sequence for pointing to a print range, when the range is the entire sheet, is END followed by HOME. This sequence is a special GOTO command that will locate the cursor at the rightmost and lowest cell in the worksheet—what Lotus Development calls the end of the "active area." This saves your having to move the cursor down manually or remember the appropriate cell address for a GOTO (F5).

Setting Print Options

Aside from designating print ranges, the only other task that requires any kind of detailed explanation in printing reports is setting print options. Several print Options will be designated for the Bank Loan Report, whereas only a few options will be used for the Meatloaf Consumption Report (to get everything on one page).

When you select Options from the / Print menu, you can choose from the following selections:

Header   Footer   Margins   Borders   Setup   Page-Length   Other

Setting Headers and Footers

For the Bank Loan Report, the first step after a print range is designated is to set the Header and Footer options. These options allow you to specify up to 240 characters of text in each of three positions—left, center, and right—in the header and footer. In reality, however, you should use only enough text to fit on an 8.5″ page.

You could enter all of the text yourself, but 1-2-3 offers some special characters that control page numbers, the current date, and where the text is printed in the header and footer lines. These special characters are

Automatically prints page numbers starting with 1

@   Automatically includes the current date in the form 29-Jun-83. Takes the date from what you entered when you loaded DOS—that is, the current date.

| Headers and footers have three separate segments: left-justified, centered, and right-justified. Use this character to separate one segment from another.

Figure 8.6, at the end of this chapter, shows how the *Header* and *Footer* options are set up with the special characters for the Bank Loan Report.

Although no headers or footers will be used for the Meatloaf Consumption report, two things should be noted about them. First, 1-2-3 always places two blank lines below the header and two above the footer line. Second, if you use the # special character for page numbers and you want to print a report a second time, you must *Clear* the *Print Options* and respecify them before the second printing. (See the "Clearing Print Options" section below.) Otherwise, the page counter will pick up where it left off.

Setting Margins

Now that you have set the headers and footers, the next logical step is to set the margins of the two reports. The *Margins* option is used to override the */ Worksheet Global Default* settings for the top, bottom, left, and right margins of the page. The */ Worksheet Global Default* margin settings from the edge of the paper are

Left	5
Right	75
Top	2
Bottom	2

The / Print <Printer or File> Options Margins command allows you to override these settings temporarily for printing purposes. We'll take advantage of this in both reports.

For the Meatloaf Consumption Report, we want to get everything on an 8.5" x 11" page. But there are 11 active columns of data in the worksheet that, when combined, form a total worksheet width of 131 characters. The only way to fit everything on one page is by using compressed print on a dot-matrix printer. We can get up to 136 characters on a line with this type of print. With the 5 characters for the left margin and the worksheet width of 131, we just stay within the limit of 136. The right margin should be set at 136, and a Setup string should be sent to the printer. (See the discussion of Setup below.)

An alternative to the compressed print would be to use the current defaults. We could let the printer print up to 80 columns on one page using pica or elite type, then continue on to later pages with what was left over. This is not the ideal solution, but it is the only other choice.

For the Bank Loan Report, the top and bottom margins are set at 5 for the "Balance Sheet for 1984" schedule, the first schedule to be printed in the report. This margin setting is the distance from the top of the page to the header and from the bottom of the page to the footer and should give us a good appearance.

The left margin is set at 4 for this report, and the right margin at 76. You may have to try several different combinations to get the setup you want.

Repeating Headers on Multipage Printouts

One of 1-2-3's special features allows you to print column and/or row headings on a multipage printout, such as the Bank Loan Report. For example, if you want to print a comparative income statement that has several columns of monthly figures which carry over to more than one page, you can have the row headings that usually occur in the first column of the first page (Sales, Gross Margin, etc.) repeated on each page. Borders Columns is the option used to repeat the row headings.

Another possibility is to print nonadjacent rows using the *Borders Rows* option. To show how this option works, suppose you want to separate the assets and liabilities when you print the Balance Sheet for the Bank Loan Report. To print the assets, you would first issue the */Print File Options Borders Rows* command and use A1..A5 as the *Rows* range. This range corresponds to the main captions for the Balance Sheet. Next, you would specify A6..A31 as the print range. Notice that this range does not include the main captions. If you include the main captions in the print range, they would be printed twice on the page. To print the liabilities portion with the main captions, leave the *Borders Rows* range as it is and specify A33..E50 as the print range. Figure 8.3 shows the liabilities portion of the Balance Sheet with the repeated headings.

There are two things to watch out for when you use the *Borders* option. First, you should not go to the */Print <Printer or File> Options Borders <Rows or Columns>* function in the command menu unless you actually want borders to be printed. If you go there by accident, A1 will be entered for either *Rows* or *Columns*, depending on which one you selected, because A1 is where the cursor goes when you specify the command. If this happens, you can enter */Print <Printer or File> Options Clear Borders* to remove the selection.

The second thing to watch out for is the possible duplication on the first page of the first column. When you repeat column headers, you usually want the first column of the first page to be printed on subsequent pages. However, if you specify that column as the border before you print the first page, you will get double first columns on the first page. To use this command properly, print a range corresponding to the first page without specifying a border, then specify the first column of the first page as the border for subsequent pages.

The *Borders* option is not used in printing the Meatloaf Consumption Report because everything is on one page. It is convenient, however, to use the *Columns* feature for some of the reports and schedules in the Bank Loan Report, where repetition of the row headings is necessary from one page to another.

```
           Balance Sheet for 1984
       (Figures in thousands of dollars)

                        Qtr 1     Qtr 2     Qtr 3     Qtr 4

Current Liabilities
  Accounts Payable     $18,750   $20,625   $22,500   $26,250
  Notes Payable         20,000    20,000    40,000    60,000
  Income Taxes Payable   4,065     6,321     7,632     9,805
                       -------   -------   -------   -------
Total Current Liabilities
                        22,815    46,946    70,132    96,055

Noncurrent Liabilities
  Long-Term Debt        20,000    18,000    16,000    14,000
                       -------   -------   -------   -------
Total Liabilities       42,815    64,946    86,132   110,055

Common Stock, $100 par value
                        50,000    50,000    50,000    50,000

Retained Earnings       16,394    35,357    58,251    87,664
                       -------   -------   -------   -------
Total Liabilities and Equity
                      $109,209  $150,303  $194,383  $247,719
                       =======   =======   =======   =======
```

Figure 8.3

Sending a Setup String to the Printer

Another print option that we use in our examples is 1-2-3's ability to pass a setup string to the printer. This option controls the compressed printing for the Meatloaf Consumption Report.

The *Setup* option sends a string of up to 39 characters to the printer. The string is sent every time you enter *Go* from the *Print* menu.

All printers are different, so you will have to look carefully at the manual to see what is required for your printer. The string is made up of backslashes (\\) followed by the decimal equivalent of special characters in ASCII code. For example, to initiate compressed print on a C. Itoh dot-matrix printer, you would use the decimal equivalent of ESC Q and associated backslashes. The string is \\027\\081. It will be used in printing the Meatloaf Consumption Report. You must do the actual translating of the appropiate ASCII codes into 1-2-3's \\nnn format yourself, using the "Printer Control Codes" appendix in the back of the *1-2-3 Manual*.

Like the other printing *Options* commands, the *Setup* string is a temporary override of a */Worksheet Global Default* setting. (For a more detailed description of this option, go to the *1-2-3 Manual* with your printer manual in hand and experiment.) If you don't expect to use your printer's special features and just want regular printing, then don't worry about this command.

Remember that if you are using compressed print, you should change the right margin to get the full 136 characters. Otherwise, you may not get all of the columns to print on one page.

Setting the Page Length

The */Worksheet Global Default* for the number of lines printed on one page is 66. You can change this number temporarily to any number between 20 and 100 with the *Page-Length* option. This option is useful when you use special forms, paper, or type sizes. Because we are using standard 8.5" x 11" paper for both reports, however, we will let this option default to 66 in both cases.

We set *Page-Length* to 88 for the Meatloaf Consumption Report, to take advantage of the compressed printing, and use the standard default of 66 for the Bank Loan Report.

Printing Cell Formulas

Another advantage that 1-2-3 has over earlier spreadsheet programs is that you can print cell contents in more than one way. For our two reports, the contents will be printed just as they are displayed on the screen, but we will also print a one-line-per-cell listing of the cell formulas for the Bank Loan Report.

The command /Print <Printer or File> Options Other controls the way cell formulas are printed. The choices that you are given when you enter this command are

As-Displayed   Cell-Formulas   Formatted   Unformatted

The Cell-Formulas option is used to create the one-line-per-cell listing of the contents of a worksheet. Although this option is often very convenient for debugging, it is used here to document the cell formulas in the Bank Loan Report, in case the Loan Officer asks us a tough question about how we got our numbers. Figure 8.4 shows the Cell-Formulas listing of the Bank Loan Report.

The ↖As-Displayed option works with Cell-Formulas to reverse the Cell-Formulas option. It returns to printing the format on the screen.

The other two options, Formatted and Unformatted, work together. The Unformatted option suppresses page breaks, headers, and footers and is used to create /Print Files for input to other programs that are independent of 1-2-3. The programs might be special print routines, data base management systems, or word-processing programs. The Formatted option returns things to normal. (These commands will not be used in printing our two reports.)

Clearing Print Options

If we wanted to print our two reports together one after the other, we would need a way to clear the different print options and settings between printing the reports. The Clear /Print menu option allows you to eliminate all, or just a portion, of the print options that you chose earlier. The choices displayed are

All   Range   Borders   Format

You can clear every print option, including the print range, by selecting All, or you can be more specific by using the other choices.

Balance Sheet for 1984
(Figures in thousands of dollars)

```
A1:  '
A2:  '
A3:  \-
B3:  \-
C3:  \-
D3:  \-
E3:  \-
B4:  (D1) ^Qtr 1
C4:  ^Qtr 2
D4:  ^Qtr 3
E4:  ^Qtr 4
A5:  \-
B5:  \-
C5:  \-
D5:  \-
E5:  \-
A6:  'Current Assets
A7:  '  Cash
B7:  (CO) 29693
C7:  (CO) 44895
D7:  (CO) 64973
E7:  (CO) 89458
A8:  '   Accounts Receivable
B8:  (,0) 38805
C8:  (,0) 45147
D8:  (,0) 49599
E8:  (,0) 57650
A9:  '   Inventory
B9:  (,0) 12500
C9:  (,0) 13750
D9:  (,0) 15000
E9:  (,0) 17500
A10: '
B10: (CO) ' -------
C10: (CO) ' -------
D10: (CO) ' -------
E10: (CO) ' -------
A11: 'Total Current Assets
B11: (,0) @SUM(B7..B9)
C11: (,0) @SUM(C7..C9)
D11: (,0) @SUM(D7..D9)
E11: (,0) @SUM(E7..E9)
A12: '
A13: 'Fixed Assets
A14: '   P, P, and E
A15: '      Leasehold Improvements
B15: (,0) 10000
C15: (,0) 10000
D15: (,0) 10000
E15: (,0) 10000
A16: '      Furniture and Fixtures
B16: (,0) 12500
C16: (,0) 12500
D16: (,0) 12500
E16: (,0) 12500
A17: '      Equipment
B17: (,0) 7500
C17: (,0) 7500+20000
D17: (,0) +C17+20000
```

```
E17: (,0) +D17+20000
A18: '      Office Equipment
B18: (,0) 4000
C18: (,0) 4000
D18: (,0) 4000
E18: (,0) 4000
B19: (CO) ' -------
C19: (CO) ' -------
D19: (CO) ' -------
E19: (CO) ' -------
A20: '   Gross P, P, and E
B20: (,0) @SUM(B15..B18)
C20: (,0) @SUM(C15..C18)
D20: (,0) @SUM(D15..D18)
E20: (,0) @SUM(E15..E18)
A21: '   Accumulated Depreciation
B21: (,0) 6700
C21: (,0) 8400
D21: (,0) 10100
E21: (,0) 11800
B22: (CO) ' -------
C22: (CO) ' -------
D22: (CO) ' -------
E22: (CO) ' -------
A23: '   Net P, P, and E
B23: (,0) +B20-B21
C23: (,0) +C20-C21
D23: (,0) +D20-D21
E23: (,0) +E20-E21
A25: '   Deposits
B25: 611
C25: 611
D25: 611
E25: 611
A26: '   Other
B26: 300
C26: 300
D26: 300
E26: 300
B27: (CO) ' -------
C27: (CO) ' -------
D27: (CO) ' -------
E27: (CO) ' -------
A28: 'Total Fixed Assets
B28: (,0) @SUM(B23..B26)
C28: (,0) @SUM(C23..C26)
D28: (,0) @SUM(D23..D26)
E28: (,0) @SUM(E23..E26)
A30: 'Total Assets
B30: (CO) +CA+B28
C30: (CO) +C11+C28
D30: (CO) +D11+D28
E30: (CO) +E11+E28
B31: (CO) '========
```

Figure 8.4

*R*ange	Removes the previous print range specification
*B*orders	Cancels *C*olumns and *R*ows specified as borders
*F*ormat	Clears out *M*argins, *P*age-Length, and *S*etup string settings. Everything that is *C*leared returns to the default setting. This option is very useful when you make mistakes or want to print reports with different formats one after the other.

Controlling the Printer

1-2-3 gives you a great deal of control over the printer from within the program itself. In fact, you get so much control that you hardly ever have to touch the printer, except to turn it on just prior to printing a report and turn if it off when you are done.

This feature will be used to great advantage in printing the Bank Loan Report. In between some of the different schedules and text that we will print for this report, we will need to space down several lines. The */ Print Printer Line* command makes the printer skip a line each time the command is entered. This command will be used several times in a row to skip between some of our schedules.

We will also need to skip often to a new page. The command to do this is */ Print Printer Page*. Like the *Line* command, the *Page* command causes the printer to skip to a new page each time you enter the command. When *Page* is used at the end of a printing session, the footer will be printed on the last page. If you *Quit* from the */ Print* menu before issuing the *Page* command, you won't get the last footer.

Finally, when we start printing the report, we will need a way to signal to the printer where the top of the page is. The command used to align the page is */ Print Printer Align*. Again, this command saves you from having to touch the printer control buttons.

The *Go* command must be entered from the */ Print* menu to start the printer. (This command also allows you to send a range to a */ Print File*.)

If you want to interrupt the printing of a report in midstream, simply hold down the CTRL key and simultaneously hit the BREAK key. It may take some time for the print buffer to clear, depending on its size, but the print menu will appear almost immediately. In the meantime, you can perform another menu function.

Now that you understand how to set print options, let's take a look at the two example reports. Figure 8.5 shows the commands that were used to do the printing. Figure 8.6 shows the actual reports as they appear when printed. The entire Meatloaf Consumption Report and the first page of the Bank Loan Report are shown.

Figure 8.5

Commands to print the Meatloaf Consumption Report

```
/ Print Printer Range A1..M15~
              Options Margins Right 136~
                      Setup \027\081~
                      Quit

           Go
           Quit
```

Commands to print the first schedule in the Bank Loan Report

```
/ Print Printer Range A1..E50~
              Options Header |0| Tuna Manufacturing Company |@~
                      Footer |Page #~
                      Margins Top 5~
                      Margins Bottom 5~
                      Margins Left 4~
                      Margins Right 76~
                      Quit

           Go
           Quit
```

Nationwide Meatloaf Consumption for 1982 (thousand tons)

	Jan-82	Feb-82	Mar-82	Apr-82	May-82	Jun-82	Jul-82	Aug-82	Sep-82	Oct-82	Nov-82	Dec-82
North Atlan	97,149	101,170	97,286	92,828	92,487	95,905	100,817	96,878	91,245	90,668	95,305	100,708
Mid Atlanti	108,016	109,643	106,770	108,870	108,506	107,571	109,316	105,167	107,825	107,022	105,767	108,464
South Atlan	132,193	134,364	131,445	133,790	135,555	131,385	133,315	130,887	132,475	135,524	131,107	131,607
North Centr	106,702	108,324	104,855	107,893	107,823	104,993	106,696	103,959	107,747	106,317	104,717	106,563
Mid Central	161,595	164,303	159,834	163,483	170,532	160,238	162,598	158,757	163,406	168,778	159,532	162,132
South Centr	196,134	198,656	195,993	198,595	198,414	195,409	196,920	195,820	197,906	198,025	193,700	195,091
North Pacif	199,610	202,264	201,444	201,725	201,127	198,061	201,726	200,604	200,530	199,497	197,819	200,327
Mid Pacific	110,710	112,563	108,211	112,475	112,008	109,675	112,386	106,346	111,219	111,842	109,426	112,160
South Pacif	171,703	173,138	171,601	172,877	172,784	170,693	171,385	169,821	171,307	172,541	169,363	170,508
Total	1,283,810	1,304,425	1,277,438	1,292,536	1,299,236	1,273,929	1,295,160	1,268,238	1,283,659	1,290,215	1,266,736	1,287,560

Figure 8.6A

Balance Sheet for 1984
(Figures in thousands of dollars)

	Qtr 1	Qtr 2	Qtr 3	Qtr 4
Current Assets				
Cash	$29,693	$44,895	$64,973	$89,458
Accounts Receivable	38,805	45,147	49,599	57,650
Inventory	12,500	13,750	15,000	17,500
Total Current Assets	80,998	103,792	129,572	164,608
Fixed Assets				
P, P, and E				
Leasehold Improvements	10,000	10,000	10,000	10,000
Furniture and Fixtures	12,500	12,500	12,500	12,500
Equipment	7,500	27,500	47,500	67,500
Office Equipment	4,000	4,000	4,000	4,000
Gross P, P, and E	34,000	54,000	74,000	94,000
Accumulated Depreciation	6,700	8,400	10,100	11,800
Net P, P, and E	27,300	45,600	63,900	82,200
Deposits	611	611	611	611
Other	300	300	300	300
Total Fixed Assets	28,211	46,511	64,811	83,111
Total Assets	$109,209	$150,303	$194,383	$247,719
Current Liabilities				
Accounts Payable	$18,750	$20,625	$22,500	$26,250
Notes Payable		20,000	40,000	60,000
Income Taxes Payable	4,065	6,321	7,632	9,805
Total Current Liabilities	22,815	46,946	70,132	96,055
Noncurrent Liabilities				
Long-Term Debt	20,000	18,000	16,000	14,000
Total Liabilities	42,815	64,946	86,132	110,055
Common Stock, $1.00 par value	50,000	50,000	50,000	50,000
Retained Earnings	16,394	35,357	58,251	87,664
Total Liabilities and Equity	$109,209	$150,303	$194,383	$247,719

Figure 8.6B

9

Creating and Displaying Graphs

A picture tells me at a glance what it takes dozens of pages of a book to expound.

—Turgenev

Next to the spreadsheet, graphics is the most used element of 1-2-3. The integration of graphics with 1-2-3's exceptional spreadsheet is a major step forward in the development of analysis software.

1-2-3's graphics are designed for quick and easy implementation. Because they are an integral part of the entire program, data can be represented graphically with almost no effort. There is no need to transfer data from one program to another to create a graph. Instead, the user issues two simple commands, and—presto!—the graph is drawn. 1-2-3 also offers a number of graphics options that allow titles, labels, and legends to be inserted in the graph.

Although 1-2-3 has a good set of basic graphics commands and adds a few bells and whistles, it does not offer the power or flexibility of some of the dedicated graphics programs. In other words, some graphics programs are more comprehensive than 1-2-3, just as some data management programs are more comprehensive than 1-2-3. But because 1-2-3's graphics are an integrated part of an entire management system, they offer far more than most stand-alone systems.

VisiPlot vs. 1-2-3

If 1-2-3's spreadsheet is a descendant of VisiCalc, then its graphics functions are even more closely related to another VisiCorp product: VisiPlot. Both VisiPlot and 1-2-3 were created by Mitch Kapor, now president of Lotus Development Corporation.

A good way to give you an idea of 1-2-3's graphics capabilities is to compare 1-2-3 with VisiPlot, a part of the VisiTrend/Plot graphics and statistical package. The VisiPlot portion of the program was designed just for graphics.

The major difference between the two programs is that VisiPlot is a stand-alone program that operates independently of its companion spreadsheet program VisiCalc. VisiPlot must be booted separately. The only way to transfer data between a spreadsheet and VisiPlot is through the DIF (Data Interchange Format) file. The DIF format, invented by Software Arts Corporation (creators of VisiCalc), is a simple file format standard used to transfer files between programs. Transferring data requires that the user create a separate DIF file, exit VisiCalc (or other spreadsheet program) and enter VisiPlot, load the DIF file into VisiPlot, and define and plot the graph. Although this technique works well, it is very time-consuming, especially if the user decides to change some of the data. If this occurs, the entire process must be repeated.

In contrast, 1-2-3's graphics capabilities reside on the 1-2-3 system diskette. Graphs based on spreadsheet data can be created, using a spreadsheet command (/G). Data does not have to be transferred from one program to another; all of the action occurs within the 1-2-3 program. This means that graphs can be created in a few seconds. Moreover, because the graphs are drawing directly on data in the spreadsheet and not on data in an intermediate DIF file, the effects of any changes in spreadsheet data can be passed through to a graph with a single keystroke. For the first time, graphics can be included in the "what if" process that makes spreadsheeting so valuable. 1-2-3, however, does require that graph files be transferred to another program before they can be printed.

VisiPlot offers more features than 1-2-3. VisiPlot contains such features as movable labels, more graph types (including area charts and hi-lo charts), and full color display of graphics. In addition,

VisiPlot is accompanied by a sophisticated statistical package—VisiTrend—that develops data series for analysis and forecasting techniques, performs multiple linear regression, and does trend line forecasting, etc. Although 1-2-3 has some statistical analysis capability, it does not have the power of VisiTrend.

Although VisiPlot has more graphics features, 1-2-3 offers almost all of the basic features of VisiPlot while integrating graphics with the spreadsheet. 1-2-3's graphics are designed more for immediate accessibility and ease of use than any other product of its type on the market today. This makes 1-2-3 one of the most exciting graphics programs.

The Graph Command

In 1-2-3, graphs are created and formatted through the Graph command (/G), which is one of the commands on 1-2-3's main menu. When you type /G, the following menu will appear in the control panel:

Type X ABCDEF   Reset View Save Options Name Quit

1-2-3 offers five basic types of graphs:

> Simple Bar
> Stacked Bar
> Pie Charts
> Line
> XY

Types of Graphs

Bar Graphs

Suppose that you want to create a simple worksheet containing data about steel production in the Western countries in 1979, as shown in figure 9.1. You can create many interesting graphs that will help make this data more understandable. For example, you can make a simple bar chart to illustrate the data on U.S. steel production alone. This graph is illustrated in figure 9.2.

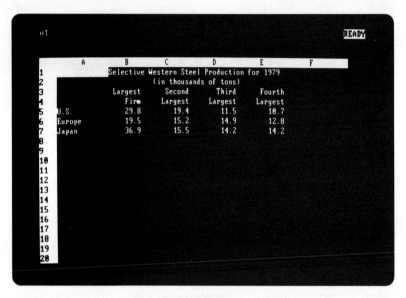

Figure 9.1

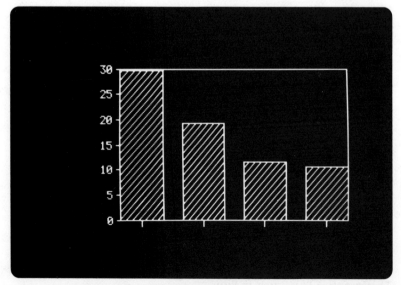

Figure 9.2

Making a Simple Bar Graph

Bar graphs are used to compare different sets of data. Typically, a bar graph consists of vertical bars that show value by height. To create a bar graph, first type /G to enter the Graphics command. At this point, the Graph menu will appear in the control panel.

Selecting the Type of Graph

You must first choose the Type of graph you want to produce. To do so, select Type from the graphics menu. The following menu will appear:

    Bar   Stack Bar   Line   Pie   XY

Because you are creating a bar graph, select the Bar option from this menu. Notice that 1-2-3 automatically returns you to the main graphics menu after the graph type is selected.

Entering Data

Now that you have told 1-2-3 what type of graph to create, you must give the program some data to use in creating the graph. This process is begun by selecting the "A" option from the main graphics menu. After this option is selected, 1-2-3 prompts for a range.

Choosing the Data Range

As usual, the range can be defined with cell references or a range name. In this case, we used the coordinates B5..E5. Remember that this reference can be entered either by actually typing the cell coordinates from the keyboard or by using the 1-2-3 Point mode.

Our simple graph requires only one range, but 1-2-3 lets you specify as many as six data ranges per graph. As you may have guessed, the letters B through F on the graphics menu represent the other ranges.

In addition, although the data range for this sample graph consists of a partial row of data, there is no reason why it can not be a partial column. The graphs at the end of this chapter include examples of both vertical and horizontal data ranges. Remember, however, that the range must be a continuous set of cells. Thus, the ranges A2..A6, D3..F3, and F14..F30 are legal ranges, but the ranges A2,A4,D7 and E5,E8,F17,L4 are not.

Viewing the Graph

The final step in producing the graph is to enter *View* from the / *Graph* menu. What happens when you enter *View* depends on the hardware you have and how you have configured the system. (For more on configuring your system, see Chapter 2.) If you have a nongraphics screen, nothing happens. All you get is a beep, but don't worry. Although you can't see the graph on the display, it still exists in your computer's memory. The graph can be saved, then printed later, using the PrintGraph program.

If you have a graphics card and either a black-and-white or color screen, you should see the bar graph displayed on the screen after you enter *View*. If you have a Hercules Graphics Card for your monochrome display, the graph will appear on that display. Notice that in both of these cases the graph replaces the worksheet on the screen. You can return to the screen by typing any key.

Finally, if you are fortunate enough to have both a graphics monitor and a monochrome display, the bar chart will appear on the graphics monitor when you select *View*. The worksheet will remain in view on the monochrome display. If your graphics monitor can display color, you can format the graph to take advantage of that capability.

Redrawing the Graph

The most exciting feature of 1-2-3's graphics capabilities is its redrawing ability. Suppose that you want to update the data in figure 9.2 to reflect a change in size of the fourth largest producer in the United States. Figure 9.3 shows the updated spreadsheet.

Now suppose that you want to graph this new data. You can do this in one of two ways. First, you can use the graphics command / *Graph View* to redraw the graph. But 1-2-3 offers an easier method.

A quick way of redrawing the graph is to press the F10 (GRAPH) key while you are in the Ready mode. This is the equivalent of *View*, but saves your having to go through the / *Graph* menu. (The F10 key does not work while you are in a graph menu.)

The F10 key makes 1-2-3's graphics mode different from any other program. The ability to redraw a graph immediately after making a change to the spreadsheet means that it is possible to perform "what

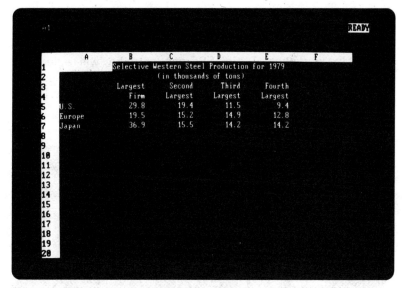

Figure 9.3

if" analysis that includes graphics. To understand the importance of this, think about the process of creating graphics with VisiCalc and VisiPlot. Because data can be transferred with an intermediate file between only these two programs, it is not practical to display graphically the result of each change in the sheet. Instead, VisiPlot commonly is used to graph only the *finished product*. Although this is very useful, it does not take advantage of the full power of graphics to make the effects of changes apparent quickly.

In 1-2-3, graphics can be an integral part of "what if" analysis. You can use graphics extensively while you fine tune projections, budgets, or other projects. You'll be amazed at how graphics will help you understand the impact of changes in your data on the results of your models.

The F10 key has another use. If you have a color graphics card and a monochrome display, you may have noticed that graphs remain on the graphics screen after they are defined until you redraw them, replace them with another graph, or turn off the system. This makes it easy to glance back and forth between the worksheet and your graph. On single-monitor systems this is not possible because the graph and the worksheet share the same space. Thanks to the F10 key, however, you don't have to redefine the graph completely to review it. You simply type F10, and the graph will appear again in place of the worksheet. Typing ESC or another key will replace the graph with the worksheet. When the F10 and ESC keys are used as toggles, you can flip back and forth between the two displays. Figure 9.4 displays this graph.

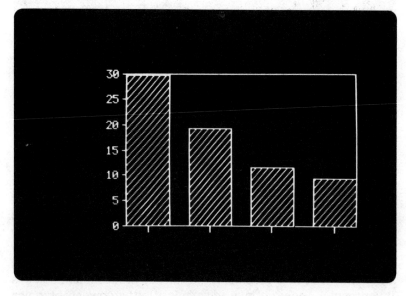

Figure 9.4

Adding Titles and Labels

Although the picture we have created is very pretty, it doesn't really offer much information. To complete the graph, we must add titles, labels, and a variety of other things. The next sections will show you how this is done.

You will probably want to enter titles for the overall graph and for the x and y axes. This is done through the / Graph Options Titles menu. It gives you the following choices:

    First   Second   X-Axis   Y-Axis

We used *X*-Axis and *Y*-Axis to enter the labels "Firm Size" and "Thousand Tons Produced," respectively, into the graph. For example, to enter the x-axis label, we selected the *X*-axis option and simply typed the title ("Firm Size") we wanted for the x axis of the graph. The y-axis label was similarly specified.

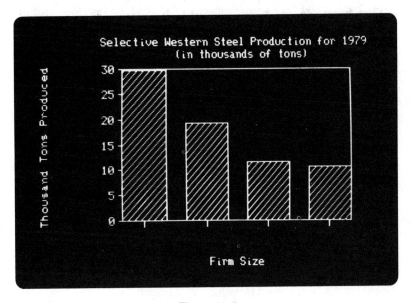

Figure 9.5

The graph titles at the top of figure 9.5 were entered using the *First* and *Second* options. *First* was used for the main title ("Selective Western Steel Production for 1979"), and *Second* was used for the subtitle below it ("in thousands of tons").

These titles are usually entered by typing the title from the keyboard. In this case, however, we used the special backslash (\) feature made available to this and other / *Graph Options* commands for entering the contents of cells instead of typing in text. To use the contents of a cell for legend text, place a backslash (\) before the actual cell address when 1-2-3 asks you for a title. We entered "\B1" for *First* and "\C2" for *Second*. The same technique can be used to enter x- and y-axis titles and legends.

A range name can also be used to create a title or label. To do this, you would enter the range name, instead of the cell references, after the backslash. The title must be 39 characters or less.

If you are working along on your computer, did you notice that after you entered a title, the options menu appeared and not the title menu? For some reason, 1-2-3 skips up two menu levels after you enter a title. To enter another title, you have to type ENTER to return to the title menu, then select the option (*First*, *Second*, *X*-axis, *Y*-axis) for the title you want to create. It would be much simpler if the title selection menu remained active after a title was entered.

You should be aware of two things about the way 1-2-3 displays titles. First, notice that 1-2-3 automatically centered the *First* and *Second* graph titles when it displayed the graph, irrespective of the label prefixes used in the worksheet. 1-2-3 will always do this.

Second, you will see that the *First* and *Second* titles look very much alike in size and intensity on the screen. 1-2-3 will always display the titles this way on the screen. The PrintGraph program, however, includes options that allow you to alter either or both titles when you print the graph. (This facility is explained in the next chapter.)

Another enhancement you may want to make to your graph is to add labels along the x axis to define the data items you are plotting. Figure 9.6 shows our basic graphs with x-axis labels added.

These labels are entered by selecting *X* from the / *Graph* menu, then pointing to the range of labels in the worksheet. In this example, the labels are located in the range B3..E3 in figure 9.3. We used 1-2-3's Point mode to simplify the process of identifying the limits of the range. 1-2-3 uses the contents of the cells in the indicated range as X labels. Notice that 1-2-3 automatically centers the X labels.

Setting Scale Limits

Automatic Scale Settings

When we created our graph for the first time, 1-2-3 automatically set the scale (lower limit and upper limit) of the y axis to fit our data. This is extremely convenient. 1-2-3 is designed to use a scale that shows all the data points in as much of the screen as possible. If 1-2-3 did not automatically set the scale in this way, creating graphs would be much more cumbersome.

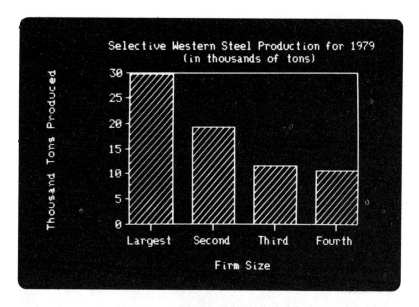

Figure 9.6

Sometimes you will want to change the scale that 1-2-3 has chosen for a graph. For example, you may want to focus attention on a certain range of values, such as those surrounding a target goal. Alternatively, you may want to create a series of graphs that all have the same scale.

Overriding the Automatic Scale

1-2-3's automatic scale can be overriden with the / Graph Options Scale. Once you have issued this command, you are given the choice of rescaling either the X-axis or the Y-axis. Once you have made a selection, you are presented with the following menu:

      Automatic   Manual   Lower   Upper   Format

Manual is used to override 1-2-3's automatic scaling, whereas Automatic is used to reinstate it. The other choices are options under the Manual selection.

Organization of the Manual Command

The organization of this command departs slightly from 1-2-3's normal command logic. If the Manual command followed the standard form, the options *Lower*, *Upper*, and *Format* would be contained in a menu one level below the *Manual / Automatic* choice. This break with the usual logic was made to avoid adding a sixth level of commands to the program.

The *Lower* and *Upper* selections are used to set the scale limits when *Manual* has been chosen. Figure 9.7 shows how this function works. This figure is a graph using the same data as that in figure 9.6, except that we have changed the scale to have an upper limit of 50 and a lower limit of -50.

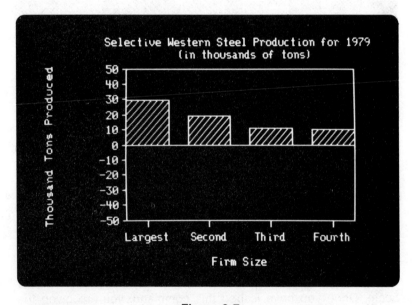

Figure 9.7

Formatting Numbers

The *Format* option allows you to change the way the numbers on the x and y axes are displayed. The alternatives under this option are the same as those for the */Range Format* and */Worksheet Global Format* commands. For example, you can specify that the numbers be displayed with a fixed number of digits, with an embedded "$" or comma, or as a percentage with an appended "%" sign. For example, figure 9.8 shows the same graph as in figure 9.7, except that the scale has been assigned the *Fixed 2* format.

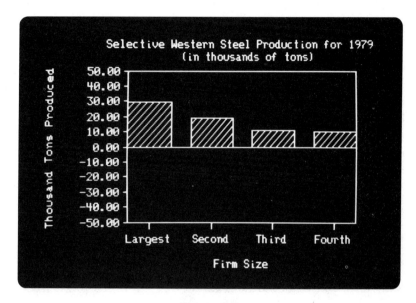

Figure 9.8

Fitting the Graph to the Scales

1-2-3 will always try to fit the graph into the scales you have specified. If you set the upper limit of a scale too low, the resulting graph will simply show as much of the data as can be squeezed into the allotted space. For example, if you set the upper limit at 5 and the lower limit at 0 and try to graph our sample data, the result will be figure 9.9.

1-2-3 will always ignore a positive *Lower* limit or a negative *Upper* limit on the y-axis scale to ensure that zero (the origin) is always on the scale. Although this may seem to reduce the flexibility of 1-2-3's Graphics mode, it is, in fact, a valuable feature. Graphs that do not display the origin can be very misleading. 1-2-3 deals with this problem by not allowing such graphs to be created.

The scale option will also not allow you to vary the spacing of the tick marks on the y axis. The program automatically places ticks at intervals along the y axis, and usually these are reasonably spaced. There may be times, however, when being able to adjust these marks would be better.

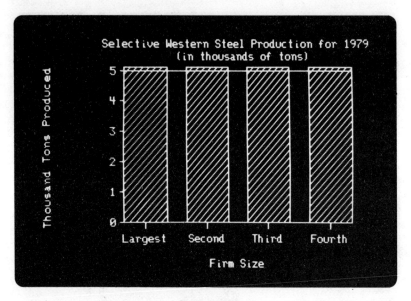

Figure 9.9

Other Scale Options

Several other options may be selected for formatting a graph. They are best applied to other types of graphs and will, therefore, be demonstrated later. For now, we are finished with the sample graph we created. Figure 9.10 shows our original graph with all of its formatting options.

Saving and Recalling Graph Settings

Only one graph at a time can be the "current" graph. Before you can build a new graph, you must store the old one.

By issuing the /Graph Name Create command, you can instruct 1-2-3 to remember the parameters used to define the current graph. With this command, you can create an eight-character graph name to represent the current graph. All of the information relating to this graph—the data range settings, the graph titles, axis titles, etc.—will be saved under this name. When you save the 1-2-3 worksheet, the name will also be saved.

You can recall a named graph at any time by issuing the /Graph Name Use command. When this command is issued, 1-2-3 presents a list of all the graph names stored in the current worksheet. You can select the graph you want to plot either by typing the name from the keyboard or by pointing to the name on the list. The /Graph Name Use command will retrieve the graph settings of the named graph and automatically redraw it.

This command is the only way a graph can be stored for later recall and display. If you don't name a graph, and either delete the graph or change the specifications, there is no way to replot it without respecifying the settings. If you forget to save the settings under a graph name before you exit, the /GNU command is of no use to you. Similarly, if you fail to save the current worksheet after you name a series of graphs in that worksheet, the names will be lost. *Be careful!* We have made this mistake several times.

It is not unusual to create several different graphs for a single worksheet. The /Graph Name Create and /Graph Name Use commands make it easy to create and use a number of graphs. For example, the settings for the various simple and stacked bar graphs

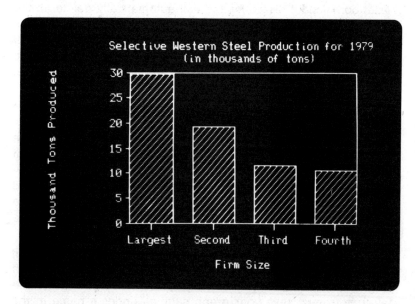

Figure 9.10

used in the "Selective Western Steel Production" examples are stored under different graph names in the same worksheet file. The / Graph Name Create and Use commands allow us to recall and draw each graph without re-entering its settings.

The / Graph Name Use command can also be used to recall a number of graphs in rapid sequence, creating what is, in effect, a slide show of 1-2-3 graphics. This feature can be used very effectively in presentations to display a large number of graphs with a minimum number of keystrokes.

Deleting Graphs

To delete a single graph name from the worksheet, you use the / Graph Name Delete command. As with the / Graph Name Create command, 1-2-3 will prompt you with a list of all of the graph names in the current sheet. You can either point to the name you want to delete or type the name from the keyboard. If you choose not to delete any graphs, simply type ESC ESC ESC (or CTRL BREAK) to return to the Ready mode.

To delete *all* the graph names, you can issue the / Graph Name Reset command. This command will automatically delete all the graph names in the current worksheet. Be Careful! When the name of a graph is deleted, the parameters for the graph are deleted also. It cannot be plotted again without being completely respecified. There is no "Yes/No" confirmation step in the / Graph Name Reset command, so once you type the R for reset, the graphs are gone.

Saving Graphs for Printing

As mentioned earlier, the main 1-2-3 program does not have the ability to print graphs. The PrintGraph program must be used to print graphics. Before a graph can be printed with PrintGraph, however, it must be saved, using the / Graph Save command. This command saves to a graph file the current graph, along with all of the formatting options you have selected. All graph files have the extension .PIC.

Once you have created a .PIC file, you can no longer access it from the main 1-2-3 menu. It is accessible from only the PrintGraph program. If you want to recreate the graph on the screen from within 1-2-3, you must save your graph settings under a name in the worksheet file.

Resetting the Current Graph

Suppose that you have named your first graph and want to begin work on a new one. The first thing to do is remove all of the information related to the first graph from 1-2-3's active memory. This can be done by issuing the /Graph Reset command.

After this command is selected, the following menu appears:

Graph   X   A   B   C   D   E   F   Quit

One of the options on this menu, Graph, lets you reset all of 1-2-3's graph parameters. If you do not want to use any of the old parameters in your new graph, this is the option you should select.

If, on the other hand, your new graph shares some parameters with the old graph, you can delete only part of the information relating to the old graph. For example, you can reset the parameters on one or more ranges by choosing options A through F. The X option resets the X labels.

Because the next example builds directly on the data from our first graph, we do not want to reset any of the settings we have defined.

Creating a More Complex Bar Graph

Before going on to discuss colors, data labels, and various other commands and features, we should first increase the complexity of the bar graph in figure 9.2 to help in further explanations. We can build a more complex graph by including the data for European and Japanese steel production alongside the data for the United States.

Adding More Data Ranges

The first thing that must be done in creating the new graph is to inform 1-2-3 that this new graph will include two additional data ranges. To do this, we enter the graphics menu by typing /Graphics. Because we've already created one data range, the next set of data will go into the B range. To enter the data range, we select the B option from the menu (either by pointing or by typing "B") and tell 1-2-3 that the data is located in the range C2..C5. Similarly, to enter the third data set, we would select the C option and indicate the location of the data: D2..D5. We are now ready to draw the graph, so we enter View because we are in the Menu mode.

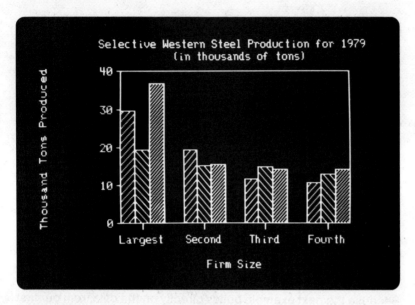

Figure 9.11

Notice the different crosshatches within the bars this time. There were crosshatches in the first graph we drew, but because there was only one set of data, we had only one pattern of crosshatches. Because this graph has several sets of data, the contrast between the crosshatches is much greater. Cross-hatching makes it very easy to distinguish between the different sets of data when they are graphed in black and white. 1-2-3 automatically controls the crosshatches.

You will also see that the data sets are grouped in the graph. The first data items from each range are grouped together; similarly, the second and third data items are grouped together. This grouping makes it easy to compare the data in each data set.

Using Legends

Whenever you have more than one set of data on a graph, it is helpful to have some method to distinguish one set from another. 1-2-3 has several ways. In line graphs, different symbols are available to mark the different data points. In bar charts, different patterns of cross-hatching are used. If the display is a color monitor, 1-2-3 can also use color to make the distinction.

With the different patterns, it is helpful to have legends to label the patterns. At the bottom of figure 9.12, below the x axis, there are three different legends corresponding to the three different ranges of data we have graphed. These legends are entered with the / *Graph Options Legends* command. Once you have selected this option, you can type the actual legend text. For example, we labeled the first data set "U.S."

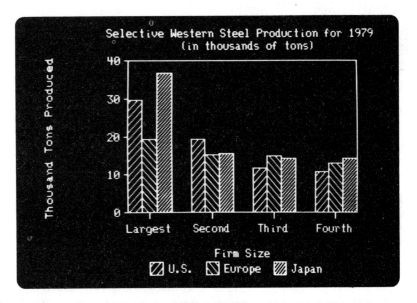

Figure 9.12

Like titles, labels can be entered with \ and a cell reference or a range name, instead of typing the label. For example, we put \A5 for / *Graph Options Legend A,* "\A6" for *B,* and so on.

Displaying the Graph in Color

If you have a color monitor, you can instruct 1-2-3 to display graphics in color. This is one of the nicest features of the program. 1-2-3 can display graphics in three colors: white, red, and blue. These are not to be confused with the larger selection of colors the program can actually use for printing graphs if you have the appropriate printer. (Printing graphs and the additional colors available are covered in the next chapter.)

To display the graph from figure 9.12 in color, you would select *Color* from the */Graph Options* menu. The bars and lines for each data range and the legend blocks take on the following colors:

A   White
B   Red
C   Blue
D   White
E   Red
F   Blue

The list of colors is obviously somewhat limited. In complex graphs, it can be easy to confuse different data ranges that are displayed in the same color. In fact, this color restriction is probably one of the biggest limitations of 1-2-3's Graphics mode.

This restriction is eased, however, by the PrintGraph program's ability to add color to your graphs when they are printed or plotted. The colors in PrintGraph are completely independent of the colors you assign with the *Color* option of 1-2-3. Even graphs that are saved with no colors can be printed in color with PrintGraph.

The */Graph Options B&W* command switches the graphics display from color to black and white.

Stacked Bar Graphs

A slight variation on the basic bar graph is the stacked bar. Stacked bar graphs are frequently used to compare different sets of data while showing the components and total of each data set. In these graphs, the totals are created by stacking the component data items one on another. In figure 9.13, you can see the total tonnage for the four largest steel producers in the U.S., Japan, and Europe.

This graph was created in much the same way as our second graph. To select the graph type, you issue the command */Graph Type Stack Bar*. There are four data ranges for this graph. You select the first by choosing the *A* option and indicating the data range B5..B7. In a similar manner, you set the second, or B range, to C5..C7. The other data ranges are selected by choosing the *C* and *D* options.

As usual, the *View* command draws the graph. Notice that we've already added legends, x-axis labels, and titles to this graph. They were added in the same way as they were in the simpler examples.

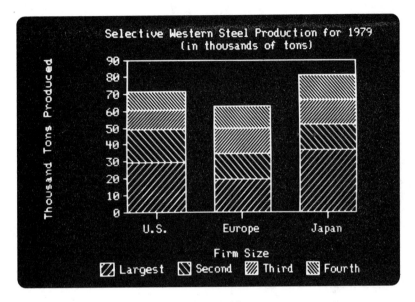

Figure 9.13

For example, the *First* and *Second* titles in figure 9.13 are the same as those in our earlier examples. The *X* and *Y* titles are different. They were entered by selecting the *X* and *Y* options and typing the title.

The legends in figure 9.13 were created by selecting the *Legend* option from the */Graph Options* menu and specifying the range B3..E3. Notice that these legends are the same as the x labels in our earlier examples.

The *X* labels in figure 9.13 are the same as the legends in the earlier graphs. These labels were entered by selecting the *X* option from the main graph menu and indicating the range A5..A7.

Line Graphs

The third type of graph offered by 1-2-3 is a line graph. Line graphs are particularly useful for showing time series data, but they are by no means restricted to this use. Consider the following data on "Interest Rate Movements for February 1983."

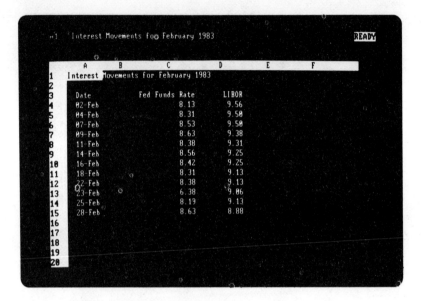

Figure 9.14

This data was taken from *The Wall Street Journal* and reflects the Federal Funds Rate and the London Interbank Offering Rate (LIBOR) for the indicated dates.

Making a Line Graph

To create a line graph of the Federal Funds Rate plotted against time, we first select the *L*ine option from the */ G*raph *T*ype menu. Next, we select the *A* option and enter the range C4..C15 as the *A* range. As always, the graph is drawn with the *V*iew option. Figure 9.15 illustrates this line graph.

Once again, notice that we've added titles to this graph. This was done by selecting the *T*itles option from the *O*ptions menu and entering the titles shown for *F*irst, *S*econd, *X*, and *Y* selections.

Notice also that our line chart has no x-axis labels. The next step is to enter the range of dates in column A as the *X* range. As with the bar graph, we enter *X* labels by selecting the *X* option from the main graphics menu. In this example, we want to use the information in column A as X labels, so we enter the range A4..A15.

If this graph is redrawn (by stepping back to the main graph menu and typing *View*), you will see (figure 9.16) that using the entire set of labels in column A causes a problem. There is simply not enough room on the graph to display all of the labels without overlapping. This can happen any time the X labels you select are unusually long, or if there are a large number of X labels, as in this case. In Version 1 of 1-2-3, there was not much you could do about this problem. Version 1A, however, offers a solution.

The */ Graph Option Scale Skip* command makes it possible to "skip" every n^{th} X label when the graph is displayed. After you type the command, 1-2-3 will prompt you for the skipping factor. In most cases, skipping every other label will be sufficient to clean up the graph. This is done by specifying a factor of 2. On some graphs, however, it may be necessary to choose a much larger factor. In our example, we've instructed 1-2-3 to skip every third label. 1-2-3 has the ability to skip as many as 2,048 X labels. Figure 9.17 shows the line graph with an x-axis skipping factor of 2.

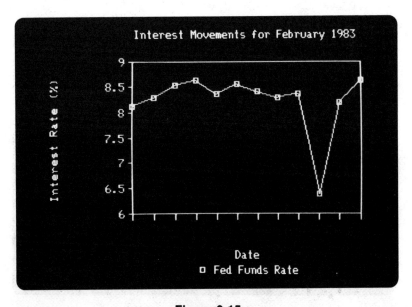

Figure 9.15

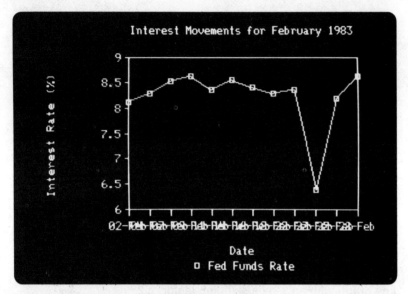

Figure 9.16

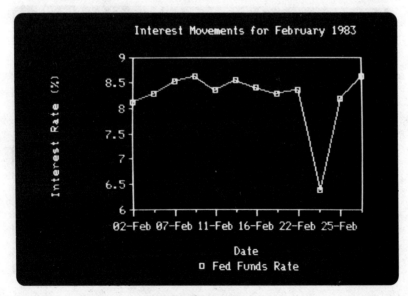

Figure 9.17

The fact that the date labels are ordered sequentially doesn't matter to 1-2-3. It could just as easily have plotted against any other set of labels. Notice that cells containing date functions were used for the x-axis labels. As with all titles or labels, 1-2-3 can use numbers, labels, or functions for these labels.

Making a More Complex Line Graph

The data set we've created suggests a second line graph that compares the variations in the Federal Funds rate to the changes in LIBOR across the same period. This graph is really a simple extension of the previous one. To continue the example, we must first create a *B* range that captures the data in the range D4..D15. Figure 9.18 illustrates our new graph.

Formatting the Line Graph

Notice the different symbols at the points of intersection on the graph ($\square$ and +). There are four ways of displaying a line graph, and

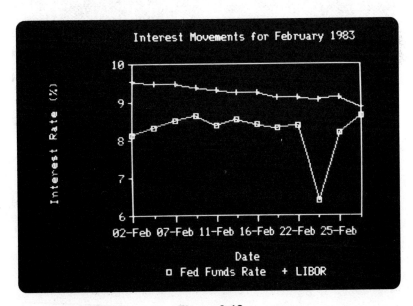

Figure 9.18

we have been using only one so far. The command used to control the lines and symbols at the points of intersection on a line graph is / Graph Options Format. This command has the following menu:

     Lines   Symbols   Both   Neither

Lines

Lines signals 1-2-3 to connect the different data points with only a straight line and no symbols. Figure 9.19 shows the graph from figure 9.18 with only lines.

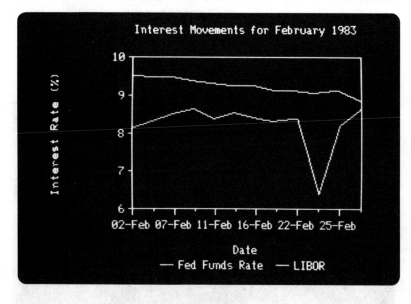

Figure 9.19

Symbols

The *Symbols* option tells 1-2-3 to leave out the straight lines and use different graphic symbols for each of up to six data ranges. The symbols used are

     A □   D △
     B +   E x
     C ◇   F ▽

Figure 9.20 shows the graph with symbols but no lines. Although this format can be used with line charts, it is more commonly used with XY plots.

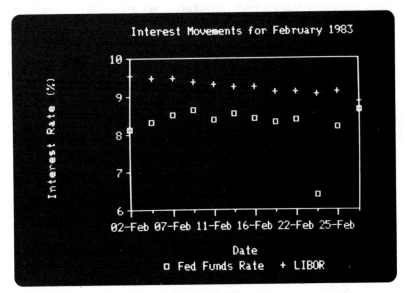

Figure 9.20

Both Lines and Symbols

The third choice in the menu is *Both*. This is actually the default used in figures 9.17 and 9.18 to get both lines and symbols. Because it is difficult to tell one data set from another without using both lines and symbols, in most cases *Both* is the preferred option.

Neither Lines nor Symbols

Neither is the final choice on this menu. It is used to suppress both lines and symbols. You may wonder how points of intersection can be shown if neither lines nor symbols appear on the graph. The answer is through *Data* Labels.

Using Data Labels

1-2-3's *Data Label* command is used to place *data* as labels from the worksheet into a graph. These labels can be placed in the graph in the vicinity of the data points on the graph. The *Data Label* option is a

part of the *Graph O*ptions menu. After this selection is made, the
following menu appears:

A   B   C   D   E   F

Notice that the options here correspond to the data ranges options:
one set of data labels for each set of data. In general, you will want to
use the same coordinates to define the data labels and the data
range. For example, in our sample graph, the data labels for data
range A are entered by entering the label range B5...I5. 1-2-3 then
presents the option of placing the data label above or below the data
point, centered on the data point, or to the left or the right.

The data labels can be numbers, values, or text. All data labels are
converted to labels before they are placed in the worksheet. In most
cases, you will want to use numbers as data labels. If you use text, be
sure to keep the strings short to avoid cluttering the graph.

Data labels can be used in a line chart that includes lines and
symbols, as well as one that contains no lines or symbols to mark the
data points. If you are not using lines or symbols (on a line graph),
you will probably want to center the data labels on the data points.
Otherwise, you'll want to choose one of the other options to avoid
cluttering the graph.

Figure 9.21 shows our first sample line graph (with only one data set)
with data labels, but without data symbols or lines. Of course, data
labels can also be used in graphs with symbols and lines. In fact, in
line charts with multiple data sets, lines or symbols are required to
differentiate the various data sets. Otherwise, the graph will look like
a jumble of numbers. Figure 9.22 shows our second line graph (with
two data sets) with data labels.

Notice that the data labels in the sample graphs are almost
unreadable because they overlap. The overlap seriously reduces
the effectiveness of data labels. Unfortunately, in the current
versions of 1-2-3, there is no way to correct this problem. Notice
also that legends are meaningless when they appear in a line chart
without lines or symbols.

Data labels also work with bar graphs. In bar graphs, the labels are
displayed as centered above each bar. As with line charts, the data
labels can be helpful in identifying the numeric value associated
with each data point.

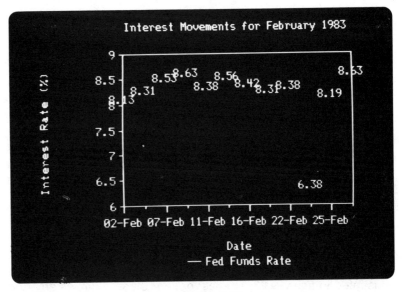

Figure 9.21

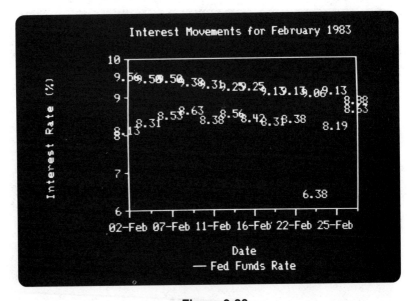

Figure 9.22

Sometimes it is easy to get confused about the difference between the x-axis titles, the X labels, and the data labels. An x-axis title usually describes the units of measure used on the x axis (like dollars or years). X labels distinguish the different data points (for example, 1981 and 1982 data) in a graph. Data labels describe each individual data item.

Using Grids

1-2-3 offers one more option for formatting graphs: grids. This option allows a grid to be interposed on a 1-2-3 graph. The command to create this grid is / Graph Options Grid. The submenu under this command offers the following options:

    Horizontal   Vertical   Both   Clear

The first option creates a horizontal grid over the graph. As you would expect, the second option creates a vertical grid. Option 3, Both, causes both type of grids to be displayed. This option is illustrated in figure 9.23. The last option, Clear, removes any grid from the current graph.

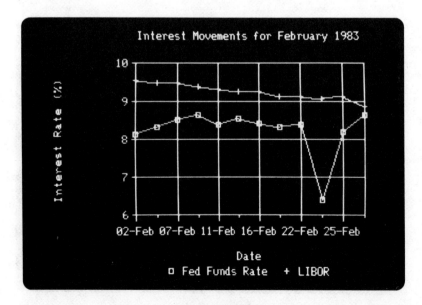

Figure 9.23

Although grids can be useful, they also can clutter the graph unnecessarily. You may find that using data labels works better than grids for many applications.

Pie Charts

Another type of graph provided by 1-2-3 is a simple pie chart. Pie charts can show relationships in a single set of data items. Each data item becomes a slice of the pie. The sum of the slices represents the entire pie.

In many ways, a pie chart is the simplest of 1-2-3's graphs. Only one data range can be represented by a pie chart, so only the / Graph A option is needed to define a pie. Because a pie chart has no axes, the x- and y-axis titles cannot be used. Similarly, grids, scales, and data labels are not used with pie charts.

One convenient way to show the advantages of a pie chart, as well as its limitations, is to add some additional data to figure 9.1. As you can see, the new data is simply the names of the four largest steel producers in the U.S., Japan, and Europe.

To create the pie chart shown in figure 9.25, we first selected the Pie option from the Type menu. Next, we entered B5..E5 for the A-range. Because pie charts do not have an x or y axis, 1-2-3 adopts the convention of using the X labels as the captions for the slices of the pie. Here B14..B17 is designated as the X label range. Figure 9.25 shows the resulting graph.

There are two things that you should notice about this pie chart: the number of slices in the pie, and the percentages next to the labels. The number of slices in the pie corresponds to the number of data items in the A range—in this case, four. The most important limitation on the number of data items used in a pie chart is that the labels tend to get awfully bunched up if you use too many. Each situation is different, but you might try collecting some of the smallest slices together into an "Other" category if you have many small data items.

The percentages next to the labels in the pie chart are calculated and automatically placed there by 1-2-3. This process is consistent with the point of a pie chart, which is to show the relationship of each data item to the whole. It would be nice, however, if there were a way to display the value of each data item in the graph next to the percentage.

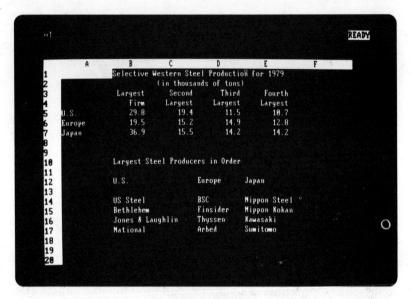

Figure 9.24

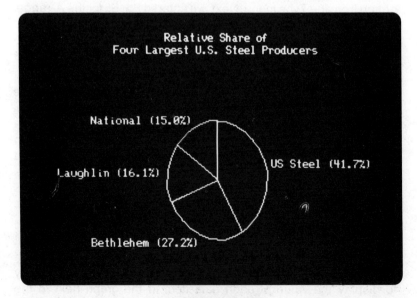

Figure 9.25

XY Graphs

The *XY* graph is the final type of graph offered by 1-2-3. An XY graph is sometimes called a scatter plot. What sets this type of graph apart from the others mentioned so far is that, in an XY graph, two or more different data items from the same data range can share the same *X* value. If you think about it for a moment, you'll realize that this is not possible with a line chart. XY graphs are not used to show time series data. Instead, they help to illustrate the relationships between different attributes of data items, like age and income or educational achievements and salary.

In an *XY* graph, the *X* labels become more than simple labels on the graph. They are, in fact, the X-axis scale. This means that an XY graph requires a minimum of two pieces of information: an *X* range and an *A* range.

In every other respect, an XY plot is similar to a line graph. In fact, a line graph can be thought of as a specialized type of XY graph. For an example of an XY graph, look at the data in figure 9.26 and the sample graph we've created in figure 9.27.

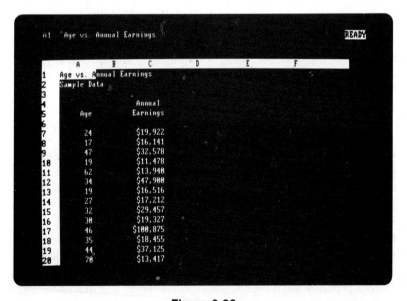

Figure 9.26

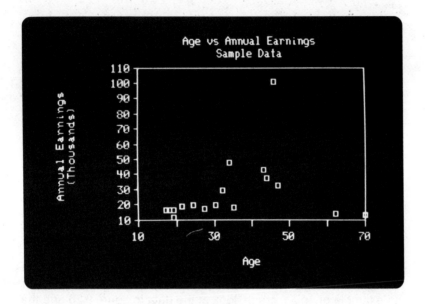

Figure 9.27

Notice that we've added titles, X labels, and a grid to this graph. Notice also that we've set the format to show only symbols instead of both lines and symbols. This was done by selecting the *F*ormat option from the *O*ptions menu and specifying the *S*ymbols alternative. Typically, XY graphs are formatted to display only symbols instead of symbols and lines. You can display the symbols, however, using any format you wish. If you format an XY graph to include lines between the data points, be sure that at least one of the data sets is sorted in either ascending or descending order. Otherwise, the lines that connect the data points will cross one another, making the graph very difficult to read.

Frequently, scatter plots include a line in addition to the various data points. This line, called the *regression line,* is an approximation of the trend suggested by the data in the graph. Unfortunately, 1-2-3 cannot produce such an XY graph. We'd like to see this capability added to the program.

More Examples

Now that all of the basic 1-2-3 graph types have been covered, the following six examples illustrate each type of graph, along with the commands that were used to create them.

The comprehensive model in the last chapter of this book (Chapter 13) also includes examples of a line and a pie chart. Study all of these examples for more information about 1-2-3's graphics.

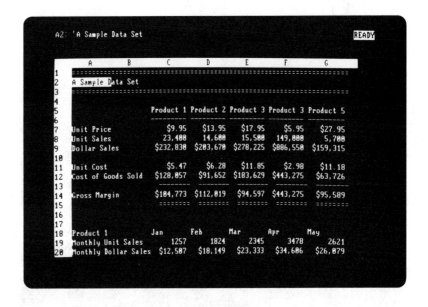

Figure 9.28

This Sample Data Set was used to create
the graphs in examples 1-6.

Commands required to produce example 1

/ Graph Type Bar
        A C8..G8~
        X C5..G5~
        Options Scale Skip 2~
                Title First A Sample Graph~
                Title Second Comparative Unit Sales~
                Title X-axis Product~
                Title Y-axis Units~
                Quit
        View

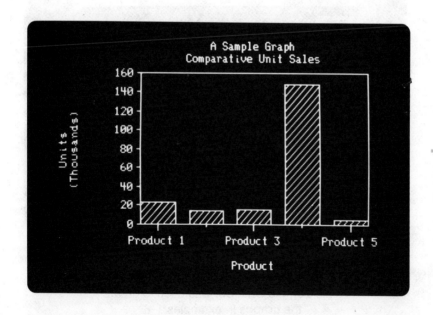

Commands required to produce example 2

/ Graph Type Stack bar
        A C12..G12~
        B C14..G14~
        X C5..G5~
        Options Scale Skip 2~
                Title First A Sample Graph~
                Title Second Components of Total Dollar Sales~
                Title X-axis Product~
                Title Y-axis Dollars~
                Legend A Cost of Goods Sold~
                Legend B Gross Margin~
                Quit
        View

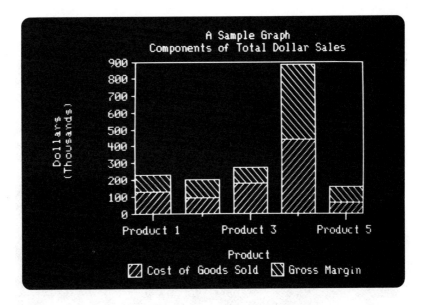

Commands required to produce example 3

```
/ Graph Type Bar
        A C7..G7~
        B C11..G11~
        X C5..G5~
        Options Scale Skip 2~
                Title First A Sample Graph~
                Title Second Unit Price to Unit Cost~
                Title X-axis Product~
                Title Y-axis Dollars~
                Legend A Unit Price~
                Legend B Unit Cost~
                Quit
        View
```

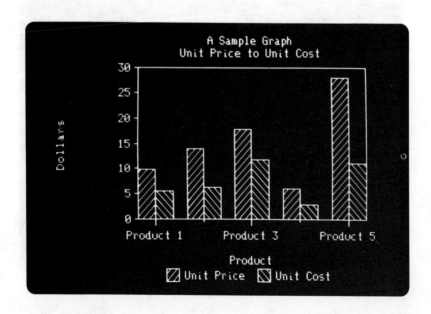

Commands required to produce example 4

/ Graph Type Pie
　　　A C9..G9~
　　　X C5..G5~
　　　Options Title First A Sample Graph~
　　　　　　　Title Second Contribution to Total Revenue~
　　　　　　　Quit
　　　View

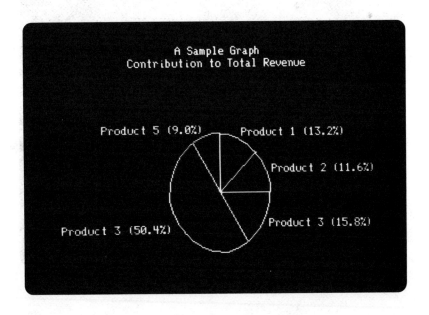

Commands required to produce example 5

/ Graph *Type XY*
        A C7..G7~
        X C8..G8~
        Options Title First A Sample Graph~
                    Title Second Price vs. Unit Volume~
                    Title X-axis Units~
                    Title Y-axis Price~
                    Format Graph Symbols Quit
                    Quit
        View

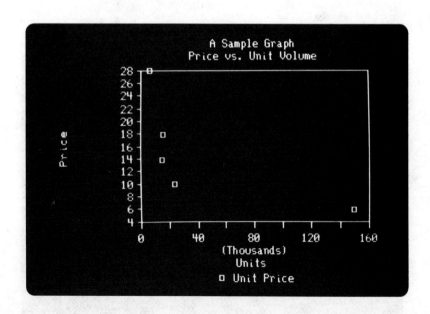

Commands required to produce example 6

/ Graph Type Line
      A C20..N20~
      X C18..G18~
      Options Title First A Sample Graph~
             Title Second Product 1 Monthly Dollar Sales~
             Title X-axis Month~
             Title Y-axis Dollars~
             Grid Both~
             Format Graph Both Quit
             Quit
    View

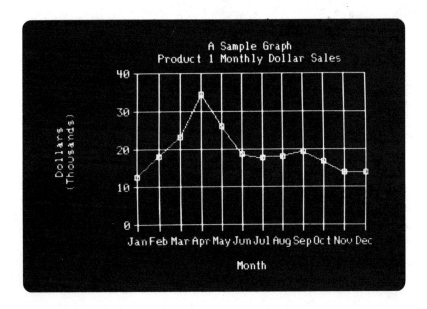

10
Printing Graphs

Printing graphs is different from creating and displaying them and is therefore treated in a separate chapter. The main 1-2-3 program cannot print graphics. To print a 1-2-3 graph, you must first save it to a graph file from within 1-2-3. Next, you must exit 1-2-3 and enter the PrintGraph program through the Lotus Access System. Finally, you select the file and set the options for printing.

This may seem like a peculiar place for 1-2-3 to deviate from its uncomplicated style, but Lotus Development had to make some compromises somewhere to keep the size of the main 1-2-3 program to a reasonable level. This is one of the places. By making the PrintGraph program separate, Lotus was able to decrease the total size of the main program. Unfortunately, a great deal of the interactive capability was removed from printing graphs.

The trade-off, however, is not severe. First, the menus and command structure of the PrintGraph program are much like the main 1-2-3 program. Second, the PrintGraph program is written for batch processing. This means that the program can print more than one graph at a time. To take advantage of this feature, you should wait to print a graph until you can print several at the same time. (In this chapter, however, we will print only one graph.)

Finally, because of its independence, PrintGraph has many special features that would not be available otherwise because of program size restrictions. These features include the ability to produce high-resolution output on special printers and plotters, enlargements and reductions, rotations, and several additional colors and font types.

Accessing the PrintGraph Program

Like 1-2-3, the PrintGraph program can be accessed through the Lotus Access System. You will probably use PrintGraph most often immediately after a 1-2-3 session. After you / Quit from 1-2-3, instead of exiting from the Access System to DOS, use the system to access the PrintGraph program. Before quitting, you will want to make sure that you have properly saved the graph file you were working on by using the / Graph Save command (as explained in the previous chapter). Once you reach the Lotus Access System, you enter P or point to the PrintGraph selection and hit RETURN. You then remove the 1-2-3 system disk, put the PrintGraph disk in its place, and hit RETURN once more.

You can also use one of two other methods to access the PrintGraph program: enter the program directly from DOS, or go through the Lotus Access System from DOS. To enter the program directly, place the PrintGraph diskette in drive A and enter GRAPH after the operating system prompt (A>). To go through the Lotus Access System, place the diskette in drive A, but this time enter LOTUS after the prompt. The advantage of using the Access System method is that it allows you to go back easily through the Access System to 1-2-3 after you finish printing graphs.

Configuring PrintGraph

Configuring PrintGraph for your particular system is the first step required to the run the program. You should use this option only once. Once the system has been configured, you will not need to change it unless you change printers or buy a plotter or other special graphics device.

The configure option assumes that your printer has graphics capability. If you are not sure whether your printer has this ability, either look at the manual that came with the printer or ask your dealer.

To configure the system, select *Configure* from among the Print-Graph main menu choices:

> Select   Options   Go   Configure   Align   Page   Quit

The slash (/) character is not required before PrintGraph commands because the menus are always active. The status of all the current settings appears on the screen when you return to the main menu.

When you have selected *Configure*, the following menu choices will appear:

> File   Device   Page   Interface   Save   Reset   Quit

First, choose *Device* to indicate to PrintGraph the appropriate output device for your system. Although *Device* is not the first item in this menu, it is probably the most important because it will determine whether or not you should continue.

Once you have chosen *Device*, all the output devices currently supported by PrintGraph will be listed down the left-hand side of the screen, and the directions for making a selection on the right. Be sure that you scroll to the next page for all the options. If your printer or plotter is not on the list, you may want to call Lotus Development to see if a later release of the program supports it, or if there is a way to create a special driver for it.

The *Device* default is an Epson MX-80 printer with single-density (120 X 72) dots (per inch). The default is used for the examples in this chapter.

Once you have made a choice from the list of available printers and plotters, or taken the default, there are other options to configure.

Specifying Drives for Graph and Font Files

The *Files* option tells the PrintGraph program which drives to search for graph and font files. Because the normal default drive for writing files is B in 1-2-3, B is also the default drive here. In contrast, drive A is where the font files are located because this drive is where the PrintGraph diskette normally resides. You will usually let this option default.

Page Size

The *Page* option is used to set the length and width of the pages to be printed. The defaults are

    Length   11.000
    Width   8.000

These settings were chosen as the default because they are the page sizes of the Epson MX-80 printer. To change them, you would enter the values that correspond to your printer's specifications for maximum page size. For example, if you are using an Epson MX—100, you might want to set the width at 14.000.

Parallel or Serial Interface

The *Interface* option specifies what type of interface card you have on your system, parallel or serial. You are given four choices:

1   A parallel interface from the IBM Monochrome Display and Printer Adapter—default

2   A serial interface from the IBM Asynchronous Communications Adapter (RS-232-C)—optional

3   A second parallel interface—optional

4   A second serial interface—optional

If you do not know what type of interface you have, check your printer manual or ask the dealer where you bought your system. If you are using a standard IBM PC with an IBM Printer, you have a parallel interface and do not need to make a change to this menu.

Saving and Resetting Configure Options

To save the *Configure* options that you have specified, select *Save* from the *Configure* menu. If you *Save* the options, they will be active from that point on, even for subsequent PrintGraph sessions.

Reset provides almost the opposite function. It will cancel all the *Configure* options set during the current session and return to either the options that were present when PrintGraph was loaded or those *Saved* during the current session, whichever occurred last.

Both of these commands require that you remove the write-protect tab from the PrintGraph diskette. If you do not, the error message "Disk is write protected" will appear on the screen. If this occurs, type ESC to acknowledge the error, remove the write-protect tab, and begin the command again. Be sure to replace the tab when you are finished changing the default settings.

Selecting Files for Printing

After you have configured PrintGraph, you should return to the main menu and choose *Select*. After you use the program for the first time, *Select* will be the first step. When you choose this option, you get a list of all the .PIC files on disk B. (If you changed the default, using the *File* option of the *Configure* command, the files resident on the disk you selected will be displayed.) A typical list of graph files as it runs down the left-hand side of the display is shown in figure 10.1.

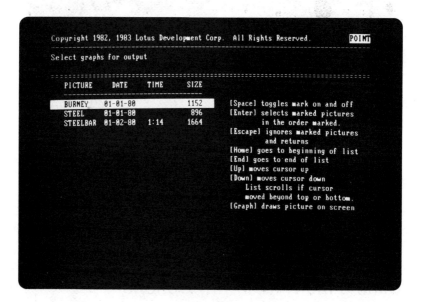

Figure 10.1

The directions for selecting files are on the right-hand side of the display.

To *Select* the graph file that you want to print, use the ↑ (Up) and ↓ (Down) keys to position to the appropriate entry, then hit the space bar to point to it. (A # will appear next to the file name.) Finally, you would hit RETURN. You can select as many graphs as you wish at this point. A # will appear next to each title you select. To confirm your choices, press the F10 (GRAPH) key to see the graphs as they were created and displayed in 1-2-3.

The graph file that we have chosen to print is Steelbar. Because this file was selected, its title will appear below "Selected Graphs" when we return to the main PrintGraph display. The display should look like figure 10.2.

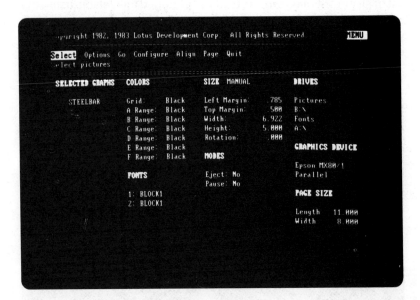

Figure 10.2

Setting Individual Print Options

Now that we have selected a graph to print, we need to set the options for printing it. Note that the options selected will apply to all the graphs printed in a batch. If you want different options to apply to different graphs, you must select and print the graphs one at a time.

To specify the options, select *Options* from the main PrintGraph menu. The following choices are displayed:

Color   Font   Size   Pause   Eject   Quit

By selecting *Color* from this menu, you can set the colors for printing or plotting different parts of graphs on a color device. If the device you are using does not support color graphics (most printers, including the Epson MX-80 that we used, do not), you are not given a choice of colors. For the purpose of explaining how the *Color* option works, however, we will assume that we are using an HP-7470A plotter that does support color. (We will switch back to the Epson MX-80 after explaining how the *Color* option is used.)

PrintGraph assigns a default color of black to each data range and the grid, axes, and scales. However, the program can support six other colors: red, orange, yellow, blue, purple, and brown. You may assign any of these colors to any data range. You can even assign the same color to more than one data range.

When you select the color option, the screen will look like figure 10.3. Colors are assigned by pointing to the data range you want to change, then selecting a new color from the control panel area. For

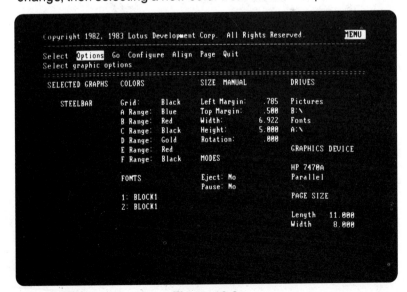

Figure 10.3

example, to change the color of range E to red, you would first point to E in the list of ranges, then select red from the color menu. Figure 10.3 shows the screen as it would appear after you made this selection.

As soon as you make a change, the new color will appear next to the range name in the list. The default color for all areas is black, and this is what we will use for our sample reports because we are using a standard printer.

Choosing Fonts

One of 1-2-3's special features allows you to choose different character types (fonts) when you are printing. (This includes printing with a dot-matrix printer.) The *Font* option allows you to choose from among eight different character types:

This is SCRIPT1 type

This is SCRIPT2 type

This is BLOCK1 type

This is BLOCK2 type

This is ITALIC1 type

This is ITALIC2 type

This is ROMAN1 type

This is ROMAN2 type

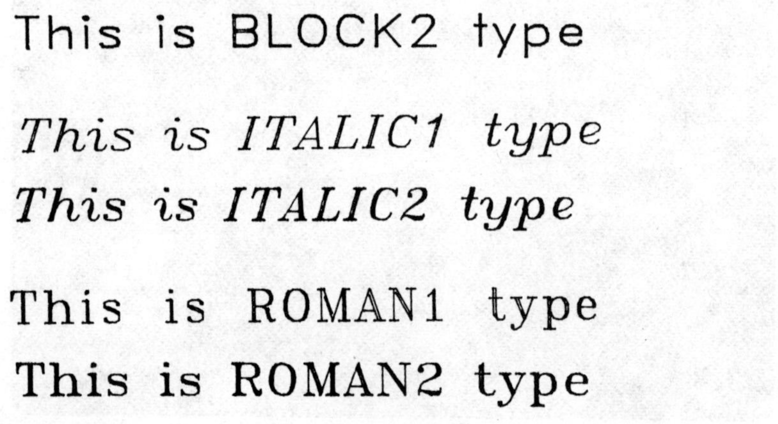

Figure 10.4

The number after the font name indicates how dark the print will appear when it is printed. The fonts whose names are followed with a 2 are identical to the fonts with the same names followed by a 1, but darker.

You have the option to set the first line of text—the graph title—to one font type and the remaining lines of text to another. If you specify only one font type, however, it will be used for all the text in the graph.

For our simple example graph, the bar chart of U.S. steel production for 1979 from figure 9.6 of the previous chapter, we will use a dark roman face for the first graph title and a lighter roman for the other lines. We will specify ROMAN2 for Font 1 (the first line of the title line), and ROMAN1 for Font 2 (everything besides the first line). Remember, if we had not specified a special font for Font 2, it would have automatically taken on the same value as Font 1. Once the fonts are specified, ROMAN2 should appear in the status display for Font 1, and ROMAN1 for Font 2.

Adjusting Graph Size and Orientation

The *Size* option allows you to make various adjustments to the size of graphs and where they will print on the page. This *Option* also allows you to rotate axes up to 90 degrees. The menu for the *Size* option gives you the following three choices:

> Full   Half   Manual

Full means that the graph will occupy an entire page, and *Half* only half a page. PrintGraph automatically handles all the spacing and margins for both of these choices. If you want to control the spacing and margins yourself, you must specify *Manual*.

The following choices will appear for *Manual*:

> Height   Width   Left   Top   Rotation

Height, *Width*, *Left*, and *Top* are used to adjust the corresponding margins in inches. *Rotation* is used to adjust the number of counter-clockwise degrees of rotation. You must choose a number between 0 and 90. On the one extreme, 0 will not cause any rotation, and the x axis will appear normally on the page. On the other, a full 90 degrees of rotation will shift the x axis perfectly upright.

Interestingly enough, 1-2-3 normally prints graphs rotated 90 degrees. In other words, graphs are printed sideways on the printer. This allows the graph to be printed with higher resolution. Nevertheless, remember that rotating the graph 90 degrees will cause it to print normally on the paper.

Rotation will require some experimentation to get the results you want. The normal default settings for *Height* and *Width* are 9.445 and 6.852, which is a ratio of about 1 to 1.378. This is called the *aspect ratio*. Whenever you change the aspect ratio, distortion can, and often will, occur as PrintGraph fits a rotated graph into the specified height and width. Distortion in bar and line graphs is usually not a problem. When pie charts are distorted, however, they usually end up looking like ellipses instead of pies. When you change the settings for height and width, the best policy is to maintain the same aspect ratio to avoid any distortion.

The Pause and Eject Options

Other main menu selections are *Pause* and *Eject*, which control the interval between printing of graphs in batch mode. *Pause* causes a pause between graphs for changing settings on the printer, and *Eject* controls whether the printer will stop for you to change paper. In our case, we will use the *Eject* option to control the paper advance.

Aligning and Advancing the Page

The *Align* selection in the main PrintGraph menu sets the program's built-in, top-of-page marker. When you choose the *Align* option, PrintGraph assumes that the paper is correctly aligned in the printer with the top of the form in the proper place. 1-2-3 then uses the page length information you provided to insert a form feed at the end of every page. NOTE: Many printers have controls that allow you to scroll the paper up one line at a time. 1-2-3 does not recognize these controls. If you, for example, scroll the paper up three lines without informing 1-2-3 by re-*Aligning*, 1-2-3 will be three spaces off when it next issues a form feed command.

Page selection is used to advance the paper one page at a time. This useful option advances continuous form paper to help you remove the printed output at the end of a printing session.

The Finished Product

To actually print the graph, you must select the *Go* option from the main PrintGraph menu. After you have done so, 1-2-3 will start printing. If you have several graphs, you may as well go have lunch while you wait for them to print because with 1-2-3's very high resolution, printing a graph takes a particularly long time. Printing the graph shown in figure 10.5 in full size on an Epson MX-80 took 4 minutes, 55 seconds.

Leaving PrintGraph

Exiting from PrintGraph is similar to exiting from any other 1-2-3 module. You simply choose the *Quit* option from the main Print-Graph menu. After you exit the program, you will be returned to the Lotus Access System.

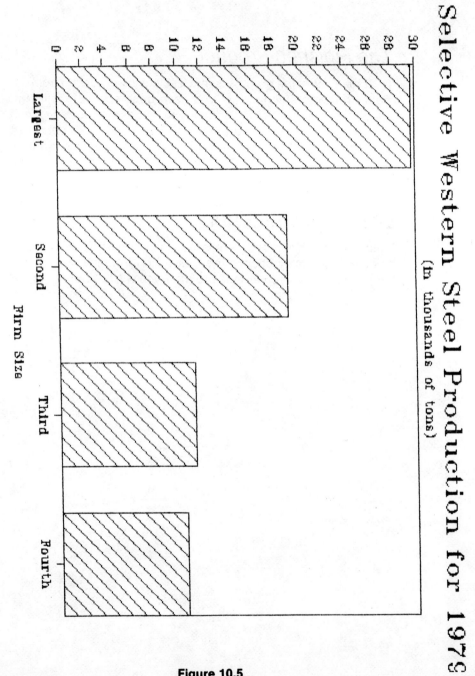

Figure 10.5

11

Data Management

Data management is the third element of 1-2-3. As mentioned earlier, Lotus Development calls this feature "data base management," but there is a problem with this term. What data base management has meant in the past is quite different from what it means in 1-2-3. Traditionally, data base management meant the management of data on disk. With the greater RAM capacity of the IBM PC, however, Lotus was able to use a new technique. In 1-2-3, the entire data base resides in the spreadsheet within main memory. There are both advantages and disadvantages to this approach.

The advantages of having the data base in RAM are speed, ease of use, and easy access. The speed is a direct result of the reduced processing time required to manipulate the data base in RAM. By doing all the work inside the spreadsheet, Lotus avoided the time required for input and output to disk. The result is an extremely fast data base manager that does most of its operations in the blink of an eye.

The ease of use is a result of the integration of data management with other spreadsheet functions and commands. The data base function meshes well with 1-2-3's other functions, including graphing and text processing. The commands for adding, modifying, and deleting items in a data base are the same ones you have already seen for manipulating cells or groups of cells within a worksheet.

Further, the overall structure for the commands specific to data base manipulation is consistent with other spreadsheet commands.

Finally, Lotus Development has made the data base entirely visible within the spreadsheet. With traditional data bases, everything except the items you have specifically searched for is hidden away on disk. In 1-2-3, all the items in the data base are easily seen by scrolling through the worksheet. This makes the data base more understandable and easier to use.

The major disadvantage of Lotus Development's approach is its limitation on the size of the data base. This limitation is a function of the maximum number of records that you can have in a data base—just over 2,000—and the more relevant limit of how much memory each record requires. If each record in the data base is large, you can quite easily run out of RAM long before you run out of potential places to put records. For this reason, 1-2-3 works best for "personal" data bases, small to medium-sized data bases that fit easily in RAM. Lists of telephone numbers, addresses, checks, etc., are all well suited to this kind of data base application.

All the commands in this chapter share the same /Data command root. Some of them, however, are not actually data base commands, but more properly belong to the spreadsheet function. The /Data Fill, /Data Table, and /Data Distribution commands all fit into this category. They are covered in their own sections at the end of this chapter.

What is a Data Base?

A data base is a collection of information. In its simplest form, a data base is merely a list. The list might contain any kind of information, from addresses to tax-deductible expenditures.

In 1-2-3, the words *data base* mean a range of cells that spans at least one column and more than one row. With this definition alone, there is really nothing unusual about a data base that sets it apart from any other group of cells. However, because a data base is actually a list, another important aspect is its method of organization. Just as a list must be properly organized to gain information from it, a data base must also be properly organized.

Remember that in 1-2-3 there is an underlying similarity between a data base and any other group of cells. This will help you as you learn about the different /Data commands that are covered in this chapter. There are many instances where these commands can be used in what might be considered "non-data base" applications.

As mentioned above, an important aspect of a data base is the way it is organized. This organization depends alot on the composition of the data base. To understand the composition, certain general definitions are needed.

First, data bases are made up of *records*. Each record corresponds to an item in a list. For example, if you made up a list of all the things you have to do in the next week and next to them put the day of the week you hoped to have them completed, each item and associated day of the week would correspond to a record in a data base.

Records are made up of *fields*. Using the list in figure 11.1, one field corresponds to the name of what you want to accomplish, and another field is the day of the week on which you want to complete the task. Sometimes the term field refers to the entire column of days of the week, or to names of things to accomplish.

1-2-3 has its own definitions for records and fields. A *record* is a row of cells within a data base, and a *field* is a single cell (or column) within a record. Figure 11.2 shows two typical 1-2-3 data bases with examples of our new buzzwords.

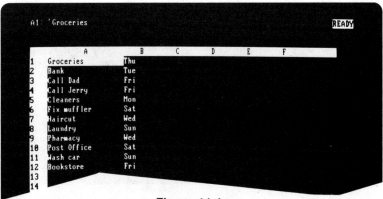

Figure 11.1

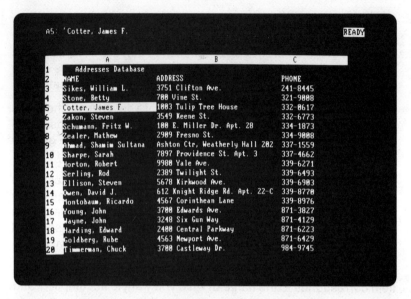

Figure 11.2A

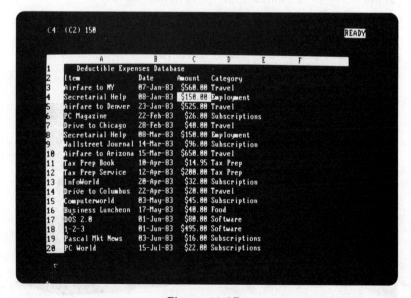

Figure 11.2B

in the Addresses data base, the third record is "Cotter, James F." in row 5. In the Deductible Expenses data base, the amount field for the "Secretarial Help" record is $150.00 (cell C4).

Notice the labels at the top of the columns. These are *field names* that are necessary in some cases for data base manipulation.

What Can You Do with a Data Base?

The mailing list shown in figure 11.3 is an example of a very simple 1-2-3 data base.

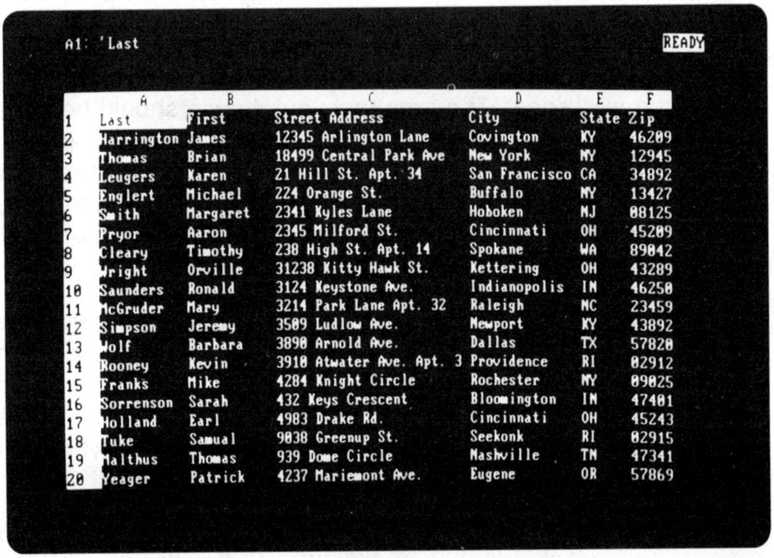
A1: 'Last READY

	A	B	C	D	E	F
1	Last	First	Street Address	City	State	Zip
2	Harrington	James	12345 Arlington Lane	Covington	KY	46209
3	Thomas	Brian	18499 Central Park Ave	New York	NY	12945
4	Leugers	Karen	21 Hill St. Apt. 34	San Francisco	CA	34892
5	Englert	Michael	224 Orange St.	Buffalo	NY	13427
6	Smith	Margaret	2341 Kyles Lane	Hoboken	NJ	08125
7	Pryor	Aaron	2345 Milford St.	Cincinnati	OH	45209
8	Cleary	Timothy	238 High St. Apt. 14	Spokane	WA	89042
9	Wright	Orville	31238 Kitty Hawk St.	Kettering	OH	43289
10	Saunders	Ronald	3124 Keystone Ave.	Indianopolis	IN	46250
11	McGruder	Mary	3214 Park Lane Apt. 32	Raleigh	NC	23459
12	Simpson	Jeremy	3509 Ludlow Ave.	Newport	KY	43892
13	Wolf	Barbara	3890 Arnold Ave.	Dallas	TX	57820
14	Rooney	Kevin	3910 Atwater Ave. Apt. 3	Providence	RI	02912
15	Franks	Mike	4284 Knight Circle	Rochester	NY	09025
16	Sorrenson	Sarah	432 Keys Crescent	Bloomington	IN	47401
17	Holland	Earl	4983 Drake Rd.	Cincinnati	OH	45243
18	Tuke	Samual	9038 Greenup St.	Seekonk	RI	02915
19	Malthus	Thomas	939 Dome Circle	Nashville	TN	47341
20	Yeager	Patrick	4237 Mariemont Ave.	Eugene	OR	57869

Figure 11.3

If this were your own data base, what would you use it for? You might want to *sort* it by last name to help you find an address. You might also want to sort the items by Zip Code to create a list of mailing labels that take advantage of the special bulk mailing rates for sorted mail.

Besides sorting the list, you might also want to *query* it for a name or group of names. For example, you could search out the address for a particular person, or select all the people in the data base that live in the state of New York.

Sorting and querying are the main methods used in 1-2-3 to extract information from a data base. Both of these methods have one or more special /*Data* commands associated with them.

Creating a Data Base

The appearance of a data base is really no different from that of any other list in a 1-2-3 worksheet. In fact, you enter data into cells in the same manner as you do for all applications.

The first step in creating a data base is to select an out-of-the-way area of the worksheet. The area that you choose should be large enough to accommodate the number of records that you plan to enter in current as well as future sessions. The number of records you intend to add in the future may be difficult to gauge. In many cases, the best alternative is to enter the data base at the foot of the active area of the worksheet, where there is room for expansion.

After you have selected the appropriate area of the worksheet for the data base, enter the field names across a single row. You can use more than one row for the field names, but 1-2-3 uses only the values in a single row. In addition, all the field names should be unique. If you repeat field names, 1-2-3 may get confused when you attempt to search items in the data base.

After the field names are entered, you enter the records in the data base. To enter the first record, position the cursor to the row directly below the field name row (do not leave any blanks if you plan to search values in the data base). You can then enter data across the row in the normal manner.

The consistency between entering data base information and other worksheet data is one of 1-2-3's simplest, yet most elegant, features. It is also one of the main reasons why data base manipulation in 1-2-3 is so much easier than it is in specialty programs, such as dBASE II.

In these other programs, you must specify the length and type of record in significant detail before entering it, because you are actually telling the program how to store the values on disk. As you will recall from Chapter 2, the way that data is stored on disk in 1-2-3 is controlled internally by the program. You control the format for display purposes only. Recall that 1-2-3 offers the *F*ormat and *C*olumn-width options for controlling the way cells are displayed on the screen.

Adding, Deleting, and Modifying Records

The first thing you will want to know after you have created a data base is how to change it. To add and delete records in a data base, you use the same row commands as you do for any other application in 1-2-3. Because records correspond to rows, you begin inserting a record with the / *W*orksheet *I*nsert *R*ow command. This command was used earlier to insert blank rows in a worksheet. You then fill in the various fields in the rows with relevant data. Figure 11.4 shows an example of inserting a record in the middle of a data base.

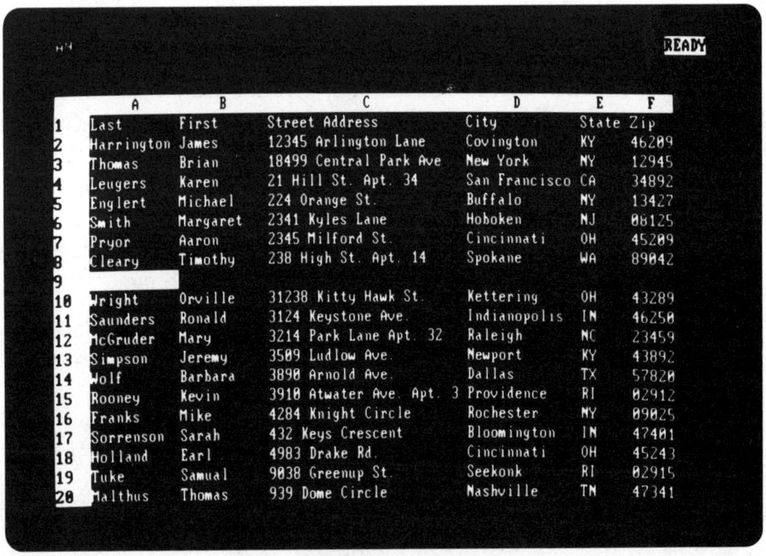
READY

	A	B	C	D	E	F
1	Last	First	Street Address	City	State	Zip
2	Harrington	James	12345 Arlington Lane	Covington	KY	46209
3	Thomas	Brian	18499 Central Park Ave	New York	NY	12945
4	Leugers	Karen	21 Hill St. Apt. 34	San Francisco	CA	34892
5	Englert	Michael	224 Orange St.	Buffalo	NY	13427
6	Smith	Margaret	2341 Kyles Lane	Hoboken	NJ	08125
7	Pryor	Aaron	2345 Milford St.	Cincinnati	OH	45209
8	Cleary	Timothy	238 High St. Apt. 14	Spokane	WA	89042
9						
10	Wright	Orville	31238 Kitty Hawk St.	Kettering	OH	43289
11	Saunders	Ronald	3124 Keystone Ave.	Indianapolis	IN	46250
12	McGruder	Mary	3214 Park Lane Apt. 32	Raleigh	NC	23459
13	Simpson	Jeremy	3509 Ludlow Ave.	Newport	KY	43892
14	Wolf	Barbara	3890 Arnold Ave.	Dallas	TX	57820
15	Rooney	Kevin	3910 Atwater Ave. Apt. 3	Providence	RI	02912
16	Franks	Mike	4284 Knight Circle	Rochester	NY	09025
17	Sorrenson	Sarah	432 Keys Crescent	Bloomington	IN	47401
18	Holland	Earl	4983 Drake Rd.	Cincinnati	OH	45243
19	Tuke	Samual	9038 Greenup St.	Seekonk	RI	02915
20	Malthus	Thomas	939 Dome Circle	Nashville	TN	47341

Figure 11.4A

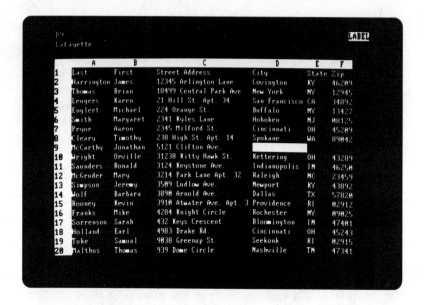

Figure 11.4B

To delete records, use the / Worksheet *Delete Row* command.

Modifying fields in a data base is really no different than modifying the contents of cells in any other application. As outlined in Chapter 3, to modify a field in a single record, you can either retype the cell entry or use the F2 (EDIT) key. To add a new field to a data base, you use the / Worksheet *Insert Column* command to insert a blank column. You then fill in the field with values for each record. Figure 11.5 illustrates how a new field is added to a data base.

All the other commands for moving cells, formatting cells, displaying the contents of a worksheet, etc., are the same for both data base and other spreadsheet applications.

Sorting Records

1-2-3's data management ability allows you to change the order of records by sorting them according to the contents of the fields. Suppose that you wanted to sort the Addresses data base in figure

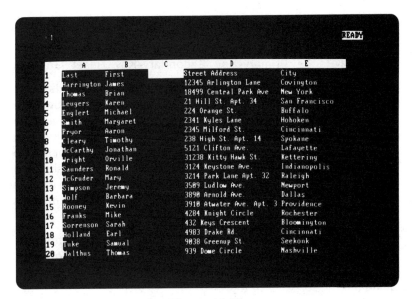

Figure 11.5A

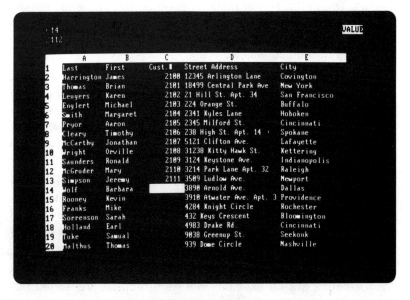

Figure 11.5B

11.3 in alphabetical order by last name. / *Data Sort* is the command used to sort the records. It has the following command menu:

Data-Range Primary-Key Secondary-Key Reset Go Quit

To sort the data base, start by designating a *Data-Range*. This range corresponds to the records to be sorted. One rule to remember here is that when you name the *Data-Range*, you must be careful not to include the addresses of the field names or they will be included in the sort. If you are unfamiliar with how to designate ranges or how to name them, see Chapter 4. For this example, we have designated the *Data-Range* as A2..F20. Remember that we can indicate a range by either pointing to the proper cells or entering their addresses from the keyboard.

The *Data-Range* does not necessarily have to be the entire data base. If part of the data base already has the organization you want, or if you don't want to sort all the records, you can sort just a portion of the data base.

The / *Data Sort* menu remains displayed even after you have entered the addresses of the *Data-Range*. This is one of 1-2-3's "sticky" menus. The / *Print Printer* menu is another. Sticky menus remain displayed until you enter Quit. The sticky menu is really an advantage here because you avoid having to enter / *Data Sort* at the beginning of each command.

After you have chosen the *Data-Range*, you must specify the keys for the sort. *Keys* correspond to fields in the records to which you attach the highest precedence when you sort the data base. The field with the highest precedence is the *Primary-Key*, and the field with the next highest precedence is the *Secondary-Key*. You must set a *Primary-Key*. The *Secondary-Key*, however, is optional.

One of the simplest examples of a data base sorted according to a primary key (often called a single-key data base) is the white pages of the telephone book. All the records in the white pages are sorted in ascending alphabetical order using the last name as the primary key. This is precisely what we are trying to recreate here.

A double-key data base has both a primary and secondary key. The yellow pages are an example. Here the records are sorted according to business type, then further sorted by business name. In this case, the business type is the primary key, and the business name is the secondary key.

For the Addresses data base example, the primary key was set to be the name column. To do this, enter *Primary-Key* from the command menu, then point to, or enter, the address of any entry in column A (including blank or field name cells). In this case, we point to cell A1 as the *Primary-Key*. 1-2-3 will then ask you to "Enter sort order (A or D)," "A" for Ascending and "D" for Descending. In our example, we chose Ascending order. Finally, we enter *Go* from the menu to execute the sort. Figure 11.6 shows the results of the sort.

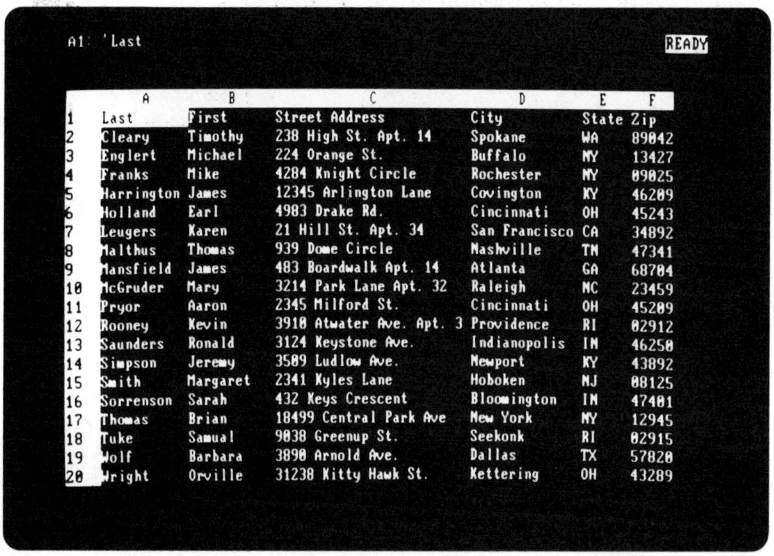

```
A1: 'Last                                                         READY

          A           B          C                      D          E     F
1   Last        First      Street Address          City       State Zip
2   Cleary      Timothy    238 High St. Apt. 14    Spokane     WA    89042
3   Englert     Michael    224 Orange St.          Buffalo     NY    13427
4   Franks      Mike       4284 Knight Circle      Rochester   NY    89025
5   Harrington  James      12345 Arlington Lane    Covington   KY    46289
6   Holland     Earl       4983 Drake Rd.          Cincinnati  OH    45243
7   Leugers     Karen      21 Hill St. Apt. 34     San Francisco CA  34892
8   Malthus     Thomas     939 Dome Circle         Nashville   TN    47341
9   Mansfield   James      483 Boardwalk Apt. 14   Atlanta     GA    68784
10  McGruder    Mary       3214 Park Lane Apt. 32  Raleigh     NC    23459
11  Pryor       Aaron      2345 Milford St.        Cincinnati  OH    45289
12  Rooney      Kevin      3910 Atwater Ave. Apt. 3 Providence RI    82912
13  Saunders    Ronald     3124 Keystone Ave.      Indianapolis IN   46250
14  Simpson     Jeremy     3589 Ludlow Ave.        Newport     KY    43892
15  Smith       Margaret   2341 Kyles Lane         Hoboken     NJ    88125
16  Sorrenson   Sarah      432 Keys Crescent       Bloomington IN    47481
17  Thomas      Brian      18499 Central Park Ave  New York    NY    12945
18  Tuke        Samual     9038 Greenup St.        Seekonk     RI    82915
19  Wolf        Barbara    3890 Arnold Ave.        Dallas      TX    57820
20  Wright      Orville    31238 Kitty Hawk St.    Kettering   OH    43289
```

Figure 11.6

The speed of the sort is surprising. It takes only a split second for this example, and only slightly longer for sorts on much larger data bases. Again, the main reason for the speed is that the data base resides in RAM.

For another example, we will use the Deductible Expenses data base as a double-key data base. Our goal is to sort the data base alphabetically by category and by date within each category.

To enter the parameters for the sort, we begin by designating the *Data*-Range as A3..D20. For the *Primary-Key*, we enter the address of any entry in the Category column and A for ascending. For the *Secondary-Key*, we use the address of any entry in the Date column, and again A for ascending. Finally, we enter *Go*. Figure 11.7 shows the results.

The order in which the records appear after the sort depends on the ASCII equivalents of the contents of the primary and secondary keys. For this reason, you do not want the *Data*-Range to be improperly designated and include blank rows at the end. Because blanks have precedence over all the characters in a sort, all the blank rows appear at the top of the data base.

The ascending order of precedence that 1-2-3 uses for sorting text strings is

> Blank spaces
> Special Characters (!, #, $, etc.)
> Numeric Characters
> Alpha Characters
> > (Upper-case characters precede lower-case
> > characters.)

Another rule is that text string cell entries precede number cell entries. For example, the text string cell entry "George" precedes the number cell entry 456. Also, formulas are evaluated first for their numeric result, then sorted as numbers. For example, @DATE (80,1,1) is sorted according to its numeric equivalent (29221).

To understand the order of precedence that 1-2-3 uses in sorting, try a simple experiment. Start by making various text, number, and formula entries down a column of cells. Then sort the range of cells you have created and see what happens. Performing a simple experiment like this will help you avoid making mistakes later.

Comments on Sorting

Remember that sorting is not reserved for data bases alone. Any list of adjacent rows can be sorted according to primary and secondary keys, even though it may not look like a data base in the strict sense. For example, as you will recall from our discussion of lookup tables

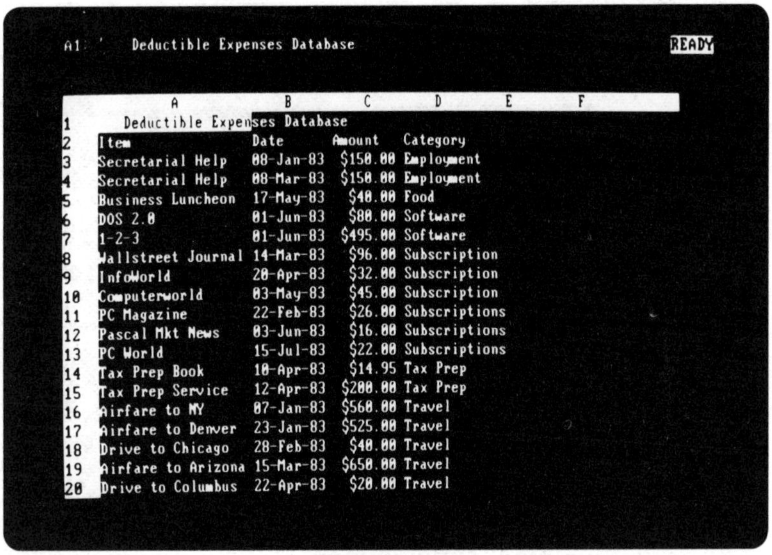

A1: ' Deductible Expenses Database READY

	A	B	C	D	E	F
1	Deductible Expenses Database					
2	Item	Date	Amount	Category		
3	Secretarial Help	08-Jan-83	$150.00	Employment		
4	Secretarial Help	08-Mar-83	$150.00	Employment		
5	Business Luncheon	17-May-83	$40.00	Food		
6	DOS 2.0	01-Jun-83	$80.00	Software		
7	1-2-3	01-Jun-83	$495.00	Software		
8	Wallstreet Journal	14-Mar-83	$96.00	Subscription		
9	InfoWorld	20-Apr-83	$32.00	Subscription		
10	Computerworld	03-May-83	$45.00	Subscription		
11	PC Magazine	22-Feb-83	$26.00	Subscriptions		
12	Pascal Mkt News	03-Jun-83	$16.00	Subscriptions		
13	PC World	15-Jul-83	$22.00	Subscriptions		
14	Tax Prep Book	10-Apr-83	$14.95	Tax Prep		
15	Tax Prep Service	12-Apr-83	$200.00	Tax Prep		
16	Airfare to NY	07-Jan-83	$560.00	Travel		
17	Airfare to Denver	23-Jan-83	$525.00	Travel		
18	Drive to Chicago	28-Feb-83	$40.00	Travel		
19	Airfare to Arizona	15-Mar-83	$650.00	Travel		
20	Drive to Columbus	22-Apr-83	$20.00	Travel		

Figure 11.7

in Chapter 6, the items in a table must be arranged in ascending order prior to executing a lookup. Figure 11.8 shows how to sort a lookup table in ascending order.

Another general comment about sorting records in a data base is that it is often hard to reconstruct the original order of the records after you have sorted them. If you think that you may want to get back to the original order, take a simple precautionary step before you sort. Add an additional field containing a number that signifies the original order of the records to the data base. If there are several records in the data base, you may want to use the */Data Fill* command to help you fill in the numbers in this field.

If you forget the precautionary step of adding an additional field and have sorted the data base into an order that you simply cannot live with, you can always get the original data base back from the disk. The */File Retrieve* command will bring the original version into the spreadsheet again and write over the unwanted data base. You can reclaim the original version this way until you *Save* an updated version of the data base.

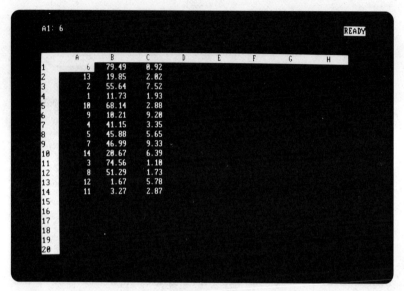

Figure 11.8A

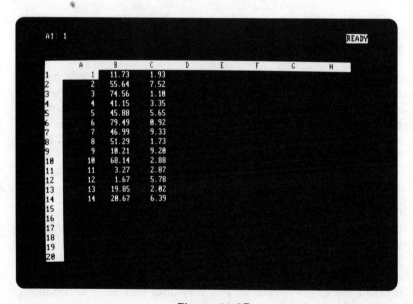

Figure 11.8B

The *Reset* command is another option in the */Data Sort* menu. This command eliminates the keys and *Data*-Range that were previously specified in the */Data Sort* settings. This is a convenient option to use if you want to change the settings for sorting items in another area of the worksheet.

Searching for Records

In addition to sorting a data base, 1-2-3's */Data* commands allow you to search for records. They cover all the steps necessary to find certain records individually or in groups. For example, with 1-2-3 you could find all the customers in a telephone number data base who have a certain area code. Another example would be to make a copy of all the names of people to whom checks for more than $100.00 were written in a checking account data base. Still another example is to purge the records that have been paid from an overdue accounts data base.

The data base used in the first example appears in figure 11.9.

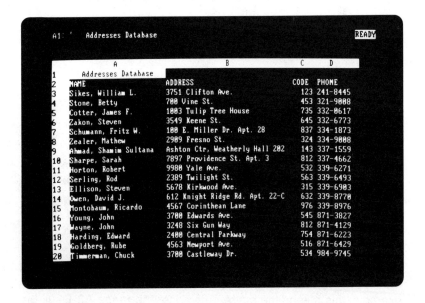

Figure 11.9

We want to locate the cursor at all the records that have area code 812. The command used to perform the search is /Data Query. Query is just another word for search.

/Data Query is actually the host command for a series of *sub-commands*:

Find
: Moves down through a data base locating the cursor at records that match given criteria

Extract
: Creates copies in a specified area of the worksheet of all or some of the fields in certain records that match given criterion

Unique
: Similar to extract, but recognizes that some of the records in the data base may be copies. Includes only unique records

Delete
: Deletes all the records in a data base that match a given criterion and shifts the remaining records to fill in the gaps that are left

In our first example, the *Find* option is used. Before we can execute the command, however, three things must be done:

1. The criteria for searching records must be set.

2. The input range to be searched must be set.

3. Where the output will be written in the worksheet must be defined (not required for *Find* or *Delete*).

In response to the three items listed above, the /Data Query command requires that three ranges be specified: the *Input* range, the *Criterion* range, and the *Output* range.

Input Range

The *Input* range for the /Data Query command is the range of records in the data base that you want to search. In our area code example, this means the entire data base (the range A2..D20), but this is not always the case.

There may be times when you will want to search just a portion of a data base, especially if that data base already has a certain measure of organization. For example, suppose that you had already sorted a data base according to check number and wanted to find all the checks for more than $150.00 which were written prior to check number 300. You would have to specify as the *Input* range only the area of the data base that includes check number 300 and below.

The *Input* range for the area code example is similar to the *Data-Range* that might be specified for a / *Data Sort* operation. However, the field names *must* be included in the input range, whereas they *cannot* be included in the *Sort Data-Range*. Again, the *Input* range for our area code example is A2..D20, as shown in figure 11.10.

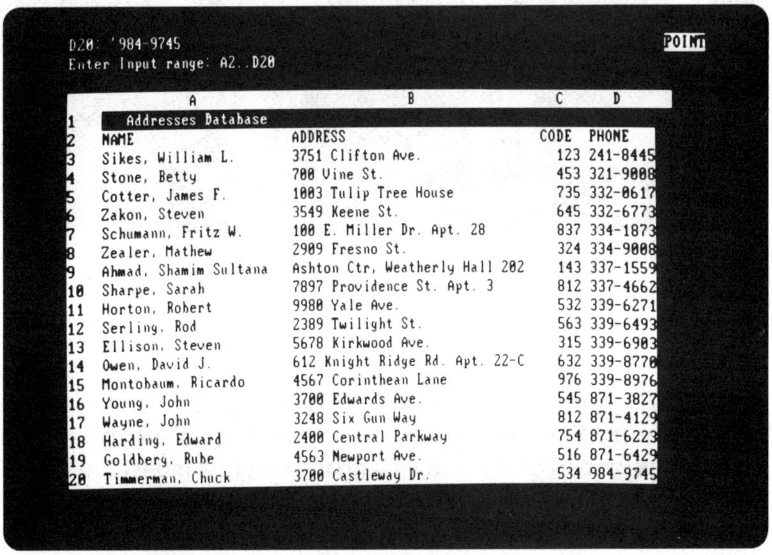

```
D20: '984-9745                                                    POINT
Enter Input range: A2..D20

          A                      B                    C     D
 1  Addresses Database
 2  NAME                  ADDRESS                    CODE  PHONE
 3  Sikes, William L.     3751 Clifton Ave.           123 241-8445
 4  Stone, Betty          700 Vine St.                453 321-9008
 5  Cotter, James F.      1003 Tulip Tree House       735 332-0617
 6  Zakon, Steven         3549 Keene St.              645 332-6773
 7  Schumann, Fritz W.    100 E. Miller Dr. Apt. 28   837 334-1873
 8  Zealer, Mathew        2909 Fresno St.             324 334-9008
 9  Ahmad, Shamim Sultana Ashton Ctr, Weatherly Hall 202  143 337-1559
10  Sharpe, Sarah         7897 Providence St. Apt. 3  812 337-4662
11  Horton, Robert        9980 Yale Ave.              532 339-6271
12  Serling, Rod          2389 Twilight St.           563 339-6493
13  Ellison, Steven       5678 Kirkwood Ave.          315 339-6903
14  Owen, David J.        612 Knight Ridge Rd. Apt. 22-C  632 339-8770
15  Montobaum, Ricardo    4567 Corinthean Lane        976 339-8976
16  Young, John           3700 Edwards Ave.           545 871-3827
17  Wayne, John           3248 Six Gun Way            812 871-4129
18  Harding, Edward       2400 Central Parkway        754 871-6223
19  Goldberg, Rube        4563 Newport Ave.           516 871-6429
20  Timmerman, Chuck      3700 Castleway Dr.          534 984-9745
```

Figure 11.10

Criterion Range

The *Criterion* range is used to specify the search criteria. As mentioned above, we want to find all records with an area code equal to 812. Our search criteria is thus 812. We need to find a way to express this in terms that 1-2-3 can understand. Figure 11.11 shows the *Criterion* range for our area code example.

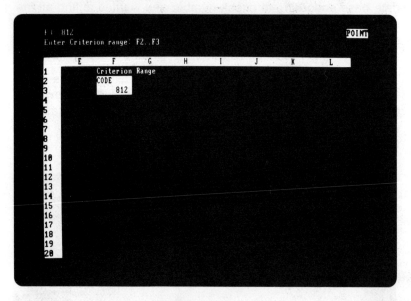

Figure 11.11

This *Criterion* range conforms to the general rules set out in 1-2-3. These rules are that a range can have a maximum width of 32 fields and a length of two or more rows, and the first row must contain the field names of the search criteria. As mentioned earlier, the field names must be unique. The rows below the field names contain the actual criteria. The area code *Criterion* range conforms to the minimum standards for all these rules.

The criteria used can be numbers, labels, or formulas. In general, numbers and labels are straightforward. In figure 11.11, the position of the label "812" below the field name "Code" in the *Criterion* range is one example. With numbers and labels, the criteria must be positioned directly below the field name to which they correspond in the *Criterion* range. In figure 11.11, the *Criterion* range is F2..F3.

The last range usually required for a /Data Query command is the Output range. However, an output range is not required in a Find operation.

Figure 11.12 shows what happens after you have specified all the appropriate ranges and finally selected Find from the /Data Query command menu.

```
A10: 'Sharpe, Sarah                                                  FIND

          A                        B                   C     D
1     Addresses Database
2    NAME                    ADDRESS                   CODE  PHONE
3    Sikes, William L.       3751 Clifton Ave.          123  241-8445
4    Stone, Betty            700 Vine St.               453  321-9088
5    Cotter, James F.        1003 Tulip Tree House      735  332-8617
6    Zakon, Steven           3549 Keene St.             645  332-6773
7    Schumann, Fritz W.      100 E. Miller Dr. Apt. 28  837  334-1873
8    Zealer, Mathew          2909 Fresno St.            324  334-9088
9    Ahmad, Shamim Sultana   Ashton Ctr, Weatherly Hall 202  143  337-1559
10   Sharpe, Sarah           7897 Providence St. Apt. 3 812  337-4662
11   Horton, Robert          9988 Yale Ave.             532  339-6271
12   Serling, Rod            2389 Twilight St.          563  339-6493
13   Ellison, Steven         5678 Kirkwood Ave.         315  339-6903
14   Owen, David J.          612 Knight Ridge Rd. Apt. 22-C  632  339-8778
15   Montobaum, Ricardo      4567 Corinthean Lane       976  339-8976
16   Young, John             3700 Edwards Ave.          545  871-3827
17   Wayne, John             3248 Six Gun Way           812  871-4129
18   Harding, Edward         2400 Central Parkway       754  871-6223
19   Goldberg, Rube          4563 Newport Ave.          516  871-6429
20   Timmerman, Chuck        3700 Castleway Dr.         534  984-9745
```

Figure 11.12

Notice that the cursor appears under the first record that conforms to our search criterion. By using the ↓ cursor key, we can position the cursor at the next record that conforms to the criterion, as shown in figure 11.13.

The ↓ and ↑ cursor keys let you position the cursor to the next and previous records that conform to the search criteria set out in the Criterion range. The HOME and END keys can be used to position the cursor to the first and last records in the data base, even if they do not fit the search criteria. To end the *Find* operation and return to the */Data Query* menu, you can use either RETURN or ESC.

```
A17: 'Wayne, John                                              FIND

              A                    B                 C    D
1         Addresses Database
2    NAME                    ADDRESS                 CODE PHONE
3    Sikes, William L.       3751 Clifton Ave.       123  241-8445
4    Stone, Betty            700 Vine St.            453  321-9008
5    Cotter, James F.        1003 Tulip Tree House   735  332-0617
6    Zakon, Steven           3549 Keene St.          645  332-6773
7    Schumann, Fritz W.      100 E. Miller Dr. Apt. 28  837  334-1873
8    Zealer, Mathew          2909 Fresno St.         324  334-9008
9    Ahmad, Shamim Sultana   Ashton Ctr, Weatherly Hall 202  143  337-1559
10   Sharpe, Sarah           7897 Providence St. Apt. 3  812  337-4662
11   Horton, Robert          9980 Yale Ave.          532  339-6271
12   Serling, Rod            2389 Twilight St.       563  339-6493
13   Ellison, Steven         5678 Kirkwood Ave.      315  339-6903
14   Owen, David J.          612 Knight Ridge Rd. Apt. 22-C  632  339-8770
15   Montobaum, Ricardo      4567 Corinthean Lane    976  339-8976
16   Young, John             3700 Edwards Ave.       545  871-3827
17   Wayne, John             3248 Six Gun Way        812  871-4129
18   Harding, Edward         2400 Central Parkway    754  871-6223
19   Goldberg, Rube          4563 Newport Ave.       516  871-6429
20   Timmerman, Chuck        3700 Castleway Dr.      534  984-9745
```

Figure 11.13

More Complicated Criterion Ranges

Figure 11.14 shows an example of a slightly more complicted *Criterion* range that is used with a different data base which stores checking account records.

Notice the label "Laura Mann" below the field name "Name" and the formula "+E4>100" below the field name "Amount" in figure 11.14. (This formula is displayed in *Text* format.) The formula combined with the actual value indicates that we want to search for all the checks made out to Laura Mann that were written for an amount greater than $100.00.

You should also notice that the formula is written using relative addressing with reference to the first row of the data base. This is the

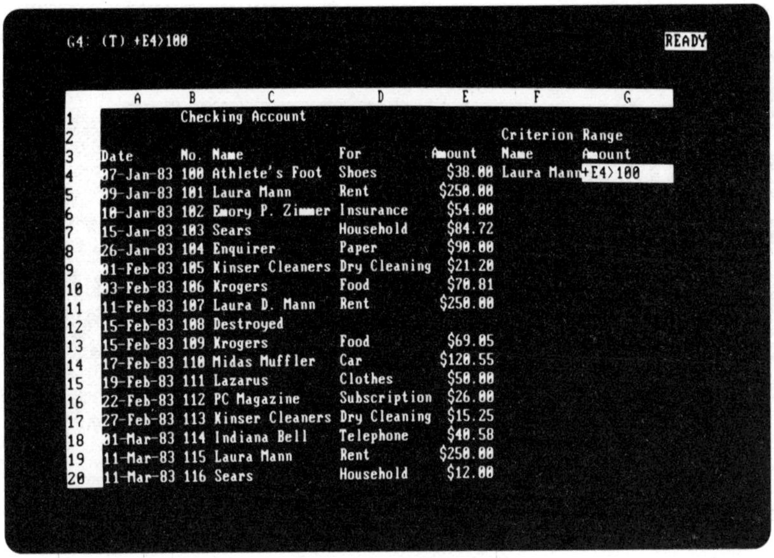

G4: (T) +E4>100 READY

	A	B	C	D	E	F	G
1		Checking Account					
2						Criterion Range	
3	Date	No.	Name	For	Amount	Name	Amount
4	07-Jan-83	100	Athlete's Foot	Shoes	$30.00	Laura Mann	+E4>100
5	09-Jan-83	101	Laura Mann	Rent	$250.00		
6	10-Jan-83	102	Emory P. Zimmer	Insurance	$54.00		
7	15-Jan-83	103	Sears	Household	$84.72		
8	26-Jan-83	104	Enquirer	Paper	$90.00		
9	01-Feb-83	105	Kinser Cleaners	Dry Cleaning	$21.20		
10	03-Feb-83	106	Krogers	Food	$70.81		
11	11-Feb-83	107	Laura D. Mann	Rent	$250.00		
12	15-Feb-83	108	Destroyed				
13	15-Feb-83	109	Krogers	Food	$69.05		
14	17-Feb-83	110	Midas Muffler	Car	$120.55		
15	19-Feb-83	111	Lazarus	Clothes	$50.00		
16	22-Feb-83	112	PC Magazine	Subscription	$26.00		
17	27-Feb-83	113	Kinser Cleaners	Dry Cleaning	$15.25		
18	01-Mar-83	114	Indiana Bell	Telephone	$40.58		
19	11-Mar-83	115	Laura Mann	Rent	$250.00		
20	11-Mar-83	116	Sears	Household	$12.00		

Figure 11.14

way all *C*riterion range formulas should be written. If you want to refer to values outside the *I*nput range, however, you must use absolute addressing. Figure 11.15 shows how relative and absolute addressing are used in the *C*riterion range.

Referring back to figure 11.14, notice that one of the checks in the data base was made out to Laura *D.* Mann. We will not get a match with our *C*riterion range if we don't have a way of handling this discrepancy.

Wild Cards

1-2-3 has some special "wild card" provisions for matching labels. The characters *?*, ***, and ~ have special meaning when used in the *C*riterion range. The *?* character instructs 1-2-3 to accept any character in that position. For example, if we wanted to select all the checks written for insurance in figure 11.14 and knew that we were prone to forgetting to capitalize the "I" in insurance, we could enter ?nsurance below "For" in the *C*riterion range. This way we could

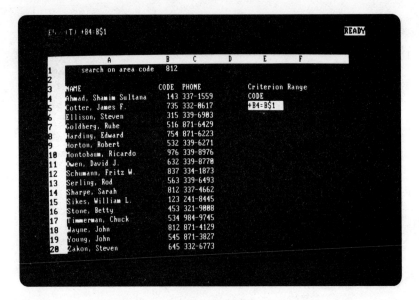

Figure 11.15

make sure that we got all the checks for insurance, including those entered as "Insurance" and "insurance."

The * character tells 1-2-3 to accept any and all characters that follow it. In the example in figure 11.14, if we entered Laura* below "Name" in the *Criterion* range, we would get all the checks for Laura Mann and Laura D. Mann. However, you must be sure that you are getting what you bargained for when you use this wild card character. In this same example, you may also get the checks for Laura Manfredi, Laura Mars, Laura Anybody, etc., if there are any in the data base.

The ~ character is the last wild card character. When placed at the beginning of a label, it indicates that all the values *except* those that follow it are to be selected. For example, if we wanted all the checks except those written for food, we could enter "~Food" below "For" in the *Criterion* range.

The Position of Formulas

As mentioned earlier, the position of numbers and labels below the appropriate field name in the *Criterion* range is important, but it is

irrelevant for formulas. In formulas, the addresses are important, not
what field names they fall under. The label "Laura Mann" must be in
the same column as "Name" in figure 11.14 to get the desired
results. If we wanted all checks written for amounts over $100.00,
regardless of to whom they were written, we could enter either of the
following:

Name	Amount	Name	Amount
	+E4>100	+E4>100	

Compound Criteria

When more than one criterion is used in the second line of the
Criterion range, you are making an explicit statement about how you
want the criteria to be used. For the example in figure 11.17, when
you place both "Laura Mann" and "+E4>100" on the same line, you
are saying that you want to search for checks that were made out to
Laura Mann *and* were written for over $100.00. If you added a third
line to the *Criterion* range and moved the formula down to the third
line, you would be saying that you want to search for checks that
either were made out to Laura Mann *or* were written for over
$100.00. These two *Criterion* ranges are completely different and
will give very different results.

Name	Amount	Name	Amount
Laura Mann	+E4>100	Laura Mann	
			+E4>100

If they were used in figure 11.14, the *Criterion* range on the left would
select check numbers 101, 107, and 115, and the *Criterion* range on
the right would select numbers 101, 107, 110, and 115 from the data
base.

There are two simple rules to remember: criteria placed on the same
row are combined with AND, and criteria placed on different rows
are combined with OR. You can make many different kinds of
Criterion ranges by combining ANDs and ORs.

Name	Amount
Laura Mann	+E4>100
Laura D. Mann	+E4>100

The *Criterion* range above gets us out of trouble with the problem of
some checks being made out to Laura Mann and others to Laura D.

Mann. This format allows us to get both. The criteria state specifically that we want all the checks made out to Laura Mann *and* written for over $100.00 *or* those made out to Laura D. Mann *and* written for over $100.00.

Complex Criterion Ranges

Criterion ranges can become complex when you combine complicated formulas with AND and OR criteria. Consider the example below that selects parts from two different suppliers whose prices have increased more than 12 percent from 1982 to 1983.

Supplier	Price
J&L	(Price83>(Price82*1.12))
Bearings Inc.	(Price83>(Price82*1.12))

Notice that in this *Criterion* range, Price82 and Price83 are range names that correspond to the cell addresses of the prices for 1982 and 1983 for the first record in the data base.

Remembering that you can create a *Criterion* range of up to 32 different fields, consider the *Criterion* range in figure 11.16 that uses six fields. This range could be used to select specific stocks from a data base that includes one week's data from all the stocks on the American and New York Stock Exchanges.

This *Criterion* range selects those stocks that had a high greater than or equal to 50 and a low greater than or equal to 10 in the last fifty-two weeks, a name beginning with "N," sales of between 1,000 and 10,000 shares in the last week, a high value between 35 and 40 in the last week, and a positive net change in the last week. As you can see, selection criteria can be made much more complex than those for the "personal" data bases that are best used in 1-2-3.

The best way to become comfortable with *Criterion* ranges is to experiment with them.

Output Range

The results of a /*Data* Query are sometimes written to a special area of the worksheet. This special area is called the *Output* range. All you need to specify for the *Output* range is a single row containing the names of the fields that you want copied. You can specify a

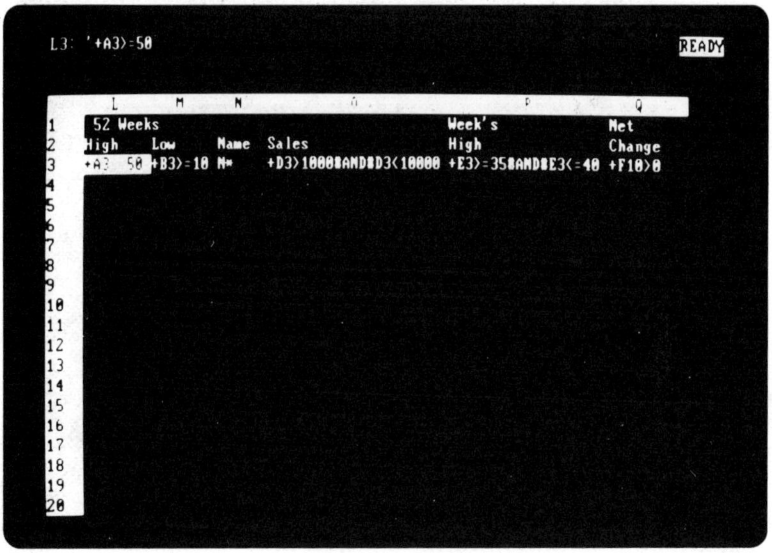

Figure 11.16

larger area for the *Output* range, but all 1-2-3 actually needs is the field names. Figure 11.17 shows the output range for the example we used above to select all the checks made out to Laura Mann for over $100.00. In this example, we have chosen *Extract* for the kind of */Data Query* operation to perform. Figure 11.18 shows the results.

As you can see, the *Extract* operation copies to the area below the field names all the records that conform to the selection criterion. In figure 11.17, the *Output* range was F8..I8.

The advantage of the *Extract* option is that it allows you to do some fairly detailed analysis on a data base. You can use *Extract* to pull data from one or more records in a data base and perform special processing on the subset. For example, by setting up the proper *Criterion* range, you can ask the question, "For what have we written checks for over $1,000.00?" The results are shown in figure 11.19.

Once you have made copies of the appropriate records, you can analyze them further by setting up new *Criterion* and *Output* ranges. For example, you could ask the question, "Of those checks

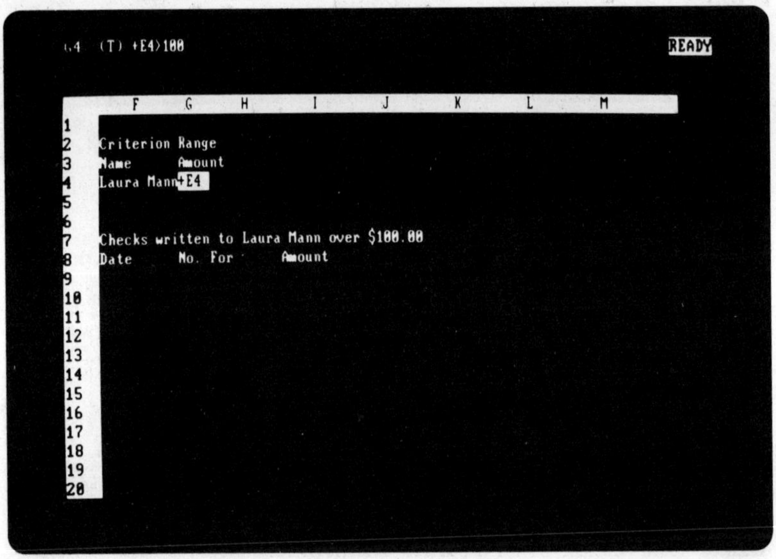

G4 (T) +E4)100   READY

```
       F      G     H     I     J     K     L     M
 1
 2   Criterion Range
 3   Name     Amount
 4   Laura Mann +E4
 5
 6
 7   Checks written to Laura Mann over $100.00
 8   Date     No. For     Amount
 9
10
11
12
13
14
15
16
17
18
19
20
```

Figure 11.17

G4 (T) +E4)100   READY

```
        F      G     H     I     J     K     L     M
 1
 2    Criterion Range
 3    Name     Amount
 4    Laura Mann +E4
 5
 6
 7    Checks written to Laura Mann over $100.00
 8    Date     No. For     Amount
 9   09-Jan-83 101 Rent     $250.00
10   11-Mar-83 115 Rent     $250.00
11
12
13
14
15
16
17
18
19
20
```

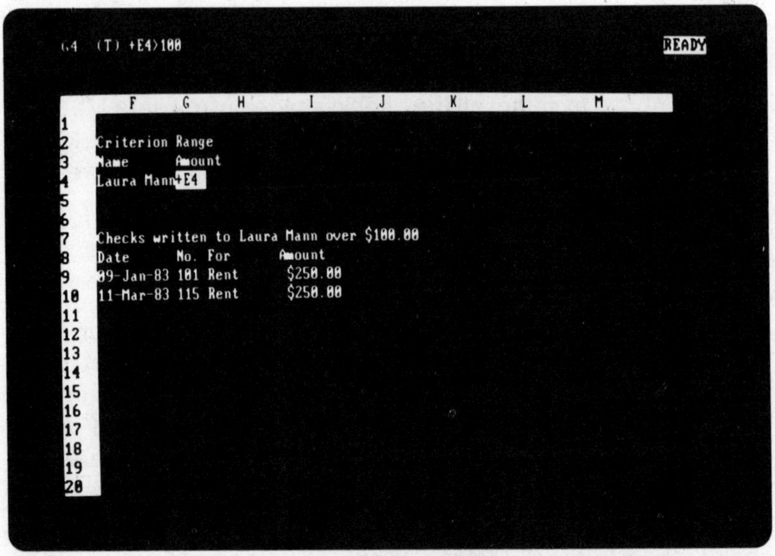

Figure 11.18

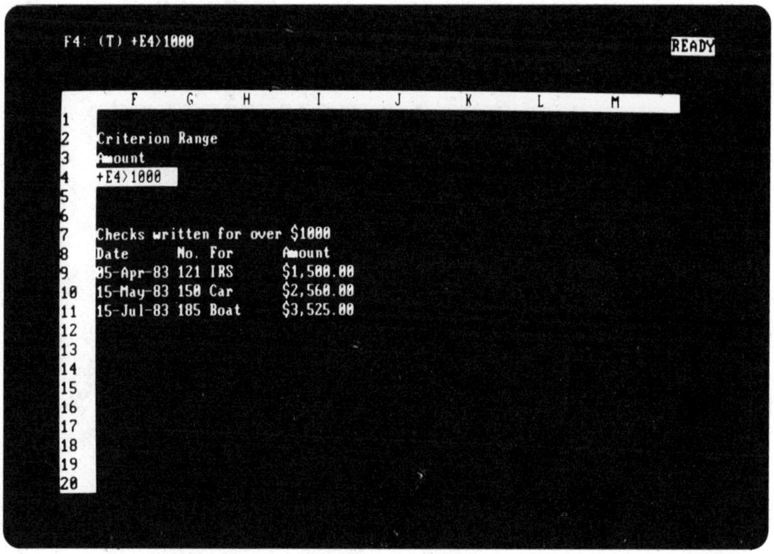

Figure 11.19

mentioned above, which ones were written in the last 15 days?"
Figure 11.20 shows the answer.

We could have gotten the same results in figure 11.20 by performing
a single / Data Query operation and combining the selection criteria
from the two Criterion ranges, as shown in figure 11.21.

Depending on the size limitations you face and your personal
preference as to how you would like to perform the Extract, you can
either combine the selection criteria or use them separately. There
is rarely one best answer.

Notice that none of the Output ranges in figures 11.17 through 11.21
contains all the field names that occur in the data base. For example,
in figure 11.17, by placing only the "Date," "No.," "For," and
"Amount" fields in the Output range, we copy only those fields.
Because we have already determined by the selection criteria who
the checks were made out to, we can eliminate that field from the
Output range. Instead, we put a single label in cell A7 above the
Output range to tell us to whom the checks were made out.

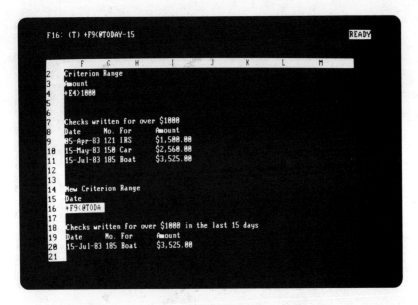

Figure 11.20

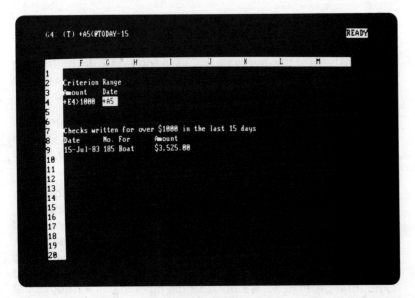

Figure 11.21

You can set up the *Output* range in any area of the worksheet. However, an out-of-the-way area that has room for expansion is best because 1-2-3 uses all the space from the row just below the field names to the bottom of the worksheet to make copies of the records that fit the selection criteria. Any cells whose contents might be in the way are written over. Be careful!

A convenient way to execute a search a second time, or as many times as you like, is to use the F7 (QUERY) key. 1-2-3 remembers the latest *Input*, *Criterion*, and *Output* ranges, and if you have not substantially modified them, you can use F7 to re-execute */Data Query* operation. This operation allows you to make changes to the criteria selections in the *Criterion* range and immediately search the data base again for the new values. This saves your having to re-enter all the ranges each time you make a small change to the *Criterion* range. You also avoid having to enter and *Quit* the command menu to execute the */Data Query* command.

The F7 key is much like the F10 (GRAPH) key (covered in detail in Chapter 9). F10 lets you draw a graph, using the latest graph settings. You can make small changes to the settings and immediately review their effect. In the same way, you can make small changes to the range settings for searching a data base and immediately see their results by pressing F7.

As mentioned earlier, the maximum theoretical limit on the number of records you can have in a data base is about 2,000. If you are performing an *Extract* operation, however, you will require additional space for the *Output* range. This further restricts the space you can devote to the data base. If the *Output* range that you are extracting could reach the size of the data base itself, the effective limit on the size of the data base is actually half the number of rows in the spreadsheet, or about 1,000 records.

If you plan to perform an *Extract* operation, consider the requirements for the *Output* range and how they might limit the kind of *Extract* you can perform. With fairly small data bases, this is not a problem. The larger a data base gets, however, the more you should keep a careful eye on the amount of RAM available. A frequent check of the */Worksheet Status* will tell you how much RAM is left and allow you to gauge what kinds of *Extract* operations are possible given the available RAM.

Other Types of Searches

Another type of search, which can be performed using a variation of
the */ D*ata Query command, selects all the *unique* records in a data
base. This option can be used to copy all the unique records from an
address data base to a separate part of the worksheet. Another, more
popular, way to use the option is to have it focus on specific fields in a
data base. To illustrate how this process works, suppose that you
want to get a listing of all the companies which are represented in
your customer data base. Suppose further that your customer data
base is organized in the manner shown in figure 11.22, where all the
records have a "Name" field and a "Company" field.

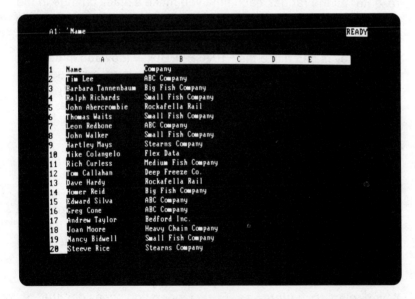

Figure 11.22

As you can see, there are several companies represented more than
once in the data base. To avoid copying duplicate records to the
*O*utput range, we use the *U*nique option. The *U*nique option is set up
like the *E*xtract option, but the results can be quite different. Figure
11.23 shows how the *E*xtract and *U*nique options work on the same
*C*riterion range (J2..J3).

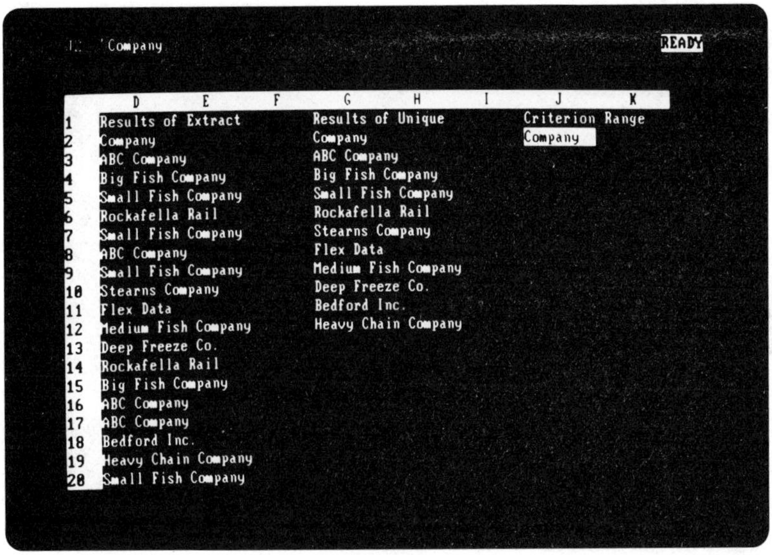

Figure 11.23

In this example, the *C*riterion range has only one file name in it ("Company"), and the cell below the field name has been deliberately left blank. For the *E*xtract operation, this allows all the records in the data base to meet the criterion. Therefore, the results of the *E*xtract show copies of the company fields from each record in the data base. For the *U*nique operation, however, all the duplicate listings of the companies are eliminated. The results of the *U*nique operation show a list of all the companies represented in the customer data base.

The last method used to search records is the *D*elete option. It removes unwanted records from data base files. Suppose that you want to purge all the paid accounts from your Overdue Accounts data base, but only after you have verified that they have in fact been paid. Figure 11.24 shows a portion of the Overdue Accounts data base.

First, you would extract all the records that have been paid to verify their accuracy. To do this, use the *E*xtract function with the *C*riterion range shown in figure 11.25. This figure also shows the results of the *E*xtract.

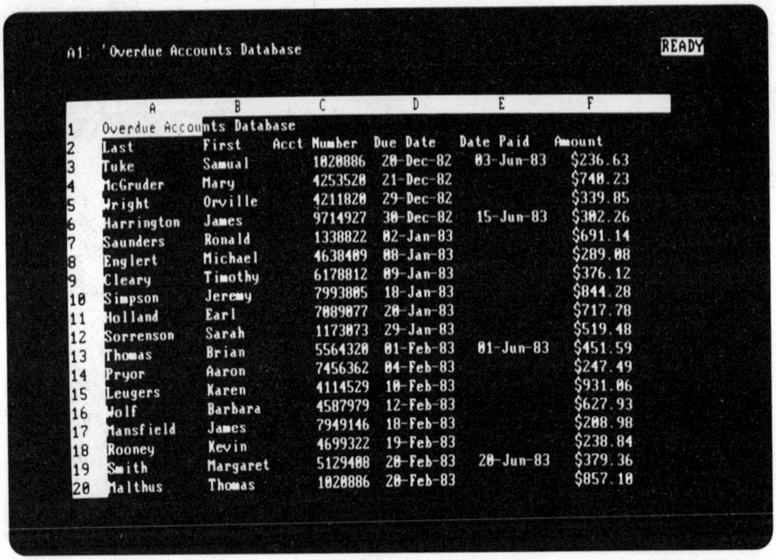

```
A1: 'Overdue Accounts Database                                    READY

          A          B         C         D         E         F
1   Overdue Accounts Database
2   Last        First     Acct Number  Due Date  Date Paid  Amount
3   Tuke        Samual    1820886   20-Dec-82  03-Jun-83  $236.63
4   McGruder    Mary      4253520   21-Dec-82             $740.23
5   Wright      Orville   4211820   29-Dec-82             $339.85
6   Harrington  James     9714927   30-Dec-82  15-Jun-83  $302.26
7   Saunders    Ronald    1338822   02-Jan-83             $691.14
8   Englert     Michael   4638409   08-Jan-83             $289.08
9   Cleary      Timothy   6178812   09-Jan-83             $376.12
10  Simpson     Jeremy    7993805   18-Jan-83             $844.28
11  Holland     Earl      7809077   20-Jan-83             $717.78
12  Sorrenson   Sarah     1173073   29-Jan-83             $519.48
13  Thomas      Brian     5564320   01-Feb-83  01-Jun-83  $451.59
14  Pryor       Aaron     7456362   04-Feb-83             $247.49
15  Leugers     Karen     4114529   10-Feb-83             $931.06
16  Wolf        Barbara   4587979   12-Feb-83             $627.93
17  Mansfield   James     7949146   18-Feb-83             $208.98
18  Rooney      Kevin     4699322   19-Feb-83             $238.84
19  Smith       Margaret  5129408   20-Feb-83  20-Jun-83  $379.36
20  Malthus     Thomas    1820886   20-Feb-83             $857.10
```

Figure 11.24

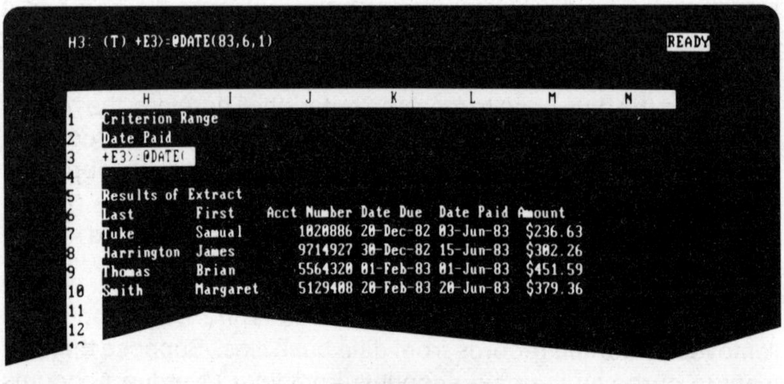

```
H3: (T) +E3>=@DATE(83,6,1)                                        READY

          H          I         J         K         L         M         N
1   Criterion Range
2   Date Paid
3   +E3>=@DATE(
4
5   Results of Extract
6   Last        First     Acct Number Date Due  Date Paid  Amount
7   Tuke        Samual    1820886   20-Dec-82  03-Jun-83  $236.63
8   Harrington  James     9714927   30-Dec-82  15-Jun-83  $302.26
9   Thomas      Brian     5564320   01-Feb-83  01-Jun-83  $451.59
10  Smith       Margaret  5129408   20-Feb-83  20-Jun-83  $379.36
11
12
```

Figure 11.25

After you perform the *Extract* operation and review the results shown in figure 11.25, you can use the same *Criterion* range for the *Delete* operation. After a confirmation step, the results appear in figure 11.26.

Notice that when the *Delete* option is executed, the records that meet the criteria are removed and the gaps that are left in the data base are closed up behind them. Like the *Find* operation, the *Delete* operation does not require an *Output* range.

When you use the *Delete* option, make sure that you are deleting the proper records. An initial precautionary step of *Extracting* them first is not a bad idea. This way you can verify that you have the proper *Criterion* range set up. Once you have deleted the records, they are gone from RAM. If you make a mistake with the *Delete* option and have not yet saved the file, you can still regain the original data base by bringing the file back from storage with the */File Retrieve* command and writing over the current worksheet.

Data Base Statistical Functions

1-2-3's data base statistical functions are similar to the standard statistical functions, but have been modified to manipulate data base fields. These functions are another unique feature of 1-2-3.

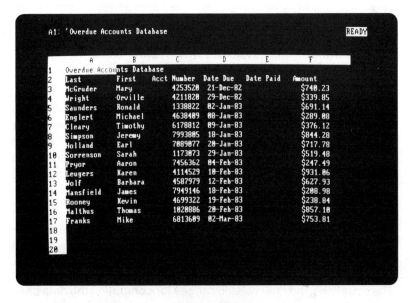

Figure 11.26

Like the standard statistical functions, the data base statistical functions perform in one simple statement what would otherwise take several statements to accomplish. It is because of this efficiency and ease of application that you should take advantage of them. The functions include:

@DCOUNT	Gives the number of items in a list
@DSUM	Sums the values of all the items in a list
@DMIN	Gives the minimum of all the items in a list
@DMAX	Gives the maximum of all the items in a list
@DSTD	Gives the standard deviation of all the items in a list
@DVAR	Gives the variance of all the items in a list
@DAV	Gives the arithmetic mean of all the items in a list

The general form of these functions is

@DFUNC(Input range, offset, Criterion range)

The *Input* and *Criterion* ranges are the same as those used by the */ Data Query* command. The *Input* range specifies the data base to be scanned, and the *Criterion* range specifies which records to select from it. The offset indicates which field to select from the data base records and is either zero or a positive integer. A value of zero indicates the first column; a 1 indicates the second column, etc.

An example that uses the data base statistical functions involves computing the mean, variance, and standard deviation of the average interest rates offered by money market funds for a given week. If you are unfamiliar with the concepts of mean, variance, and standard deviation, they are covered in Chapter 6. At this point, we assume that you know what they mean and will simply show you how to use them for data base applications here.

Figure 11.27 shows the Money Market Returns data base and the results of the various data base functions. Notice that the functions to find the maximum and minimum rates of return are also included.

The equations and their related ranges for computing the data base statistics are

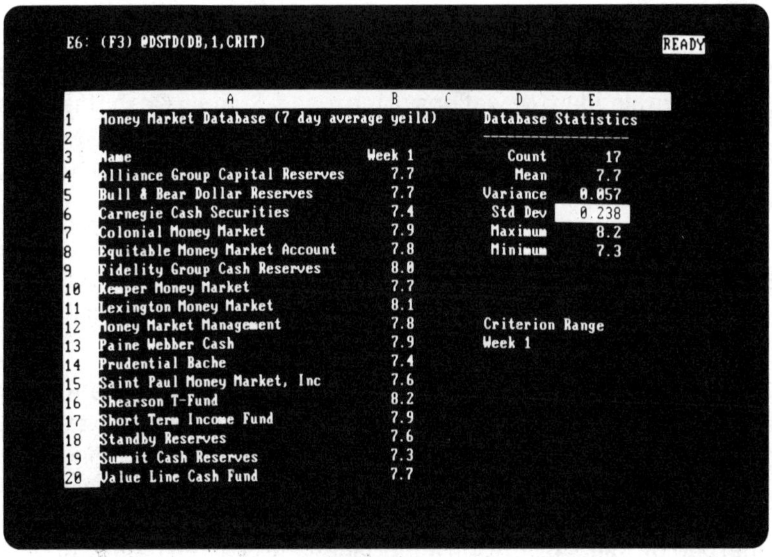
E6: (F3) @DSTD(DB,1,CRIT) READY

	A	B	C	D	E
1	Money Market Database (7 day average yeild)			Database Statistics	
2					
3	Name	Week 1		Count	17
4	Alliance Group Capital Reserves	7.7		Mean	7.7
5	Bull & Bear Dollar Reserves	7.7		Variance	0.057
6	Carnegie Cash Securities	7.4		Std Dev	0.238
7	Colonial Money Market	7.9		Maximum	8.2
8	Equitable Money Market Account	7.8		Minimum	7.3
9	Fidelity Group Cash Reserves	8.0			
10	Kemper Money Market	7.7			
11	Lexington Money Market	8.1			
12	Money Market Management	7.8		Criterion Range	
13	Paine Webber Cash	7.9		Week 1	
14	Prudential Bache	7.4			
15	Saint Paul Money Market, Inc	7.6			
16	Shearson T-Fund	8.2			
17	Short Term Income Fund	7.9			
18	Standby Reserves	7.6			
19	Summit Cash Reserves	7.3			
20	Value Line Cash Fund	7.7			

Figure 11.27

Count	@DCOUNT(A3..B20,1,D13..D14)
Mean	@DAVG(A3..B20,1,D13..D14)
Variance	@DVAR(A3..B20,1,D13..D14)
Std Dev	@DSTD(A3..B20,1,D13..D14)
Maximum	@DMAX(A3..B20,1,D13..D14)
Minimum	@DMIN(A3..B20,1,D13..D14)

The results in figure 11.27 indicate that the mean return for the week for the seventeen different money market funds is at an annual percentage rate of 7.7 (cell E4). The variance is approximately .057 (cell E5), yielding a standard deviation of approximately .238 (cell E6). This means that about 68% of the money market funds are returning a rate of between 7.46 and 7.94 percent annually.

One Std Dev below mean = 7.7 - .238 = 7.46
One Std Dev above mean = 7.7 - .237 = 7.94

Summit Cash Reserves returns the lowest rate at 7.3. The 7.3 figure comes from the @DMIN function used in cell E8. This value is approaching two standard deviations below the mean. Two standard deviations below the mean is computed as follows:

Two Std Devs below mean = 7.7 - (2 x .238) = 7.22

Because approximately 95% of the population falls within plus or minus two standard deviations of the mean, Summit Cash Reserves is very close to being in the lower 2.5 percent (5 percent divided by 2 because the population is assumed to be normal) of the population in money market funds for that week.

Conversely, the Shearson T-Fund returns the highest rate: 8.2. The @DMAX function was used to determine the highest rate (cell B16), which is just over two standard deviations above the mean, or the highest 2.5 percent of the population.

Obviously, the data base statistical functions can tell you a great deal about the data base as a whole and how to interpret the values in it. If you add several more weeks' data to the example in figure 11.27, you can use the data base functions to perform analysis on all or part of a larger data base. Figure 11.28 shows some of the data that can be used to perform a further analysis of the money market funds.

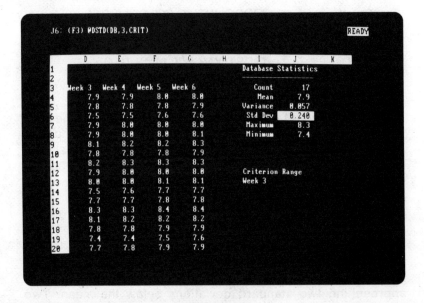

Figure 11.28

You can use the methods detailed above to interpret the results in figure 11.28. The following table gives examples of the *Input*, *Offset*, and *Criterion* ranges used for the data from week 3 of our example.

Input range	A3..G20
Offset	3 (for the fourth column)
Criterion range	I13..I14

From this information, you can determine how the formulas were set up for each week. The *Criterion* range displayed in figure 11.28 shows the criteria used to select the values for the third week.

Table Building

The table building function has the same / *Data* command root as all the other commands covered in this chapter. Table building is an extended version of the "what if" process. In fact, all the functions performed by the table building feature could be duplicated by repeated "what if" statements. However, the time required to do the latter would be prohibitive. Table building automates the "what if" process to the point where you can make a very extensive analysis with a minimal amount of effort. It allows you to perform the kind of thorough analysis that you might not do otherwise.

Table building automates the "what if" process through iteration. That is, 1-2-3 takes sets of values and substitutes them one at a time into the worksheet. The results of the substitution are automatically recorded by 1-2-3. You provide 1-2-3 with the values to substitute and also tell it where to substitute them.

This may sound mysterious, but it is actually very simple. Most of the the work is done internally by 1-2-3. All you have to know is how to set up the appropriate ranges; 1-2-3 takes care of the rest. The / *Data Table* command is the host command for the table building function and enables 1-2-3 to run circles around the competition in "what if" analysis.

The / *Data Table* command may seem difficult to use at first. Once you have learned how to use it, however, you will find that it is one of the most powerful commands in 1-2-3. In fact, the power of this command rivals similar commands in some of the most sophisticated mainframe decision support systems. When you consider the ease of implementation, the *Data Table* command really has something going for it.

The idea of the */Data Table* command is to structure the "what if" process. It allows you to build a table of input values and have 1-2-3 substitute them one at a time into a model you have developed. 1-2-3 then records the results in the table, next to the input values.

A very simple example would be to build a table of interest rates and determine their effect on the monthly payments of a thirty-year mortgage, as shown in figure 11.29.

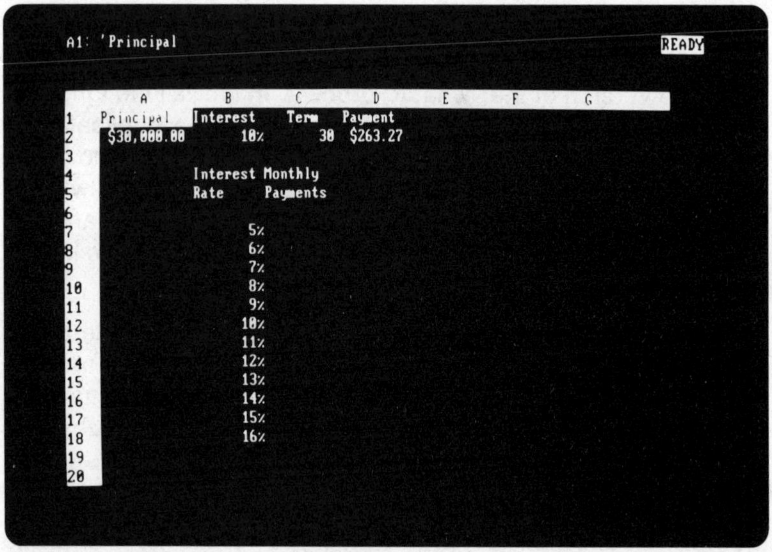

Figure 11.29

By using the */Data Table 1* command, you can have 1-2-3 substitute the interest rates you have entered in a column into the appropriate input cells above. After a short wait, 1-2-3 will list the monthly payments in the column, next to the interest rates.

Before entering the /Data Table 1 command, you must enter the interest rate values in a column. (We used the /Data Fill command here, which is covered in the next section.) Cells B7..B18 hold the interest rates. The next step is to enter the appropriate formula for calculating the results, or cell address from which to draw them, next to the column of interest rates and one row above the first entry.

In figure 11.30, we entered +D2 in cell C6, but we could have entered the actual formula used to compute the value in cell C6. The formula in that cell is @PMT(A2,B2/12,C2*12). +D2 shows up because the /Range Format Text command was used on cell C6 to override the General display format.

When the /Data Table 1 command is executed, 1-2-3 asks you to indicate an "Input Cell." This is the cell in which we plan to substitute all the values in the column of interest rates. In this example, we enter B2. Next, it asks you to enter a "Table Range." This is the range of cells that includes the column of interest rates to be substituted as well as the column where we want the results to appear. Our entry here is B6..C18. Notice that we have also been careful to include the formulas row in the range specification.

While 1-2-3 is calculating the results, a WAIT sign will flash in the upper right corner of the screen. When 1-2-3 has finished, and sometimes it takes awhile, the screen will return to the Ready mode. At this point, the table is complete with all the payment values.

If you are dissatisfied with the results of the command, or you simply want to try some other input values, you can change the values and press the F8 (TABLE) key to have the table automatically recalculated. The F8 key is similar to the F7 (QUERY) key except that it is used for table building rather than searching data bases. Pressing F8 causes 1-2-3 to recalculate the table automatically using the current command parameters that you specified for the previous /Data Table command.

A more involved example uses the /Data Table 2 command. This command requires two input variables instead of one. The advantage to this is the increased breadth of sensitivity analysis. This example is designed to show the effects on total cost of changes in order quantity and order point. We are after that combination of order point and order quantity that minimizes "Cumulative Costs to

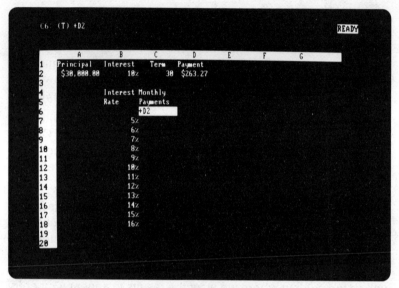

Figure 11.30A

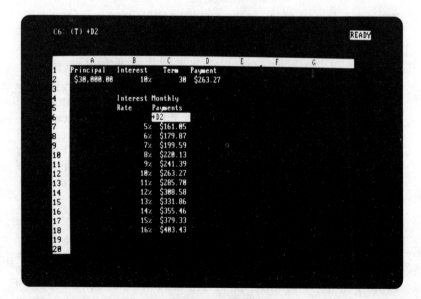

Figure 11.30B

Date" at the end of a twelve-month period. Figure 11.31 illustrates this example.

The lower left-hand portion of figure 11.31 shows how the /Data Table 1 command is used in our example and shows the effect on cost of several different order quantities. To the right is a much more extensive table, which is the result of executing the /Data Table 2 command. Here several more order points are used to make the analysis more complete. This is the advantage of the /Data Table 2 command.

To use the /Data Table 2 command, the values for Variable 2 (order point) are entered in the row just above the first entry of Variable 1 (order quantity). Notice also that +M12, the address of the formula for "Cost to Date," is entered in the row directly above the first entry of Variable 1. Again, the Text format is used to display +M12.

When executed, the /Data Table 2 command calls for "Input Cells" for Variables 1 and 2 and a "Table Range." The following information is entered for these parameters:

Input Cell Variable 1	B15
Input Cell Variable 2	B16
Table Range	F21..K47

After you enter this information, 1-2-3 begins building the table of results. The waiting time for the /Data Table 2 command is substantial, but when you consider what 1-2-3 is actually doing, it is worth it. To duplicate manually what 1-2-3 does would take quite a bit longer.

There is no one correct answer to this problem. Our limited analysis shows, however, that on average an order point of about 27 and an order quantity of about 32 are best.

The advantages of the /Data Table command are the ability to conduct extensive sensitivity analysis and to display the results in a tabular format. The /Data Table lets you do the kind of thorough analysis that you might not do otherwise, given the time required to perform it. Further, the power of the command in combination with macros and special data base statistical functions can be outstanding.

	A	B	C	D	E	F	G	H	I	J	K	L	M
1	Month	Jan	Feb	Mar	Apr	May	Jun	Jul	Aug	Sep	Oct	Nov	Dec
2	-------												
3	Beginning Inventory	43	51	35	60	42	30	46	33	45	35	59	40
4	Past Demand for Month	28	16	11	18	12	20	13	24	10	12	19	22
5	Ending Inventory	15	35	24	42	30	10	33	9	35	23	40	18
6	Quantity Ordered	36	0	36	0	0	36	0	36	0	36	0	36
7	Setup Costs ($10 per order)	10	0	10	0	0	10	0	10	0	10	0	10
8	Inventory Costs ($.2/unit)	$3.00	$7.00	$4.80	$8.40	$6.00	$2.00	$6.60	$1.80	$7.00	$4.60	$8.00	$3.60
9	Shortage Costs ($1/unit)	$0.00	$0.00	$0.00	$0.00	$0.00	$0.00	$0.00	$0.00	$0.00	$0.00	$0.00	$0.00
10	Total Costs for Month	$13.00	$7.00	$14.80	$8.40	$6.00	$12.00	$6.60	$11.80	$7.00	$14.60	$8.00	$13.60
11	Cum Cost From Last Month	$0.00	$13.00	$20.00	$34.80	$43.20	$49.20	$61.20	$67.80	$79.60	$86.60	$101.20	$109.20
12	Cumulative Costs to Date	$13.00	$20.00	$34.80	$43.20	$49.20	$61.20	$67.80	$79.60	$86.60	$101.20	$109.20	$122.80
13													
14													
15	Order Quantity Input Cell->	36											
16	Order Point Input Cell---->	28											
17													
18		Order	Cumulative			Order	Cumulative						
19		Quant	Cost			Quant	Cost						
20		-----	------			-----	------						
21			+M12			+M12	25	26	27	28	29	Average	
22		25	$137.40			15	$150.40	$150.40	$150.40	$150.40	$150.40	$150.40	
23		26	$136.00			16	$163.60	$163.60	$163.60	$163.60	$163.60	$163.60	
24		27	$144.60			17	$143.00	$149.80	$160.00	$160.00	$160.00	$154.56	
25		28	$137.60			18	$154.80	$154.80	$154.80	$154.80	$154.80	$154.80	
26		29	$140.20			19	$141.40	$145.20	$149.00	$149.00	$149.00	$146.72	
27		30	$130.40			20	$148.40	$148.40	$148.40	$152.40	$152.40	$150.00	
28		31	$131.80			21	$132.40	$136.60	$136.60	$150.80	$150.80	$141.44	
29		32	$122.80			22	$138.00	$142.40	$142.40	$142.40	$142.40	$141.52	
30		33	$130.00			23	$138.60	$138.60	$143.20	$143.20	$147.80	$142.28	
31		34	$130.40			24	$133.20	$133.20	$133.20	$138.00	$138.00	$135.12	
32		35	$123.40			25	$132.40	$137.40	$137.40	$137.40	$142.40	$137.40	
33		36	$122.80			26	$136.00	$136.00	$136.00	$136.00	$141.20	$137.04	
34		37	$129.20			27	$123.80	$134.60	$144.60	$144.60	$144.60	$138.44	
35		38	$128.00			28	$120.80	$126.40	$132.00	$137.60	$137.60	$130.88	
36		39	$124.20			29	$128.60	$128.60	$128.60	$140.20	$140.20	$133.24	
37		40	$130.40			30	$124.40	$124.40	$124.40	$130.40	$142.40	$129.20	
38		41	$128.40			31	$131.80	$131.80	$131.80	$131.80	$131.80	$131.80	
39		42	$134.40			32	$122.80	$122.80	$122.80	$122.80	$129.20	$124.08	
40		43	$123.20			33	$130.00	$130.00	$130.00	$130.00	$130.00	$130.00	
41		44	$128.80			34	$110.00	$116.80	$130.40	$130.40	$130.40	$123.60	
42		45	$134.40			35	$116.40	$116.40	$116.40	$123.40	$123.40	$119.20	
43		46	$121.60			36	$122.80	$122.80	$122.80	$122.80	$122.80	$122.80	
44		47	$126.80			37	$121.80	$121.80	$129.20	$129.20	$129.20	$126.24	
45		48	$122.00			38	$110.40	$118.00	$118.00	$128.00	$128.00	$120.48	
46		49	$127.20			39	$116.40	$116.40	$124.20	$124.20	$124.20	$121.08	
47		50	$122.40			40	$122.40	$122.40	$122.40	$130.40	$130.40	$125.60	

Figure 11.31

Filling Ranges with Numbers

The command for filling ranges is / Data Fill. One of the strengths of this command is that it is very useful when combined with the other data base commands mentioned earlier in this chapter, especially / Data Table and / Data Sort.

/ Data Fill fills a range of cells with evenly incremented or decremented numbers. One example of this command is the actual year numbers used as titles in a sales forecast shown in figure 11.32.

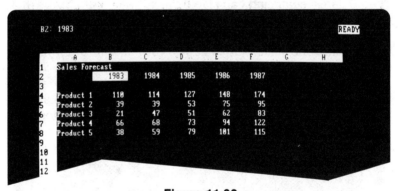

Figure 11.32

The / Data Fill command first prompts you for the number at which you want to start the sequence. It then asks for the step or incremental value you want to add to the previous value. Finally, it asks for the ending value at which to stop the filling operation.

To enter a sequence of year numbers for a five-year forecast beginning in 1983, begin by specifying the range of cells to be filled. For this example, we chose B2..F2. Then the beginning value, 1983, is entered. The incremental or step value here is 1. The ending value is 1987 for a five-year forecast.

One disadvantage of the / Data / Fill command for year numbers is that you can't center or left-justify the numbers after you have created them. As numbers, they will always be right-justified. If you like your year numbers centered or left-justified, you should not use this command. You will have to type in labels instead.

Another example of the / Data Fill command, which is particularly useful with the / Data Table command, is building a list of interest rates, as mentioned in the example in figure 11.30. In this figure, the column of interest rate values was entered with the / Data Fill command. For the range of cells to be filled, we specified B7..B18, and for starting value we entered .05. The step value entered in this case was .01. For the ending value, we let 1-2-3 default to 2047, which is far beyond the ending value we actually needed. The / Data Fill command, however, fills only the range you have specified and does not carry beyond it.

The / Data Fill command can also be used with / Data Sort. When using the / Data Fill command, if you attach consecutive numbers to each record in a data base (thereby placing the numbers in a separate field), no matter how fouled up you make the order you can always get back to the original sequence. You simply / Data Sort the filled range. This is especially useful if the data base you began with has a relational rather than a numeric order, such as the names of the months in a year. Figure 11.33 shows an example before and after a / Data Sort.

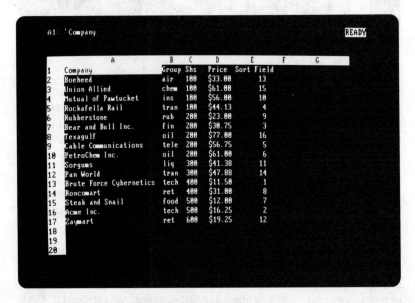

Figure 11.33A

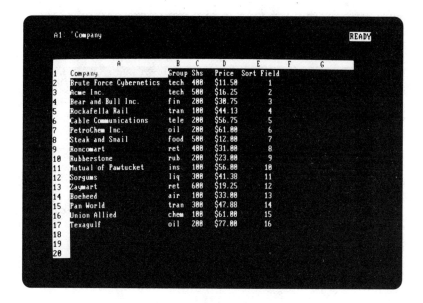

Figure 11.33B

In our examples, we have always used regular numbers for the beginning, incremental, and ending values. It is also possible, however to use formulas and commands. For example, if you want to fill a range of cells with incrementing dates, you could use the @DATE function to set the beginning value. You could also use a cell formula, such as +E4, for the incremental and ending values. 1-2-3 allows any number of different combinations.

Frequency Distributions

The command used to create frequency distributions in 1-2-3 is */ Data Distribution*. For those who are not familiar with the term, a *frequency distribution* is a representation of the relationship between a set of measurement classes and the frequency of occurrence of each class. A very simple example of a frequency distribution and the use of the */ Data Distribution* command is shown in figure 11.34. It deals with a list of consumers and their product preferences.

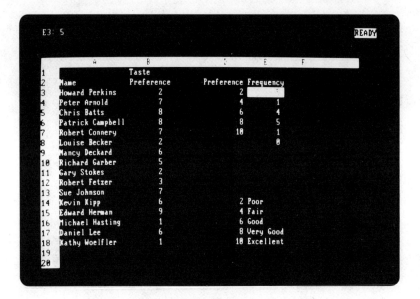

Figure 11.34

To execute the */Data Distribution* command in this example, you must first specify a "Values" range. This range corresponds to the range of numbers associated with "Taste Preference" in figure 11.34. We specified B3..B18 for the values range. The next step is to set up the range of intervals, or what 1-2-3 calls the *Bin* range. We specified D3..D7 for the Bin range. You can use the */Data Fill* command to specify the values to be included in the Bin range, but this assumes that you want evenly spaced intervals. In our example, we do not have evenly spaced intervals, so we did not use the */Data Fill* command to fill the range.

When you specify these ranges and enter the */Data Distribution* command, 1-2-3 returns the "Results" column to the right of the Bin range (E3..E8). The Results column is a frequency distribution and is always in the column segment to the right of the Bin range and extending one row down.

The values in the Results column represent the frequency of occurrence of the numbers in the Values range that fall within the interval. The first interval in the Bin range is for values greater than zero and less than or equal to one, the second for values greater than one and less than or equal to 3, etc. The last value in the Results column, in cell D6 just below the corresponding column segment, is the frequency of what is left over (that is, the frequency of anything that doesn't fit into an interval classification).

The /Data Distribution command can be used to create understandable results from a series of numbers. The results are easily graphed, as shown in figure 11.35.

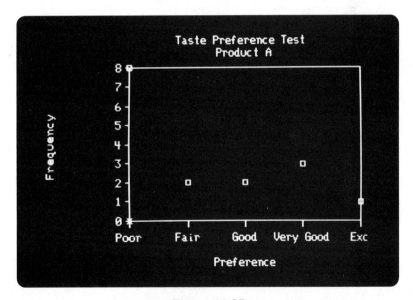

Figure 11.35

From the looks of this graph, the manufacturer of the product probably should be searching for another product, or at least improving the taste of the current one.

12

Keyboard Macros

Keyboard macros may be the most exciting element of 1-2-3. They are certainly the most innovative part of the program. Although other spreadsheets offer limited macro capability, none comes close to the power and flexibility offered by 1-2-3.

1-2-3 was not the first program to include keyboard macros. Other spreadsheet programs, such as VisiCalc and SuperCalc, have a degree of programmability through external command files.

The SuperCalc spreadsheet has a command, /eXternal, that is used to load and execute an external program file. As with 1-2-3, a SuperCalc execute file is a collection of keystrokes that can be used as an alternative to typing certain commands for the keyboard. But SuperCalc's execute files are much simpler than 1-2-3's macros. For one thing, SuperCalc has no special commands for controlling the execution of execute files. For another, in most versions of SuperCalc, there is no way to stop a macro, short of typing CTRL C, once the macro has been started.

The newest version of VisiCalc, VisiCalc Advanced Version, offers a feature called *keystroke memory* that comes close to 1-2-3's macros. VisiCalc Advanced Version does not, however, offer as many special commands or as much flexibility and ease of use as 1-2-3.

Unfortunately, macros are barely touched on in the 1-2-3 manual, which devotes only 10 pages to the entire topic. As a result, many 1-2-3 users are not using macros at all. Others are not using them as effectively as they could.

What Is a Keyboard Macro?

Before 1-2-3 was released to the general public, Lotus decided on the name *typing alternative* to describe keyboard macros. Although this name was later de-emphasized in favor of the term *keyboard macros,* it is very descriptive of the true nature of macros.

In their most basic form, macros are simply collections of keystrokes. A macro is like a storehouse of keystrokes. These keystrokes can be commands or simple text and numeric entries. Macros provide an alternative to typing commands and data from the keyboard—hence the name "typing alternative." A macro can be used instead of the keyboard to issue a command or to enter data into the 1-2-3 worksheet.

But a macro can be much more than just a simple collection of keystrokes. 1-2-3 has a number of special commands that can be used only with macros. These commands do such things as: accept input from the keyboard during a macro, perform a conditional test similar to that of the IF-THEN command of the BASIC language, and create user menus. These commands make 1-2-3's keyboard macros a simple (but increasingly complex) programming language and make 1-2-3 the first truly programmable spreadsheet.

The Complexity of Macros

Lotus calls one section of its manual *Advanced Topic: Do you Sincerely Want to Become a Programmer?* This is an appropriate question. 1-2-3's macro functions are complex. Because they can have global effects on the worksheet, they should always be used carefully.

The 1-2-3 novice may want to avoid macros until he or she is fairly comfortable with 1-2-3 in general. But you do not need to know everything about 1-2-3 before you begin to use macros. This chapter contains a number of macros that you can use right away.

Even if you are new to 1-2-3, there is no reason why you can't begin immediately to experiment with macros.

If you have experience with BASIC or another programming language, the macros will be easier to learn and use. But even the advanced programmer will find some obstacles with 1-2-3's macros. First, the macros are difficult to debug. In version 1A, a new feature that allows the macro to be executed one step at a time should alleviate this problem.

One thing we don't explain in this chapter is programming theory. If you are interested in building highly complex 1-2-3 macros, we suggest that you take some time to learn programming theory. A number of excellent books on this subject are available in your local bookstore.

A second, more serious, problem is that, although the macros are a very useful tool, they do not have enough commands and functions to be considered a full programming language. This can be frustrating to experienced programmers if they try to use macros to create a true 1-2-3 program.

The best macros are simple macros. Until Lotus expands the macro facility (which it apparently is planning to do), most users would be better off using macros to automate simple, repetitive tasks. If you want to create a sophisticated program with 1-2-3, do what you would normally do before writing a program in any other language: plan it carefully and be prepared to spend a lot of time coding and debugging.

The Elements of Macros

A macro is nothing more than a specially named *text cell.* All macros are created by entering the keystrokes (or representations of those strokes) to be stored into a worksheet cell. For example, suppose you want to create a very simple macro that will format the current cell to appear in the currency format with no decimal places. The macro would look like this:

    '/RFC0~~

You would enter this macro into the worksheet in exactly the same way that you would any other label: by typing a label prefix, followed by the characters in the label. The label prefix informs 1-2-3 that what follows should be treated as a label. If this prefix were not used, 1-2-3 would automatically interpret the next character, /, as a command to be executed immediately instead of stored in the cell. Any of the three 1-2-3 label prefixes (', ", or ^) would work equally well. (We chose ' because we're used to seeing labels aligned at the left edge of the cells.)

All macros that begin with a nontext character (/, +, -, or any number) must be started with a label prefix. Otherwise 1-2-3 will interpret the characters that follow as numbers or commands.

The next four characters represent the command used to create the desired format. If you think about it, /RFC is simply shorthand for /*Range Format Currency*. The "0" informs 1-2-3 that we want no digits to be displayed to the right of the decimal. If you were entering this command from the keyboard, you would type the 0 in response to a prompt. In the macro, the 0 is simply assumed by 1-2-3.

At the end of the macro are two characters called *tildes*. When used in a macro, the tilde represents the ENTER key. In this case, the two tildes signal that the ENTER key should be hit twice. Think about this for a moment. If you were entering this command from the keyboard, you would have to strike ENTER twice: after supplying the 0 for the number of decimals, and again to signal that the format applied to the current cell. If you have your 1-2-3 program handy, try this procedure to see what we mean.

1-2-3 uses symbols like ~ to stand for other keystrokes as well. For example, look at the following macro:

'/RFC0~.{END} {RIGHT}~

This macro is very similar to the one we just looked at, except that the command here causes the cursor to move. This command can be used to format an entire row instead of just one cell.

Once again, notice the ' at the beginning of the macro and the ~ symbol at the end. Notice also the phrase {END} {RIGHT} in the macro. The {END} in this phrase stands for the END key on the keyboard. The {RIGHT} represents the right arrow key. This phrase has the same effect in the macro as these two keys would have if they were typed in sequence from the keyboard. The cursor would move to the next boundary between blank and nonblank cells in the row.

Symbols like these are used to represent all of the special keys on the IBM PC keyboard. In every case, the name of the function key (that is, RIGHT for the right arrow, or CALC for function key F9) is enclosed in braces. For example, {UP} represents the up arrow key, the symbol {END} stands for the END key, and {GRAPH} represents the F10 graph key. If you enclose in braces a phrase that is not a function name, 1-2-3 will return the error message:

Unrecognized key name {...}

Another special key representation is {?}, which is similar to BASIC's INPUT command. When 1-2-3 encounters a {?} in a macro, it pauses and waits for the user to enter some data from the keyboard. Once data is entered, it is stored in the current cell.

Figure 12.1 shows the complete list of special key representations.

Figure 12.1

Function Keys

{EDIT}	Edits contents of current cell (same as F2)
{NAME}	Displays list of range names in the current worksheet (same as F3)
{ABS}	Converts relative reference to absolute (same as F4)
{GOTO}	Jumps cursor to cell coordinates (same as F5)
{WINDOW}	Moves the cursor to the other side of a split screen (same as F6)
{QUERY}	Repeats most recent query operation (same as F7)
{TABLE}	Repeats most recent table operation (same as F8)
{CALC}	Recalculates worksheet (same as F9)
{GRAPH}	Redraws current graph (sames as F10)

Cursor-Movement Keys

{UP}	Moves cursor up one row
{DOWN}	Moves cursor down one row
{LEFT}	Moves cursor left one column
{RIGHT}	Moves cursor right one column

Figure 12.1 *(cont'd.)*

{PGUP}	Moves cursor up 20 rows
{PGDN}	Moves cursor down 20 rows
{HOME}	Moves cursor to cell A1
{END}	Used with {UP}, {DOWN}, {LEFT}, or {RIGHT} to move cursor to next boundary between blank and non-blank cells in the indicated direction. Used with {HOME} to move cursor to lower right corner of the defined worksheet.

Editing Keys

{DEL}	Used with {EDIT} to delete a single character from a cell definition
{ESC}	ESC key
{BS}	BACKSPACE key

Special Keys

{?}	Causes macro to pause and wait for input from keyboard. Macro resumes execution after the user strikes ENTER.
~	Enter

Macro Commands

1-2-3 has a set of special macro commands. They are also called *invisible* commands because they cannot be issued from the keyboard, but only from within a macro. 1-2-3's macro command set is similar to the commands offered by most higher level programming languages, such as BASIC.

The /XI, /XQ, and XG Commands

The */XI* command is the equivalent of the BASIC language's IF-THEN-ELSE command. It allows you to build conditional tests in the middle of a macro. This very powerful tool can be used in a variety of interesting ways. The Accumulator macro below shows one example of the */XI* function. The */XQ* command tells the macro to quit execution. This macro is frequently used with /XI. For example, these two commands can be linked together to form a statement like:

'/XISales>1000000~/XQ~

This macro command says, If the contents of the cell named Sales are greater than one million, stop executing this macro. If this command were buried in a macro, it would perform this test and either continue or stop the execution of the macro.

The /XGLocation command is similar to BASIC's GOTO command. It instructs the macro to continue executing, beginning with a particular cell location. Location is usually a range name. This command is used with an /XI conditional test.

/XCrange and /XR

The /XCrange and /XR commands are similar to BASIC's GOSUB and RETURN functions. /XC causes the macro to access a macro subroutine in a separate location. When that subroutine is finished, the /XR command causes processing to resume on the next line of the original macro. The /XC command is similar to the /XG command, but offers a way to return the macro to the point of departure. /XG, however, does not—it is a one-way ticket to a different part of the sheet.

/XNmessage~range~
and /XLmessage~range~

/XNmessage~range~ and /XLmessage~range~ are input commands like {?}. They differ in that they allow a message to be displayed in the program's control panel before input is made. The message can contain up to 39 characters.

The /XN command accepts only numeric entries. Remember that numeric entries include @ functions and formulas as well as pure numbers. /XL accepts only labels, but will accept a number if it is entered in the indicated cell as a number label.

Both commands store input in the cell specified by the *range*. The range can be a cell reference or a range name. If you do not specify a range, the input will be stored in the cell where the cursor is currently located.

/XM

The last macro command, /XM, is the most exciting of all. It allows the programmer to create menus that appear while a macro is executing. These menus look like the standard 1-2-3 menus and allow the user to make choices during the execution of a macro. They can also be used during processing to give messages and warnings to the user.

The /XM command is probably the most useful, and least under-stood, macro command. But /XM is really very simple. It is just a tool that can be used to create custom menus to handle a variety of tasks.

All 1-2-3 menus are accessed by the /XMLocations command. The *location* in the /XM command points to a *menu range*, which can be up to eight columns wide and two rows deep. The entries in the first row of the menu range are called *menu options*. When the menu is executed, these entries are displayed as menu options in the control panel. The second row of the menu range may contain explanatory messages to clarify each menu option.

Below each option in the menu range is one or more lines of macro code. This code will run if, and only if, the option above it is selected.

One of the simplest uses for a menu is to allow the user to answer a yes/no question from within a macro. For example, the following macro (called the "Quit" macro, or \Q) asks you if you are sure that you want to exit from 1-2-3.

Before we look at this menu macro in detail, let's "explode" the illustration so that all of the component parts are clear. Look at figure 12.3.

The first line of the menu macro, /XMB2~, tells the macro to look for a menu range at cell B2. The actual menu is found in cells B2 to C3. This menu presents two choices: Yes and No. These two choices are found in row 2. Notice that the first choice is in column B, and the second choice is in column C. All /XM menus work this way: each choice in the menu is presented in a different worksheet column.

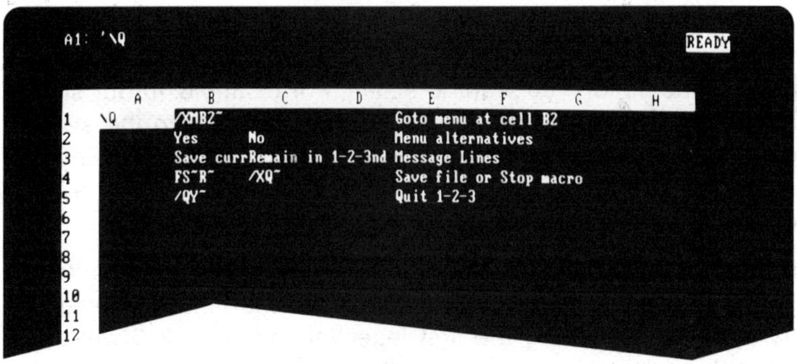

Figure 12.2

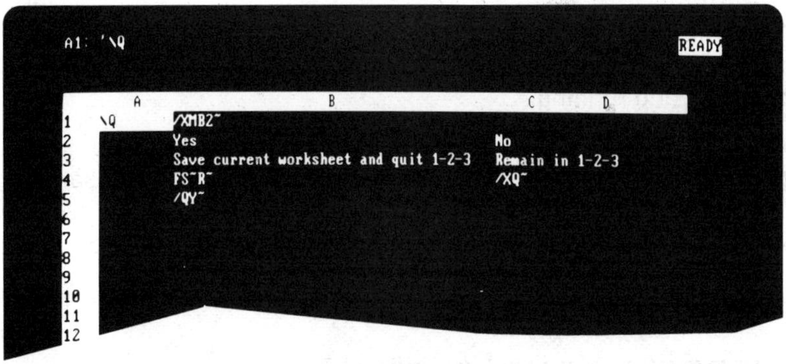

Figure 12.3

The labels in row 3 are explanatory messages that accompany each menu option. In the first illustration above, these messages seem to run together. This occurs because the first message is too long to be completely displayed in cell B3. When the columns are widened, it is clear that the full message is there. These messages help to clarify the menu options. In our example, the option "Yes" is accompanied by the message, "Save the current worksheet and quit 1-2-3." The option "No" has the message, "Remain in 1-2-3."

As with 1-2-3's standard menus, you can select an option from a macro menu in one of two ways. First, you can use the cursor to point to the option you want to select. For example, in our simple illustration, typing → would move the menu cursor to the second option, "No." The second way to select an option is to type the first character in the option's name. For example, to select the "No" option in our example, we could type N.

Be careful to choose option names that begin with different letters. If you have two or more options in a menu with the same first letter and try to select one using the first-letter technique, 1-2-3 will automatically select the first option it comes to with the letter you specified.

Suppose that we select the "Yes" option. The macro will continue to process at cell B4. The statement in this cell instructs 1-2-3 to save the current file and quit from 1-2-3. (It assumes that the file has already been saved once and, therefore, has a file name.)

If we select the "No" option, the macro will continue processing at cell C4. This cell contains a simple /XQ function that causes the macro to stop running

If you create a menu that is too long to fit in the control panel, 1-2-3 will return the error message "Illegal menu." The same message is returned if the menu has more than eight options. Similarly, the secondary messages associated with each menu option can contain 80 characters because the width of the IBM PC display is only 80 characters.

Planning Your Macro

As discussed earlier, a keyboard macro is essentially a substitute for keyboard commands. This is particularly true for the simpler macros that do not involve extensive use of /X commands, but it also applies to more complex macros.

Because a macro is a substitute for keystrokes, the best way to plan a macro is to step through the series of instructions you intend to include in the macro from the keyboard, one keystroke at a time. Do this before you start creating the macro. Take notes about each step as you go, then translate the keystrokes that you've written down into a macro that conforms to the syntax rules.

Where to Put the Macro

In most cases, you will want to place your macros outside the area that will be occupied by your main model. This will help to keep you from accidentally overwriting a macro as you create your model.

Remember that placing your macros outside the basic rectangle which contains you model can consume large amounts of memory. If you are working with a large model and a relatively small amount of memory, you should be careful about this problem. In addition, placing macros outside the normal rectangle will cause the END HOME function to place the cursor at the right corner of the overall spreadsheet, including the macro area, instead of at the lower right corner of the model. This makes the END HOME key useless.

We frequently put macros in column AA in our models. We selected this column for several reasons. First, our models rarely require more than 26 columns, so we don't have to worry about overwriting the macros area with the model. Second, column AA is not so far from the origin that it causes too much memory to be lost.

There is no rule that says you must place your macros in the same column in every model. In models that you'll use more than once, you'll want to place the macros wherever it is most convenient. In small models, there is no need to waste several columns by placing the macros way out in column AA. You may want to put your macros in column I, which lies just off the home screen when all of the columns have a width of 9.

We typically apply the range name MACROS to the area of our sheet that contains the macros. This allows us to get at the macros quickly with the GOTO command and the range name MACROS.

Documenting Your Macros

Professional programers usually write programs that are *self-documented,* or *internally documented.* This means that the program contains comments that help to explain each step in it. In BASIC, these comments are in REM (for REMark) statements. For example, in the following program, the REM statements explain the action taken by the other statements.

```
10  REM This program adds two numbers
20  REM Enter first number
30  INPUT A
40  REM Enter second number
50  INPUT B
60  REM Add numbers together
70  C=A+B
80  REM Display Result
90  Print C
```

It is also possible to document your 1-2-3 programs. The best way to do this is to place the comments next to the macro steps in the column to the right of the macro. For example, in the simple macro in figure 12.4, the macro name is in column AA, the macro itself is in column AB, and the comments are in column AC.

Including comments in your macro will make them far easier to use. Comments are especially useful when you have created complex macros that are very important to the overall design of the worksheet. Suppose that you have created a complex macro, but have not looked at it for a month. Then, you decide you want to modify the macro. Without built-in comments, you might have a difficult time remembering what each step of the macro does.

Naming Macros

Once the macro has been entered in the worksheet as a label (or a series of labels), the macro must be given a name. Ranges containing macros are assigned names just like every other range.

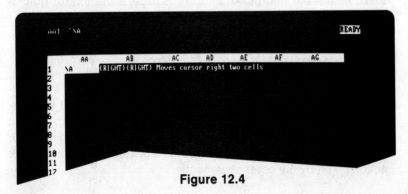

Figure 12.4

The only difference is that the name you assign to a macro must meet certain special conditions: it must be only one character, it must be an alphabetic character (or 0), and it must be preceded by a backslash (\). Table 12.1 shows several legal and illegal macro names.

Table 12.1

Legal Names	Illegal Names
\A	\ABC
\b	ABC
\0	\?
	\1

For example, suppose that you had just built the macro shown in figure 12.5.

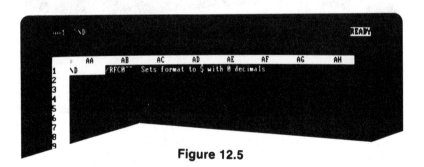

Figure 12.5

Now you need to name this macro. Although you could give the macro any one-letter name, it is always a good idea to choose a name that in some way describes the macro. Obviously, it is difficult to create descriptive one-letter names. In this case, for example, you could choose the name \D (for dollar) or \F (for format). Probably the best name for this macro would be \$—but because the symbol "$" is not a letter, it is not a legal macro name. We would like to see Lotus add some flexibility to macro names.

Suppose that we decided to name the macro \D. To assign the name, we would issue the command / *Range Name Create*. Next, we would enter the name we had selected—\D—and hit the ENTER key. Finally, 1-2-3 would prompt us for the range to name. If the cursor were currently on cell AB1, we could simply type ENTER to assign the name to the cell. Otherwise, we would type the cell coordinates from the keyboard.

Some macros require more than one row in the spreadsheet. For example, look at the simple two-row macro in figure 12.6.

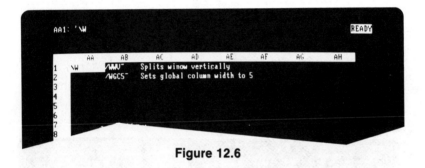

Figure 12.6

To name this macro, we need to assign a name to only the first cell in the range that contains the macro. In this case, we would assign the name \W to cell AB1. There is no reason, however, why a name cannot be assigned to the entire range AB1..AB2 (except that it takes a little more time).

1-2-3's *Range Name* command is remarkably flexible. For example, one cell can be part of several different named ranges.

There is another variation on the *Range Name* command that can be very useful when dealing with macros. The *Right* option of this command allows the user to name a range, using the contents of the cell immediately to its left. For example, suppose that you had created the macro in figure 12.7.

You could name this macro by using the *Range Name Labels Right* command, which would assign the name \A to the range AB1.

The *Range Name Labels* command can be used in a variety of ways. If you are documenting your macros properly, you will already have

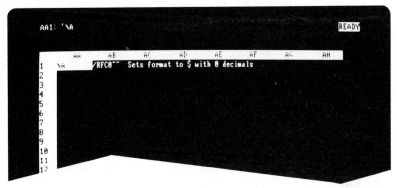

Figure 12.7

the names in the sheet; therefore, using the *Labels* option is a simple and convenient way to name the macros.

If you import macros from an external library file, you can use the *Label* command to create quickly names for the imported macros. In fact, one of the macros in this chapter automatically imports a worksheet file and names all of the macros in the file.

Executing a Macro

All macros are executed, or invoked, by typing ALT, followed by the letter name of the macro. For example, if the macro we wanted to use was named \A, it would be invoked by typing ALT A. It may help you to think of the "\" symbol in the name as a representation of the ALT key.

As soon as the command is issued, the macro starts to run. If there are no bugs or special instructions built into the macro, it will continue to run until it is finished. You will be amazed at its speed. The commands are issued faster than you can see them.

Many macros can be stored in a single cell. Some that are especially long or include special commands must be split into two or more cells, like the example shown above. This is no problem. When 1-2-3 starts executing a macro, the program continues in the first cell until all the keystrokes stored there are used. 1-2-3 then moves down one cell to continue execution. If the cell below is blank, the program stops. If that cell contains more macro commands, however, 1-2-3 will continue reading down the column until it reaches the first blank cell.

Common Errors

Like all computer programs, macros are literal creatures. They have no ability to discern an error in the code. For example, you will recognize immediately that the symbol {GOTI} is a misspelling of the word {GOTO}. But a macro can not do this. It will try to interpret the misspelled word and, being unable to, will deliver an error message.

This means that you must be extremely careful when you build your macros so that they have no errors. Even misplaced spaces and tildes can cause difficulty for 1-2-3. No matter how careful you are, however, some errors are going to slip through.

The biggest problem most beginners have with macros is forgetting to represent all of the required ENTER keystrokes in the macros. This can lead to some interesting results. For example, the missing "~" after the "V" in the macro in figure 12.8 will cause the screen to look like figure 12.9 when the macro is run.

Figure 12.8

Another big problem with 1-2-3 macros is that the cell references included in macros are always absolute. They do not change when, for example, cells are moved about or deleted from the sheet. For example, this simple macro:

'/RE~A6~

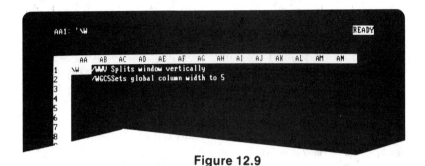

AA1: '\W   READY

    AA   AB   AC   AD   AE   AF   AG   AH   AI   AJ   AK   AL   AM   AN
1 \W   /WWV Splits window vertically
2   /WGC5Sets global column width to 5
3
4
5
6
7
8

Figure 12.9

erases the contents of cell A6. But, suppose we move the contents of cell A6 so that they now lie in cell B6. This would be done with the command / *Move A6 B6*. Because we still want to blank the same contents from the sheet, we might expect our macro to say:

'/RE~B6~

If you try this example, however, you will see that the macro has *not* changed.

If you think about it for a second, this makes perfect sense. A macro is nothing but a label. You wouldn't expect other labels to change when the sheet is changed. For example, if you created the label:

'A15A15A15A15

you wouldn't expect it to change to:

'C15C15C15C15

if you inserted two columns in the sheet to the left of column A. Macros are no different.

The absolute nature of cell references within macros is a strong argument in favor of using range names. Because a range name remains associated with the same range even if the range is moved, range names within macros (and other formulas) will follow the cells to which they apply, eliminating the kind of problem we saw above.

Debugging a Macro

Almost no program works perfectly the first time. In nearly every case, there are errors that will cause the program to malfunction.

Programmers call these problems *bugs* and the process of eliminating them *debugging the program*.

Like programs written in other programming languages, 1-2-3
macros usually need to be debugged before they can be used. In
Version 1 of the program, debugging macros could be very difficult.
Because macros run so rapidly, the user frequently had trouble
identifying the precise step that caused the problem. 1-2-3 didn't
help much—its error messages usually did not apply to the macro,
but rather only to the result of the error.

Version 1A of 1-2-3 has an extremely useful tool that helps makes
debugging much simpler: the STEP function. When 1-2-3 is in the
Step mode, all macros are executed one step at a time. 1-2-3 literally
pauses between each keystroke stored in the macro. This means
that the user can follow along step by step with the macro as it
executes.

Let's step through the buggy macro we developed in the previous
section. The macro in figure 12.8 was supposed to create a second
window on the worksheet and change the width of the columns in
one window to seven characters. If we attempted to run this macro,
we would see the screen in figure 12.9.

Once an error message appears, you must first get out of the macro
and into the Ready mode by typing ESC one or more times. When the
mode indicator says READY, you can start debugging the macro.

If we assume that we don't know what the problem is with the macro,
our next step is to enter the Step mode and rerun the macro. To
invoke the single-step mode, type ALT F1. When you do this, the
mode indicator will change to the message "SST." The macro will
start executing, but will only move forward one step at a time. After
each step, the macro will pause and wait for you to type any
keystroke before going on. Although any key can be used, we prefer
the space bar to step through a macro.

As you step through the macro, you will see each command appear
in the control panel. In our example, the control panel would look
like figure 12.10 just before the error occurs.

Thanks to the single-step mode, when the error occurs, it is easy to
pinpoint the location in the macro. Once the error is identified, you

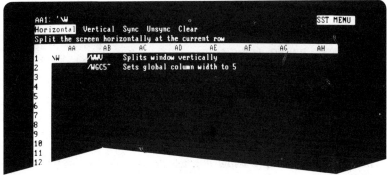

Figure 12.10

can exit the Step mode by typing ALT F1 again. Then, abort the macro by typing ESC.

Editing the Macro

You are now ready to repair the error. Fixing an error in a macro is as simple as editing the cell that contains the erroneous code. You don't need to rewrite the cell. You only need to change the element that is in error.

In our example, we would first move the cursor to cell AB1, then type F2 to enter the Edit mode. Because the error is a missing ~, the fix is easy. Just type ~, followed by ENTER, to exit from the Edit mode.

Although editing complex macros can be tougher than editing a simple one like the one above, the concept is exactly the same. Just use 1-2-3's cell editor (F2) to correct the cell that contains the error.

Sample Macros

Open-Ended Macros

Although most macros are designed to complete the task they begin, it can sometimes be useful to create *open-ended* macros. These begin a command sequence, but do not complete it. The command must be completed from the keyboard.

A Macro to Format a Range

One of the macros that we have already created makes an excellent open-ended macro. The macro:

    '/RFC0~~

can be converted to an open-ended macro by removing the second tilde from the end of the macro:

    '/RFC0~

This macro works precisely like its closed brother, except that it does not complete the formatting command. Instead, it ends, leaving the command open and waiting for a range to be provided. You would enter the range from the keyboard.

This feature can be very useful. For example, in many worksheets you will want some cells formatted as dollars and others as integers. In one case, you may have only one cell to format. In another, you'll want to format a whole row. This macro can be used in either situation. For example, if you want to format only one cell, you can place the cursor on the cell to be formatted and execute the macro. When the macro is finished, you can type ENTER to complete the command. This applies the format to the current cell. On the other hand, if you want to format an entire row, you can use the arrow keys to POINT to the range to be formatted after the macro is completed.

Open-ended macros frequently specify every part of the command except the range to which the command applies. That is provided from the keyboard.

In effect, the open-ended macro allows you to apply a format or a command to any range of the sheet you wish. Many of the /Range commands can be simplified by condensing them into open-ended macros.

A Macro to Erase a Range

For example, the following macro:

    '/RE.

starts the Range Erase command but stops prior to assigning the range for the command. The range is supplied from the keyboard.

This macro becomes a quick way to erase any portion of the worksheet.

Changing Text to Numbers

Occasionally when using 1-2-3, you will create text cells that contain only numbers. One of the most frequent uses of numeric text cells is yearly column headers, like those shown in figure 12.11.

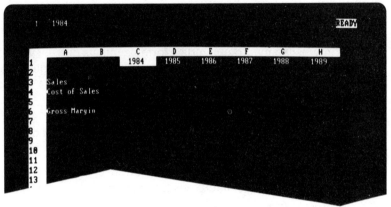

Figure 12.11

In this case, the numbers were entered as text so that they could be centered in the columns. For example, the label in cell C1 was entered as ^1984. But suppose you want to convert these numeric text entries into pure numbers so that they can be referenced by a formula elsewhere in the sheet. How can this be done? With a macro, of course! The following macro converts a numeric text entry into a pure number with one keystroke:

'{EDIT} {HOME} {DEL} ~

This macro is the equivalent of typing F2, HOME, and DEL from the IBM PC keyboard. Let's look at how it works.

The first command, EDIT, puts 1-2-3 into the Edit mode. The second, HOME, moves the edit cursor to the first position of the string being edited. The third command, DEL, deletes the label prefix character from the front of the string. The result is that the label is converted into a number. Table 12.2 illustrates the editing process.

Table 12.2

EDIT	^1983_
HOME	△1983 .
DEL	1983
~	1983

Changing Formulas to Their Current Value

Another interesting macro converts a formula into its current value. To illustrate this example, suppose we had created the following formula:

+A1+A2

Suppose further that the value of cell A1 is 5, and the value of cell A2 is 10, so that the value of the cell containing this formula is 15.

Now suppose that we want to convert this formula (+A1+A2) into the number 15. The following macro will do the trick:

{EDIT} {CALC}~

We call this macro the *formula-to-value macro*. You will see several interesting uses for this simple macro in the next few examples.

The Indent Macro

Here's an easy macro that you will be able to use all the time. If you've been spreadsheeting for any time at all, you've probably had occasions where you've created a row or column of labels, then decided to change the justification of those labels. For example, you may have created a column of row headers in column A that looks something like figure 12.12, and later decided to indent each label one character. Indenting a single label is not difficult. You simply edit the cell, move the cursor to the far left of the cell with the HOME key and one character back to the right with →, then type a space. Finally, you type ENTER to end the edit. Repeating this process 20 times, however, can be tedious. The macro in figure 12.13 will do the same

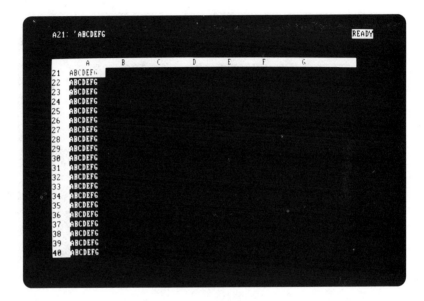

Figure 12.12

job and repeat it until you give a command to stop the macro. Figure 12.14 shows the results of the macro.

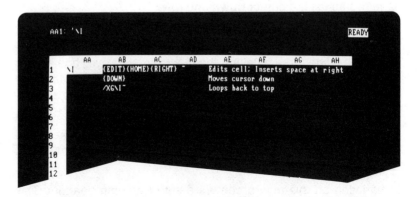

Figure 12.13

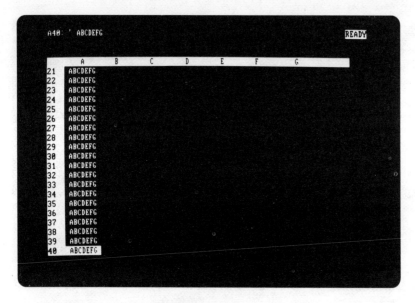

Figure 12.14

To indent all of the labels in column A, you move the cursor to cell A21 and invoke our macro by typing ALT I. The cursor will start skipping down the column, indenting each label one space as it goes. If you look at the first line of our macro carefully, you will see that it simply "macroizes" the edit process discussed in the previous paragraph. Line two jumps the cursor down one row.

The statement in line three tells the macro to continue processing at the cell named \I. If you remember that this macro is named \I, you'll realize that line three is telling the macro to start over again. This kind of device is called a *loop* in programming jargon. This loop will cause the program to continue running until you manually stop it.

Once all of the labels are indented, you stop the macro. The simplest way to do this is to type CTRL BREAK. The CTRL BREAK keys can always be used to stop a macro, but are not a very elegant way of doing it.

A variation on this macro centers a set of column headers. This macro is illustrated in figure 12.15. To understand how it works,

suppose that you built the worksheet shown in figure 12.16. You
now want to center the column headers in row 3. To do this, you
move the cursor to cell D3 and invoke our macro by typing ALT C.
The labels will immediately be centered in each of the columns, as
shown in figure 12.17.

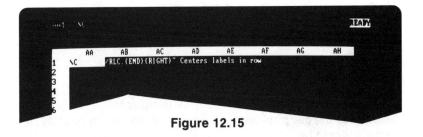

Figure 12.15

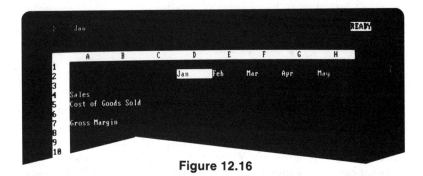

Figure 12.16

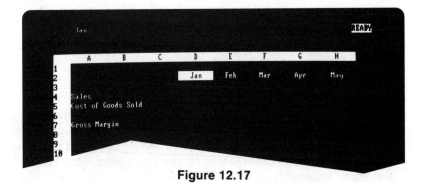

Figure 12.17

This macro points out another valuable use for macros: *editing* the worksheet. At times, we have created complex macros that added and deleted rows or columns throughout the worksheet. Editing macros is most useful when the editing task must be performed repeatedly. In this case, try to create a macro that will perform the job automatically.

A Simple Pointing Macro

One of the most useful types of macros is a pointing macro. For example,

'+{RIGHT} {RIGHT} {RIGHT}+{DOWN} {DOWN}~

inserts a formula in the current cell that is equal to the cell two cells below plus the cell three cells to the right. If we start in cell C17, the formula would be

F17+C19

Notice that this macro includes nothing but mathematical symbols and cursor-key representations.

Entering Text with Macros

Although you will normally enter the Macro utility from the Ready mode of 1-2-3, you can also invoke a macro from the Menu mode, or while you are entering a label or formula into the sheet. This allows you to create macros that enter commonly used phrases into the worksheet. For example, suppose the word "expense" will occur a number of times in a given sheet. The word will sometimes occur by itself and other times will be displayed with other words, as in "sales expense" and "office expense."

You can create a macro that enters the word "expense" in the current cell. The macro would look like this:

' expense

Notice that an extra space appears at the beginning of the macro. This space separates the word expense from any other word in the cell when the macro is invoked. You will also notice that this is an open-ended macro. Other words can be appended in the cell after the word "expense."

Suppose that you are defining cell A55 as containing the label "expense—miscellaneous." First, invoke the macro to enter the label "expense" into the cell. Next, simply complete the phrase from the keyboard. The completed cell will look like this:

'expense—miscellaneous

Type ENTER to close out the cell. To enter the label "Telephone expense (Local)," follow the macro with the word "(Local)" before typing ENTER.

This kind of macro can save time when you set up a large worksheet. You should create several "common word" macros like the one above and use them to enter labels throughout the sheet.

A Macro to Create Headers

The simple macro in figure 12.18 can be used to create a row of column headers in the worksheet. Each cell contains the abbreviation of the name of a month.

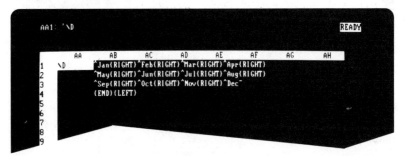

Figure 12.18

Essentially, this macro scrolls across a row, inserting the name of one month in each cell before moving on. Notice the use of the {RIGHT} key to stand for the right arrow key (→).

Dating the Worksheet

Thanks to 1-2-3's built-in date functions, you can date your worksheets with the @TODAY function. The obvious way to date a sheet is to enter the @TODAY function in an appropriate cell. But there is a problem with doing the job that way. When the sheet is reloaded into memory after being saved, the program will automatically recalculate, changing the date before you view it and defeating the purpose of dating the sheet in the first place.

There is a macro solution to this problem. The simple macro in figure 12.19 automatically dates the sheet and insures that the current date remains in the sheet.

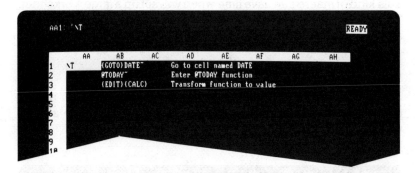

Figure 12.19

This macro assumes that the range name DATE has been assigned to a single cell somewhere in the sheet. The macro goes to the range with the name DATE and inserts the value of @TODAY there. The cell DATE can be formatted in any way you choose for the best display of the date.

The third line is our old friend, the formula-to-value conversion macro. This line converts the contents of the DATE cell from the @TODAY function to the actual numeric value of the @TODAY function. This conversion keeps the date from being updated automatically the next time the sheet is loaded.

The one problem with this macro is that it doesn't automatically return you to the point from which you started. Instead, the macro leaves the cursor on the DATE cell. This can be remedied, however, with the use of /RNCHERE in a help macro. (See figure 12.38 and the accompanying discussion below.)

There is, however, an even simpler way to enter the date in a cell, suggested by Bill Liles at Lotus Development Corporation. The macro is illustrated in figure 12.20.

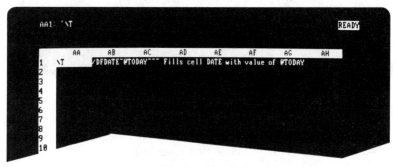

Figure 12.20

This macro uses the power of the *Data Fill* command to enter the *value* of the @TODAY function in the cell named DATE. Notice that the *Data Fill* command enters into the cell the value of the function, and not the function itself, bypassing the need for our {EDIT} {CALC} macro. The *Data Fill* command uses the value of the @TODAY function as the start value. The last two tildes after the @TODAY function select the defaults for the other *Data Fill* options, Step and Stop.

Another way to perform this task is illustrated by the macro in figure 12.21, which does essentially the same thing as the *Data Fill* command, except that the @TODAY function must be entered manually in response to the prompt "Enter today's date." The */ XN* command inserts the value of the function, and not the function itself, in the indicated cell.

Both of these macros have the advantage of not moving the cursor. Thus they can be used at any time to date the sheet without repositioning the cursor.

A Macro to Name Macros

Although using the */ Range Name Label* command is a convenient way to name macros, we can speed up the process by creating a

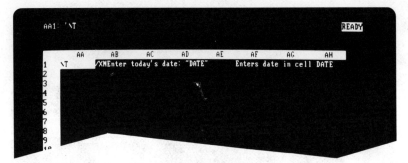

Figure 12.21

macro that automatically names another. This macro condenses the
*R*ange *N*ame command into a single keystroke:

'/RNLR~

Before you execute this macro, you must move the cursor to the cell
that contains the *name* of the macro you want to name. For example,
in the worksheet in figure 12.22, you would move the cursor to cell
AA1 before issuing the command. After the macro is complete, the
name "\W" would be assigned to cell AB1.

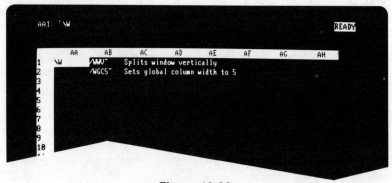

Figure 12.22

Creating a standard macro area in you worksheet will make the
naming macro even simpler to use. For example, suppose you

decide that you will always store your macros in column AB. This means that the name for the macros will lie in column AA. You could then modify our range-naming macro to look like figure 12.23.

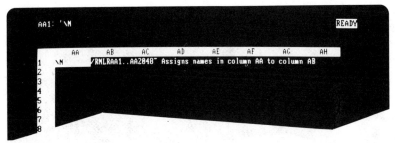

Figure 12.23

This macro names every cell in column AB with the cell references found in column AA. If you use this macro, however, make sure that there is no "garbage" in column AA, but only true macro names. Otherwise, the wrong names will be assigned to the macros in column AB.

Creating a Macro Library

Once you have become comfortable with macros and have developed a few that you find yourself using repeatedly, you will want to develop what we call a *macro library.* A macro library is a worksheet that contains several macros. It typically also includes the name labels associated with each macro and any internal documentation you have written.

If you decide to create a macro library, you will need the simple macro below. This macro loads into memory a set of macros that you have on disk and names each macro in the set. For example, suppose that you have a macro library which contains the following macros:

\A/RFC0~~

\B/RE.

and that this library is stored on disk in a worksheet file called LIBRARY.WKS. Now suppose that you are creating a new model and and want to include the library in the model. The macro in figure 12.24 will do the trick.

Figure 12.24

This macro performs two operations. First, it moves the cursor to cell AA1, then it loads the file LIBRARY.WKS. The macros will be loaded into cells AA1 and AA3.

We can now combine this macro with the one in figure 12.23 to create the macro shown in figure 12.25.

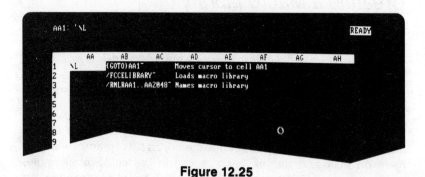

Figure 12.25

This macro will load and name the macro library. (Although columns AA and AB are used here, you can use any range you want to store your macros.)

Using the Numeric Keypad

Many 1-2-3 users (and those of other IBM PC-based programs) lament the use of the numeric keypad for both entering numeric data and moving the cursor. Because the keypad serves double duty, it really cannot be used to enter a series of numeric data. This is especially irritating to those trained in the use of a 10-key adding machine. For example, suppose you want to enter the following data into the worksheet:

123
234
345

Simple enough, right? But, to use the numeric keypad to enter the numbers into the sheet, you would have to go through the following process:

{GOTO}B1	Position cursor on cell B1
{NUM}	Convert keypad to numeric entry
123	Enter first number
{NUM}	Convert keypad to cursor movement
{DOWN}	Move down one cell
{NUM}	Convert keypad to numeric entry
234	Enter second number
{NUM}	Convert keypad to cursor movement
{DOWN}	Move down one cell
{NUM}	Convert keypad to numeric entry
345	Enter last number
{NUM}	Convert keypad to cursor movement

Obviously, the time spent toggling back and forth between cursor movement and numeric entry would eliminate any benefit that could be gained by using the keypad to enter numbers.

However, you can build a macro that will automatically move the cursor each time you strike the ENTER key. The macro illustrated in figure 12.26 will let you use the keypad to enter numbers while you move down a column or across a row.

This macro illustrates several interesting techniques. First, it prompts the user to enter some information (in this case, the number 123) in the current cell. Notice that while 1-2-3 waits for you to type

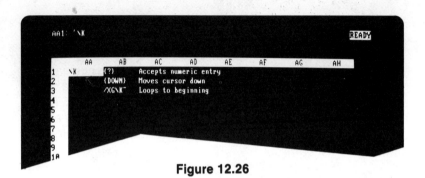

Figure 12.26

in information, the mode indicator in the upper-right corner of the
screen reads "CMD READY." This prompt reminds you that a macro
is underway and that 1-2-3 expects you to do something.

After data is entered, the macro automatically jumps down one cell.
The next line of the macro shows the /XG (or GOTO) command at
work. This line tells the macro to go to the cell named \K and
continue processing there. Because the macro itself is named \K,
the GOTO command forces the macro to repeat itself.

When the macro starts repeating, it prompts for a second number, in
this case 234. It then skips down one cell and repeats the process. It
will continue to repeat until you type CTRL BREAK to halt execution.
CTRL BREAK can always be used to stop the execution of a macro.
Notice that after you type CTRL BREAK, the mode indicator returns
to its normal READY status.

Be sure that you understand the difference between 1-2-3's GOTO
command and the /XG macro command. The GOTO command is
used to move the cursor to any location on the worksheet. The /XG
command, on the other hand, simply directs the flow of a macro.

Enhancements on the Basic Macro

We can enhance this basic macro in many interesting ways. First,
we could change the middle line so that the cursor moves up, or to
the left or right after each entry. You will probably find that two of
these (the DOWN variation we've demonstrated and the one that
moves RIGHT after each input) will be sufficient for your needs.

The basic macro we've designed is very practical, but somewhat inelegant. For example, while it is waiting for a number, the macro does not provide a prompt to the user about what is expected. This can be changed by substituting a */XN* command for the simple {?} function. The macro would look like figure 12.27.

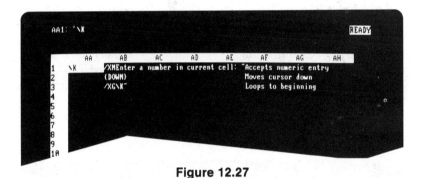

Figure 12.27

When this macro runs, it begins by prompting the user for data, as shown in figure 12.28.

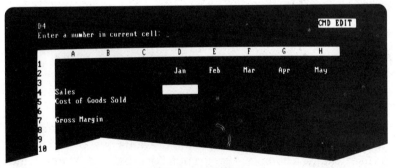

Figure 12.28

After the number is entered, it will appear in the current cell (in this case, A1). As in the simpler example, the cursor then jumps down one cell, and the macro repeats. This version of the macro is attractive because it offers a higher level of interactivity than that provided by the previous version.

Note the double tilde (~~) in the /XN statement in this example. Usually a cell reference appears in place of the first tilde. The cell reference instructs 1-2-3 to enter the number into the cell reference provided. The lack of a cell reference here instructs 1-2-3 to deposit the number in the current cell (the cell where the cursor lies).

Adding a "Menu"

We can soup up this macro even more by adding a *menu,* so called because it is created with the /XM command. It is really just a simple prompt. By adding the menu, we can move the cursor one cell in any direction after we enter the number. The macro now looks like figure 12.29.

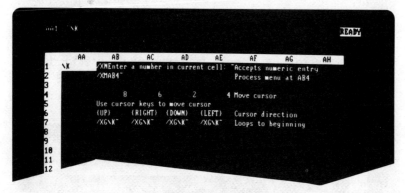

Figure 12.29

Because this is a fairly complex macro, let's go through it one step at a time. The macro begins, just like the previous one, by prompting the user to enter a number. After the number is entered, however, the macro gives control over 1-2-3 to a menu, which begins in cell AB4. The statement /XMAB4~ translates as: Begin processing the menu located at cell AB4.

Notice that the menu located in cells AB4 through AE7 is generally similar to the sample menu we illustrated earlier. The main difference is that the menu includes just one cell of explanatory text below the basic menu line. We could have included more lines, but they were not needed in this example.

When 1-2-3 begins processing the menu, the screen looks like figure 12.30.

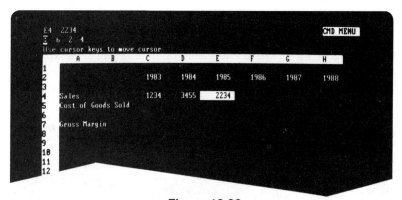

Figure 12.30

You may be puzzled by the choices offered by this menu. At first, it doesn't seem to make sense. Notice, however, that the numbers 8, 6, 2, and 4 correspond to the UP, RIGHT, DOWN, and LEFT arrow keys. This should tip you off. The menu allows 1-2-3 to convert the numbers 8, 6, 2, and 4 into their cursor-movement equivalents.

If you built this macro and are working along, you have probably noticed several of its limitations. For one thing, you can only move one cell at a time across the worksheet. For another, you must enter some number, even if it is just 0, in each cell you pass through. Another limitation is that you must type ENTER and enter a direction between entering numbers. It would be nice if you could go directly to the next cell without having to type ENTER.

You should also notice that this macro menu does not work like most macro menus. In most menus, you make your selection by using the left and right arrow keys to point to options in the menu. You can also type the first character of the option you want.

Our example, however, assumes the the keypad is being used for numeric entry and that the cursor keys are disabled. They, therefore, cannot be used to move the menu cursor. You can make selections in this menu only by typing the first (and only) character of an option. As it turns out, this is exactly what you want to do, because typing the first character simulates typing the arrow key to move the worksheet cursor.

The Accumulator Macro

Many VisiCalc users are familiar with the difficulty of creating year-to-date totals in a VisiCalc sheet. The same problem exists in 1-2-3. For example, suppose you created the sheet shown in figure 12.31.

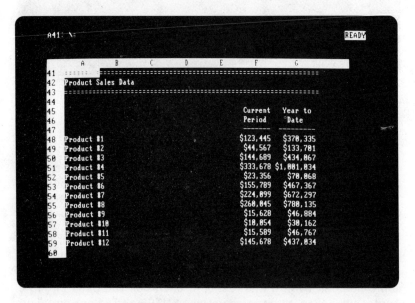

Figure 12.31

Now suppose that you want to accumulate the current period amounts into the year-to-date total. This can be done by defining each cell in column G with a formula like:

G48 = G48+F48

This circular reference adds the amount in cell F48 (the current) period number) to the amount in cell G48 (the year-to-date amount) each time the model is recalculated. For example, if we recalculate the model above, the result would be as shown in figure 12.32, which is exactly what we want. But what would happen if we accidentally typed CALC again? The sheet would look like figure 12.33, which is definitely not what we want—we've erroneously double counted the numbers in the current column. You run this risk anytime you create this type of circular reference. We can, however, create a macro that accomplishes the job of accumulating year-to-date totals.

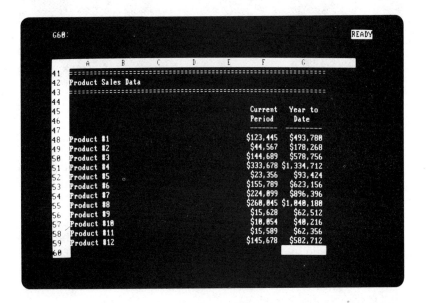

Figure 12.32

In our original example, what would happen if there were no formulas in the cells in column G, just numbers? This would eliminate the risk of accidental double counting. But we also want to add the data in the two columns, which requires some sort of formula.

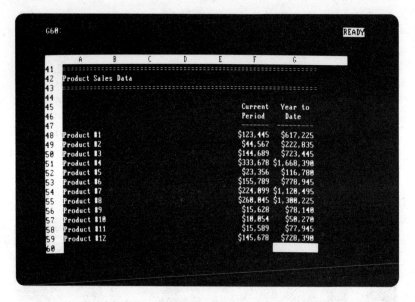

Figure 12.33

Thanks to Steve Miller of Lotus Development Corporation, the simple macro illustrated in figure 12.34 solves this problem perfectly.

Let's go through the macro one step at a time. To use this macro, place the cursor on the cell at the top of the column in which you want to accumulate the total—in this case, column G. Then the macro is executed. The first expression *edits* cell G48, then moves the cursor to cell F48 (one cell to the left) and adds the number in that cell to the number in cell G48.

Notice that the cursor was moved down one cell, left one cell, and finally up one cell ({DOWN} {LEFT} {UP}), to reach cell F48. Why was this necessary? Once you enter the Edit mode, the left and right arrow keys do not move the cursor from cell to cell, but cause the edit cursor to move along the edit line. When you are in the Edit mode and want to point to a cell, you must always move the cursor *up* or *down* with the arrow keys before you can move it left or right. Try the procedure to see what we mean.

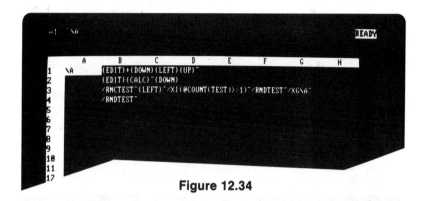

Figure 12.34

You will recognize the next step as our simple formula-to-number conversion macro. This formula converts the results from a simple addition of two numbers to an even simpler single number.

The third line moves the cursor down one row; then the magic begins. The fourth line can be translated as: Create a range name called TEST. Assign that name to the range that includes the current cell and the cell immediately to the left of the current cell; then determine the value for the @COUNT function for that two-cell range. The statement beginning with /XI... contains a logical test. The function can be translated as: If the value of the @COUNT function is greater than or equal to one, then delete the name TEST, go to the cell named \A, and continue processing. (This is a simple loop.) If the value of @COUNT for the range TEST does not meet the condition, then delete the name TEST and stop processing.

You may be thinking "Whoa!" Having gone through this macro once, let's go back through it again in a little more detail to explain why we did some of the things we did. For example, notice that the TEST range was defined as *two* cells wide. We did this to get around a strange characteristic of the @COUNT function.

This macro checks each cell in column F to see if the cell is empty. If it is, then the macro assumes that the end of the column of numbers has been reached. If the cell is not empty, the macro continues until it reaches the bottom of the column. Why don't we test the value of @COUNT for each cell in column F? You may remember from Chapter 6 that the @COUNT of a single cell is *always* one, whether or not it contains data. But the count of a two-cell range is always one if one of the cells is empty, and always zero if both cells are empty. The @COUNT function in this macro uses a two-cell range to get an accurate reading on the status of the cells in column F.

This macro can be started another way. The method used assumes that the formula-to-value macro is already in the worksheet, allowing you to include the formula in the larger macro without having to put it in two places in the same worksheet.

Figure 12.35

In the version of the macro shown in figure 12.35, the {EDIT} {CALC} statement in the first example is replaced by an /XC command. This command, called a *subroutine* or *function call,* lets the macro skip to another location to continue processing. Notice the /XR statement in row 8 above. This is the return function that sends the macro back to the point just beyond the /XC command to continue processing.

Subroutines are commonly used in programming to simplify large, complex programs. Many large programs use certain routines repeatedly in different parts of the program. In addition, many common routines are used by most programs. These routines can be broken out into subroutines, which are miniature programs in their own right. They can be accessed by subroutine calls in the larger program. The /XC and /XR commands allow 1-2-3 users to take advantage of this style of programming.

Unfortunately, Lotus decided that whenever 1-2-3 comes upon an */XR* function that is not preceded by an */XC*, an error message will be given. This prevents you from appending the */XR* function to the end of a simple macro to create a library of subroutines for your larger macros. The simple macros will work despite the error messages, but the errors are very irritating.

Putting Instructions in Your Worksheets

Like 1-2-3, many of the new and exciting commercial programs come with on-line help. Thanks to 1-2-3's macro capabilities, you can add help screens to your 1-2-3 worksheets.

The macro that allows you to create on-line help screens is fairly simple. It relies on 1-2-3's *Range Name* and GOTO commands. Before the macro is built, you must create a *help screen* in your worksheet. You can do this by entering the message, or messages, you want to convey to your users in a series of cells anywhere in the sheet. The help screen in this example is confined to one window of data.

After the help screen is created, you must give the upper-left corner of the range a name. We suggest "Help," because it is simple and to the point. Figure 12.36 shows a sample help screen. Notice that we've placed the screen at cell A100 in the worksheet. Although this is a convenient place for the help screen, you can put it anywhere you want on the worksheet. Remember, cell A100 in our example is named "Help." The macro in figure 12.37 takes us to the help screen.

The first statement creates a range name, HERE, and assigns it to the current cell. The second line of the macro moves the cursor to the range named HELP—in this case, to cell A100. The {?} in the third line causes the macro to pause and wait for input from the keyboard.

At this point, the help screen would be visible on the computer display. You can take your time reading the messages on the screen, then press ENTER when you are finished. When any key is struck, the {?} command will be satisfied, and the macro will resume processing.

This macro not only brings us help, but also automatically returns us to where we were. The statement in the fourth line of the macro,

Figure 12.36

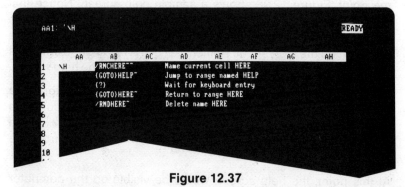

Figure 12.37

{GOTO} HERE, returns the cursor to the cell that was named HERE a moment before. In other words, the macro automatically returns us to the point where we started.

The final step in this macro erases the name HERE from 1-2-3's memory. This housekeeping step is taken so that there will be no conflict between the old HERE area and the new HERE area when the macro is used again.

Deleting the range name HERE is very important. Whenever you create a range name in the 1-2-3 worksheet, 1-2-3 will automatically insert the range name in place of the cell reference that defines the same cell in any formulas that refer to the cell. In other words, if you named cell A15 HERE, the formula:

   +A15+A16

would change to:

   HERE+A16

Now, suppose that you go ahead with your work and do not delete the range name and that, at some later time, you decide to use the help macro again. In the course of accessing the help screens, the macro names the current cell HERE. This new cell—which could be anywhere in the sheet—will now be used instead of A15 in our formula. This could mess up a carefully planned worksheet.

Although this macro is very useful, you could use menus to create even more sophisticated help. For example, suppose that you had more help messages than could be squeezed on one screen. You would need a macro that allows you to view more than one screen before returning to the origin.

By slightly modifying our original macro, you could accomplish this change. The new macro is shown in figure 12.38.

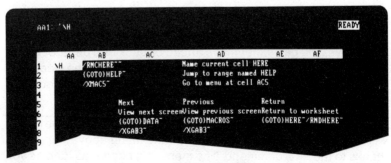

Figure 12.38

Notice that this macro includes a fairly complex menu that can be used to select one of three options: View Next Page, View Previous Page, or Return to Worksheet. (The complete messages are not visible in the example because they overlap the boundaries of the cells.) The first two steps of the macro work precisely as before. Once the help is in view, however, the macro changes significantly. Assuming that the HELP area is located at cell A100, when the first help screen is displayed, the control panel of the worksheet will look like figure 12.39.

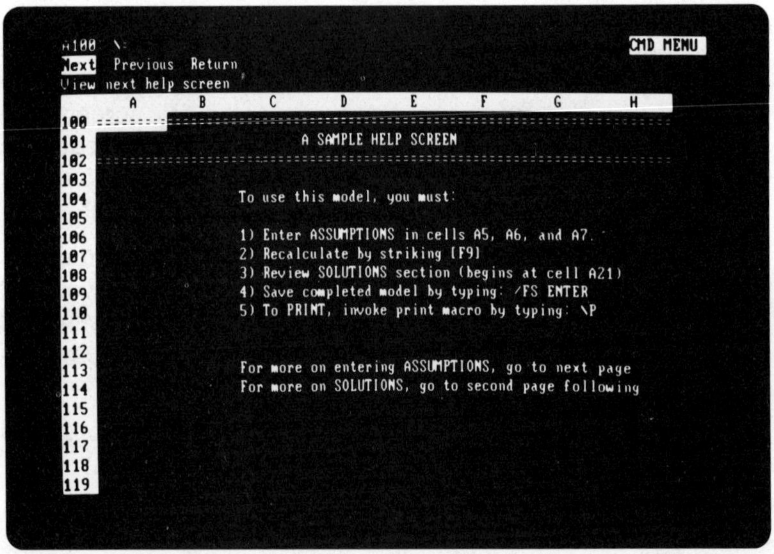

Figure 12.39

By pointing with the cursor, or by typing the first letter of the desired alternative, you can either move ahead or back one page, or return to the main worksheet. If you return to the worksheet, the macro will be completed the same way as in the simpler example—by returning to the range named HERE, then deleting that range name.

If, however, you choose to go forward or back one screen, the cursor will move in the desired direction, and the menu above will repeat, thanks to the /XG command. The menu will appear as long as you choose the Next or Previous options.

This macro could be revised even more to accommodate a more complex set of help screens. For example, suppose that you have four help screens in your current model, covering the topics DATA ENTRY, MACROS, PRINTING, and SAVING. You could create the macro illustrated in figure 12.40 that would allow the user to select directly any of the four options.

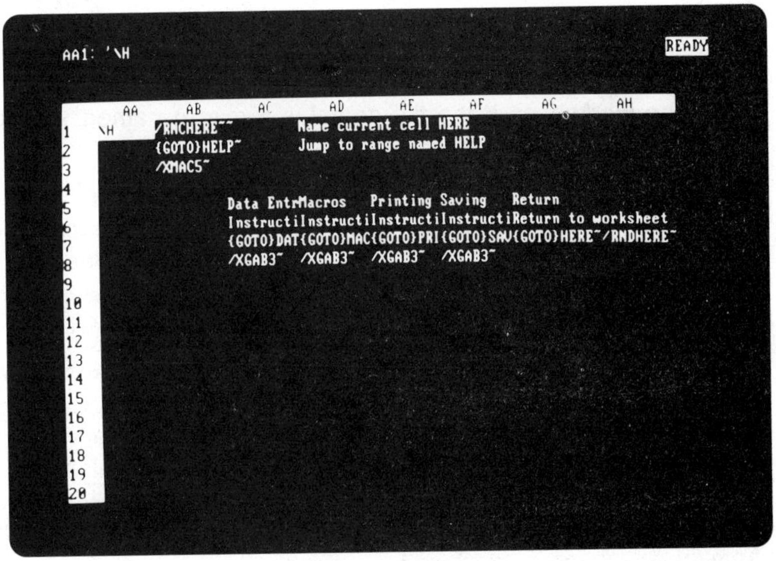

Figure 12.40

This macro is essentially the same as the macro in the previous example, except that this one gives the user the choice of one of four specific areas of help, instead of just offering the "Page back" and "Page forward" options. This kind of indexed help comes close to that offered by the 1-2-3 program itself.

Wouldn't it be nice if we could name these help macros "\?" Using the "?" would closely parallel many other programs that use this symbol to call for help, but as we have seen, 1-2-3 allows only letter names for macros.

Automatic Macros

The latest version of 1-2-3 (Version 1A) offers a new and exciting macro feature called *automatic macro execution.* This technique allows the user to create a special macro that will automatically execute when the sheet is loaded. This macro is created just like any other macro. The only difference is in its name. The macro that you want to execute automatically must have the name "\0."

An even more powerful feature of Version 1A of 1-2-3 is its ability to load a model automatically into the 1-2-3 worksheet. In this version of the program, when 1-2-3 loads, it automatically searches the current disk drive for a special worksheet file named AUTO123.WKS. If this file is on the disk, 1-2-3 will automatically load it into the worksheet. If the file contains a macro named \0, the macro will automatically execute.

You can use these features of 1-2-3 to create completely self-contained programs in the 1-2-3 worksheet. An ALT command is not required to start the macro in this case. When combined with menus and the other useful /X commands, the automatic execution feature makes macros a remarkably user-friendly tool.

One thing to note about the automatic macro—it cannot be executed by typing "ALT 0" from the keyboard. If you need to be able to execute the macro from the keyboard, however, there is no reason why the macro you've named "\0" could not also have another name, such as "\A." One macro then becomes, in effect, two: one that executes automatically, and one that can be executed from the keyboard.

There can be only one automatic macro in each worksheet. However, this macro can be as large as you want and can include as many steps as you wish. It can also include /XC (function call) commands that access other macros in the sheet.

Printing with a Macro

Macros can be used to automate complex tasks that are repeated frequently. Printing a large worksheet is such a task. There are several steps involved in readying the worksheet for printing: specifying the print range; aligning the paper in the printer; and specifying such options as borders, headers, footers, and margins. Although the design of a printing macro will vary from application to application, the sample model in figure 12.41 demonstrates many of the ways a macro can help with this task.

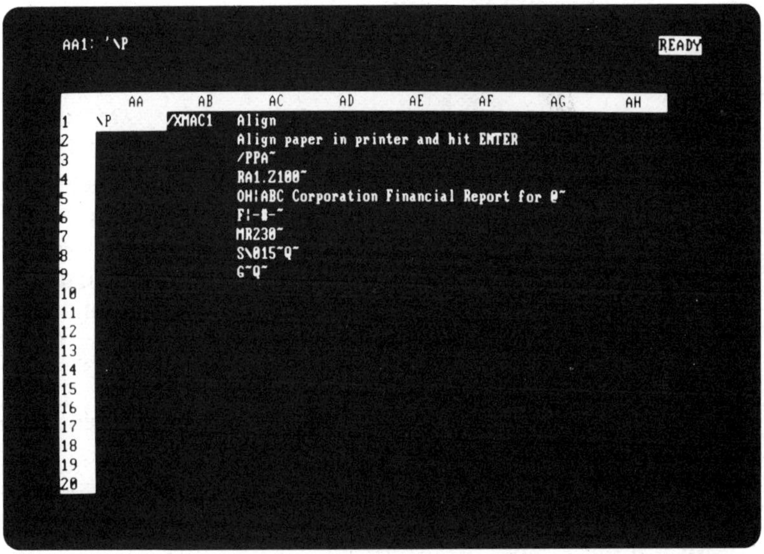

Figure 12.41

This macro looks complex, but it is really very simple. The first line sends control of the macro to a menu that directs the user to align the paper in the printer and type ENTER. The next line invokes the 1-2-3 / Print Printer Align command, which informs 1-2-3 about the location of the top of form. The fourth line supplies the range for the print job. This range must be predetermined and entered in the macro. There is no way to leave this part of the macro open if you want it to continue processing.

The next lines assign values to the 1-2-3 print options. Line five inserts a centered title (including the current date) in the report. Line six adds a footer that supplies the page number. The next command sets the right margin to 230, and the following line instructs the printer (in this case an Epson FX-100) to print in a compressed mode. The "Q~" command makes the macro step up one level in the print menu so that the "G~" (Go) command in the next line can be issued. The final "Q~" returns 1-2-3 to the Ready mode after the report is printed.

Note that this macro cannot be used for every model, but you can create a macro like it to print your frequently used reports.

Creating Graphs

In much the same way, you can use macros to issue quickly the commands required to produce common graphs. For example, 1-2-3 can be used to perform monthly financial analysis. This job includes producing a few graphs. We have created a simple macro that calls the graph by name for plotting. The comprehensive example in the following chapter shows a macro that creates a graph from financial data.

In Chapter 13, you will also find a complex macro that copies data from one part of the worksheet into a data base.

13

A Comprehensive Model

The comprehensive model in this chapter integrates all the main elements of 1-2-3—spreadsheet, data base, macros, and graphics—in one worksheet. It demonstrates how all the main elements discussed earlier work together to create a unified whole.

The model is designed for a corporate controller, Mr. Dudley Eyeshade, who finds that he must frequently answer questions from the president and sole proprietor, Mr. John Paul Gherkins, about trends in the financial status of Mr. Gherkins' pickle business—Gherkins, Inc. For example, Mr. Gherkins may ask him to prepare reports that show the fluctuation in net income from one month to the next over the course of the year. He may also ask Mr. Eyeshade about fluctuations in such items as current assets, working capital, gross sales, etc. Along with these items, Mr. Eyeshade finds that he must report from time to time on the status of several key financial ratios and how they relate to prior status from months and years past.

A General Description of the Model

This model is called the "Financial Ratio Model," but this title does not tell the whole story. The model does much more than just compute financial ratios.

	A	B	C	D	E	F	G	H
1	===
2	Balance Sheet
3	===
4								Common
5	Assets						31-Jul-83	Size
6	
7	Cash						$275,000	8%
8	Marketable Securities						35,000	1%
9	Accounts Receivable			1,256,000				
10	Allowance for Doubtful Accounts			8,000				
11	Net Accounts Receivable						1,248,000	39%
12	Inventory						359,000	11%
13	Prepaid Expenses						70,000	2%
14	Other						23,000	1%
15							-----------	
16	Total Current Assets						2,010,000	62%
17	
18	Property, Plant, and Equipment			956,700				
19	Accumulated Depreciation			123,700				
20	Net Property, Plant, and Equipment						833,000	26%
21	Investment-Long-term						396,000	12%
22							-----------	
23	Total Noncurrent Assets						1,229,000	38%
24							-----------	
25	Total Assets						$3,239,000	100%
26							==========	
27	
28	Liabilities
29	
30	Notes Payable						$276,000	9%
31	Accounts Payable						378,000	12%
32	Accrued Expenses						98,000	3%
33	Other Liabilities						25,000	1%
34							-----------	
35	Total Current Liabilities						777,000	24%
36	
37	Long-Term Debt						333,000	10%
38	
39	Stockholder's Equity
40	
41	Common Stock, $1.00 par value						440,000	14%
42	Paid-in Capital						361,000	11%
43	Retained Earnings						1,328,000	41%
44							-----------	
45	Total Stockholder's Equity						2,129,000	66%
46							-----------	
47	Total Liabilities and Net Worth						$3,239,000	100%
48							==========	

Figure 13.1A

	A	B	C	D	E	F	G	H	I
50	===
51	Income Statement
52	===

		31-Jul-83	Y-T-D	Common Size
56	Gross Sales	$732,730	$5,656,407	100%
57	Less: Returns and Allowances	4,167	70,833	1%
58		-------------------
59	Net Sales	728,563	5,585,574	99%
60	Cost of Goods Sold	468,947	3,855,667	68%
61		-------------------
62	Gross Margin	259,616	1,729,907	31%
63	Operating Expenses	201,042	1,306,667	23%
64	Depreciation	12,016	84,112	1%
65		-------------------
66	Earnings before Interest and Taxes	46,558	339,128	6%
67	Interest Expense	7,043	53,578	1%
68		-------------------
69	Earnings before Taxes	39,515	285,550	5%
70	Income Taxes	10,342	73,158	1%
71		-------------------
72	Earnings after Taxes	29,173	212,392	4%
73	Cash Dividends	0	76,389	1%
74		-------------------
75	Net Income	$29,173	$136,003	2%
76		===================

	A	B	C	D	E	F	G	H	I
79	===
80	Financial Ratios
81	===
82	INDICATORS OF SOLVENCY
83	Debt/Equity Ratio						0.52
84	Times Interest Earned						6.61 Times
85	
86	INDICATORS OF LIQUIDITY
87	Net Working Capital						$1,233,000
88	Net Working Capital/Assets						0.38
89	Current Ratio						2.59
90	Quick Ratio						2.12
91	Cash Ratio						0.40
92	
93	FUNDS MANAGEMENT RATIOS
94	Receivables/Sales						0.14
95	Days Sales Outstanding						51 Days
96	Payables/Cost of Goods Sold						0.07
97	Days Purchases in Payables						24 Days
98	Inventory Turnover						15.68 Times
99	Days Sales in Inventory						23 Days
100	Sales/Fixed Assets						0.88
101	
102	PROFITIBILITY RATIOS (Annualized)
103	Return on Sales						0.48
104	Return on Total Assets						0.11
105	Return on Shareholder's Equity						0.16

Figure 13.1B

The sequence of events for using the model is very simple. First, the data for the model is supplied by Mr. Eyeshade, who enters Balance Sheet and Income Statement figures on the last day of each month. After entering a month's data, he invokes an *accumulator* macro that adds the monthly Income Statement figures to the year-to-date totals in the column to the right of the monthly figures.

After the Income Statement figures have been accumulated, the controller invokes a second keyboard macro. This macro saves certain key financial ratios that Mr. Eyeshade believes he may want to use later in a data base.

These records are kept in a data base so that Mr. Eyeshade can evaluate trends in the key ratios and financial statement items. For example, he may want to search the data base for the net income value for December, 1982, and compare it to the level of net income for the current month. He may also want to search the data base for twelve months of net income values and evaluate the movement in the values.

After Mr. Eyeshade has selected information from the data base, he can use graphics to enhance the information before presenting it to Mr. Gherkins. He can use any number of different graph types to do this. In our example, he uses simple line and bar graphs and a pie chart.

After each graph is created, Mr. Eyeshade saves it in a graph (.PIC) file. Once all the .PIC files have been created, Mr. Eyeshade exits from 1-2-3 and enters the PrintGraph program where he prints the graphs one after the other.

The Spreadsheet

The *spreadsheet* refers to the portion of the model that is used to enter the Balance Sheet and Income Statement figures for a given month. Figure 13.1 shows the figures for the last month entered: July, 1983.

Notice that in column H, the rightmost column of the Balance Sheet, and in column I, the rightmost column of the Income Statement, there are columns of percentages labeled "Common Size." In the Balance Sheet portion, the common size column represents each item as a percent of total assets. In the Income Statement portion, the column size represents each item as a percent of gross sales. The term *Common Size* is used because it gives the financial analyst a way to evaluate trends over time in financial statements even though the amount of total assets and sales may have changed. The analyst can get an idea of the underlying movements of funds.

Common size figures allow Mr. Eyeshade to perform a quick visual inspection of the percentages to see if he incorrectly entered any balance-sheet or income-statement items. He can also review these percentages against any past percentages that he might remember. None of these percentages is actually saved in the data base.

You should also notice the Y-T-D column to the left of the common-size column (column H) in the Income Statement. This is where the year-to-date values for the various items in the Income Statement are stored. Again, none of these values is stored in the data base. However, they do allow the controller to compare data from a given month against the accumulated total for the year so far.

A final point to notice about this part of the model is the distinction between *Currency* and *, (Comma)* format. 1-2-3 allows you to conform to the accounting convention of using dollar signs in the first and last entries of financial statement entries and omitting them everywhere else.

Macros

There are two macros in this model: one accumulates totals in the year-to-date column of the Income Statement, and the other automatically enters records into the data base. The name of each macro appears to the left of its first cell entry.

For example, if you glance at cell I28 in figure 13.2, you will see the label \A.

The "\A" in cell I28 has two purposes. First, by using the */ Range Name Labels Right* command, \A becomes the range name for cell J28, the first cell of the macro. Second, the appearance of \A right next to the macro serves as documentation of the macro's name.

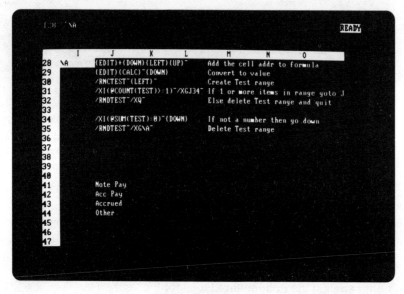

Figure 13.2

\A is the first macro that is actually used by Mr. Eyeshade. It is the accumulator macro. This macro takes the monthly income statement values supplied by Mr. Eyeshade in column G and adds them to the year-to-date values in column H.

To use this macro, Mr. Eyeshade must position the cursor in cell H56, which is the first value in the year-to-date Income Statement. The macro stops automatically when it reaches the end of the list of Income Statement values.

The macro begins by having 1-2-3 enter the Edit mode. You may think that the next step is to move immediately the cell pointer left and point to the cell to be added to the year-to-date value, but this is not the case. If you use the ← and → cursor-movement keys when you first enter the Edit mode, 1-2-3 thinks that you want to move the cursor left or right in the second line of the control panel and not in the worksheet. To get around this problem, you begin by using the ↑ cursor-movement key. This causes 1-2-3 to move the cell pointer up one cell and shift to the Point mode. Now we can point to the appropriate cell entry.

Once the appropriate cell address has been added to the year-to-date Income Statement value, the next step is to convert this newly created entry from a formula to a value. This avoids any mis-references when the values are copied to the data base. For example, if you leave the cell entry as a formula and copy it to a cell in the data base, the relative addresses used in the formula will change as you copy the formula from one location to the other. You could avoid this problem by using absolute addressing in the cell formula, but it is much easier just to use EDIT followed by CALC to convert the entry immediately.

The next step in the accumulator macro is to create a new range called "Test." *Test* is just a device for testing whether there are any values in the monthly Income Statement cells that still need to be added; the "Test" range is created and deleted with each loop of the macro. If there are any numeric values in the range, they are added to the year-to-date column. If the values encountered are not numbers but labels, however, then these items are passed over and not added to the year-to-date column. Finally, when two blank cells are encountered side-by-side, one a monthly cell and the other a year-to-date cell, the macro stops.

The second macro, /D, is shown in figure 13.3. This macro takes specific values from the Income Statement and Balance Sheet and copies them to fields within the data base. The first step in the macro is to position the cursor to the very top of the data base. The statement in cell J2 uses a range name called "Database" that represents the cell A111. This cell is the first cell in the first row of the data base. Figure 13.4 shows the data base portion of the spread-sheet.

The next step in the macro is to position the cell pointer down one row below the last entry in the data base to begin entering the next record. The next statements in the macro are used to copy certain items, such as the Record Date, Total Assets, Current Assets, Working Capital, etc., one at a time to the data base. The documentation in column M to the right of the macro indicates the values that are copied. After each value is copied, you would use EDIT followed by CALC. This method is used by the accumulator macro to convert cell entries from formulas to actual values.

	I	J	K	L	M	N	O
1							
2	\D	{GoTo}Database~			Position to dbase area		
3		{End}{Down}{Down}			1 line below last entry		
4		/cG5~~			Copy Date		
5		{Edit}{Calc}~{Right}			Convert from formula to value		
6		/cG25~~			Total Assets		
7		{Edit}{Calc}~{Right}			Convert to value		
8		/cCA~~			Current Assets		
9		{Edit}{Calc}~{Right}			Convert to value		
10		/cG87~~			Working Capital		
11		{Edit}{Calc}~{Right}			Convert to value		
12		/cG56~~			Monthly Gross Sales		
13		{Edit}{Calc}~{Right}			Convert to value		
14		/cG70~~			Monthly Earn After Taxes		
15		{Edit}{Calc}~{Right}			Convert to value		
16		/cG89~~			Current Ratio		
17		{Edit}{Calc}~{Right}			Convert to value		
18		/cG83~~			Debt to Equity Ratio		
19		{Edit}{Calc}~{Right}			Convert to value		
20		/cG104~~			Return on Assets Ratio		
21		{Edit}{Calc}~{Right}			Convert to value		
22		/cG95~~			Days Sales Outstanding		
23		{Edit}{Calc}~			Convert to value		
24		/dsd{Down}~			Expand Data-Range for Sort...		
25		pA1~d~g			Set primary key and go		

Figure 13.3

	A	B	C	D	E	F	G	H	I	J
107	===
108	Database
109	===
110					Month					
111	Record			Working	Gross	Month		Debt to	Return	
112	Date	Tot Assets	Cur Assets	Capital	Sales	EAT	Cur Ratio	Equity	On Assets	DSO
113	31-Jul-83	$3,239,000	2,010,000	$1,233,000	$732,730	29,173	2.59	0.52	0.11	51
114	30-Jun-83	$3,202,976	1,907,543	$1,160,483	$729,652	26,612	2.55	0.52	0.10	53
115	31-May-83	$3,192,286	1,893,724	$1,167,836	$726,572	24,269	2.61	0.53	0.09	53
116	30-Apr-83	$3,181,407	1,843,487	$1,118,712	$722,683	24,833	2.54	0.53	0.09	53
117	31-Mar-83	$3,175,632	1,875,261	$1,091,880	$717,947	25,481	2.39	0.54	0.10	54
118	28-Feb-83	$3,158,517	1,888,461	$1,154,019	$714,820	22,582	2.57	0.55	0.09	55
119	31-Jan-83	$3,142,910	1,821,474	$1,085,296	$713,267	23,201	2.47	0.55	0.09	57
120	31-Dec-82	$3,118,964	1,810,432	$1,131,818	$709,580	22,898	2.67	0.56	0.09	58
121	30-Nov-82	$3,084,112	1,758,559	$1,094,167	$705,182	22,137	2.65	0.56	0.09	59
122	31-Oct-82	$3,081,261	1,762,365	$1,072,725	$704,854	23,101	2.56	0.57	0.09	60
123	30-Sep-82	$3,043,640	1,867,870	$1,092,085	$704,000	26,308	2.41	0.58	0.10	61
124	31-Aug-82	$3,028,681	1,844,625	$1,071,413	$701,632	26,541	2.39	0.58	0.11	63
125	31-Jul-82	$3,013,676	1,764,898	$1,059,416	$700,554	27,008	2.50	0.59	0.11	63
126	30-Jun-82	$2,991,601	1,768,636	$1,061,479	$697,503	24,048	2.50	0.59	0.10	63
127	31-May-82	$2,962,020	1,701,132	$1,006,475	$693,041	25,537	2.45	0.59	0.10	65
128	30-Apr-82	$2,939,631	1,814,346	$1,056,518	$692,004	21,674	2.39	0.60	0.09	65
129	31-Mar-82	$2,936,500	1,675,854	$1,015,673	$690,824	26,006	2.54	0.60	0.11	66
130	28-Feb-82	$2,922,458	1,684,678	$1,033,158	$690,289	23,351	2.59	0.61	0.10	68
131	31-Jan-82	$2,903,961	1,682,436	$1,002,948	$688,450	21,269	2.48	0.62	0.09	68
132	31-Dec-81	$2,891,879	1,779,420	$1,095,574	$686,639	22,339	2.60	0.62	0.09	69
133	30-Nov-81	$2,889,668	1,720,860	$1,026,998	$685,821	27,259	2.48	0.63	0.11	71
134	31-Oct-81	$2,868,248	1,654,943	$972,434	$685,073	26,496	2.42	0.63	0.11	73
135	30-Sep-81	$2,864,642	1,696,249	$1,042,317	$684,348	23,122	2.59	0.64	0.10	74
136	31-Aug-81	$2,831,978	1,695,018	$1,004,192	$681,827	22,862	2.45	0.64	0.10	75
137	31-Jul-81	$2,830,797	1,644,616	$986,548	$680,687	21,246	2.50	0.64	0.09	77
138	30-Jun-81	$2,799,154	1,607,371	$957,749	$680,000	20,470	2.47	0.64	0.09	77
139	31-May-81	$2,788,738	1,601,230	$963,565	$679,317	22,278	2.51	0.64	0.10	78
140	30-Apr-81	$2,759,173	1,575,963	$947,576	$677,506	20,832	2.51	0.65	0.09	79
141	31-Mar-81	$2,737,433	1,572,624	$972,634	$675,798	26,529	2.62	0.65	0.12	80
142	28-Feb-81	$2,715,848	1,612,148	$958,375	$673,293	26,051	2.47	0.66	0.12	82
143	31-Jan-81	$2,710,753	1,587,850	$985,838	$670,182	24,985	2.64	0.66	0.11	83

Figure 13.4

The formats of the cells for all the items copied to the data base are determined by the cell they are copied from. As you will recall, when a value is copied from one cell to another, the format of the source cell is copied along with the value.

Finally, the last two lines of the /D macro are used to sort the data base automatically in descending order according to the date. In the second to last line (cell J24), the statement reads, "/dsd {Down}~." This statement automatically resets the Data-Range to include the record just added. The last line in the macro sets the primary key to the first column of the data base and initiates the sort.

The Data Base

The data base refers to the area of the spreadsheet that contains the monthly records of key ratios as well as the Balance Sheet and the Income Statement items. To illustrate how Mr. Eyeshade might want to manipulate the data base, let's look at three different examples.

In the first example, suppose that Mr. Eyeshade is asked by Mr. Gherkins, the president, to find the gross sales and earnings after taxes for January 31, 1982. A logical way to get this information is by using the / Data Find command. Figure 13.5 shows part of the Input range (which corresponds to the entire data base—A112..J143) and the Criterion range (L112..L113). The single record found as the result of the command is highlighted in reverse video.

In the second example, Mr. Gherkins wants to know the trend in working capital throughout the first six months of 1983. The controller chooses the / Data Extract command for this application. Again, the Input range is the entire data base (A112..J143). Figure 13.6 shows the Criterion range (L119..L120) used to select the records. Notice that the criteria are shown in the Text format. The Output range for this Extract operation is the range L124..M124. Figure 13.6 also shows the values in the Output range (L125..M130) that are copied as a result of the command.

Mr. Eyeshade might want to print the results of the Extract as they appear in the worksheet. To do this, he would specify the Range to be printed for the / Print Printer command. The range he uses is L124..M130. At this point, he enters Go from the / Print Printer menu, and the results of the Extract are printed on the printer.

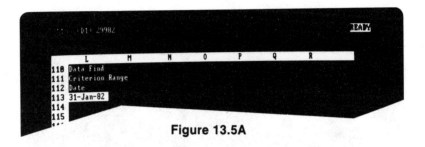

Figure 13.5A

	A	B	C	D	E	F	G
121	30-Nov-82	$3,084,112	1,758,559	$1,094,167	$705,182	22,137	2.65
122	31-Oct-82	$3,081,261	1,762,365	$1,072,725	$704,854	23,101	2.56
123	30-Sep-82	$3,043,640	1,867,870	$1,092,085	$704,000	26,308	2.41
124	31-Aug-82	$3,028,681	1,844,625	$1,071,413	$701,632	26,541	2.39
125	31-Jul-82	$3,013,676	1,764,898	$1,059,416	$700,554	27,008	2.50
126	30-Jun-82	$2,991,601	1,768,636	$1,061,479	$697,503	24,048	2.50
127	31-May-82	$2,962,020	1,701,132	$1,006,475	$693,041	25,537	2.45
128	30-Apr-82	$2,939,631	1,814,346	$1,056,518	$692,004	21,674	2.39
129	31-Mar-82	$2,936,500	1,675,854	$1,015,673	$690,824	26,006	2.54
130	28-Feb-82	$2,922,458	1,684,678	$1,033,158	$690,289	23,351	2.59
131	31-Jan-82	$2,903,961	1,682,436	$1,002,948	$688,450	21,269	2.48
132	31-Dec-81	$2,891,879	1,779,420	$1,095,574	$686,639	22,339	2.60
133	30-Nov-81	$2,889,668	1,720,860	$1,026,998	$685,821	27,259	2.48
134	31-Oct-81	$2,868,248	1,654,943	$972,434	$685,073	26,496	2.42
135	30-Sep-81	$2,864,642	1,696,249	$1,042,317	$684,348	23,122	2.59
136	31-Aug-81	$2,831,978	1,695,018	$1,004,192	$681,827	22,862	2.45
137	31-Jul-81	$2,830,797	1,644,616	$986,548	$680,687	21,246	2.50
138	30-Jun-81	$2,799,154	1,607,371	$957,749	$680,000	20,470	2.47
139	31-May-81	$2,788,738	1,601,230	$963,565	$679,317	22,278	2.51
140	30-Apr-81	$2,759,173	1,575,963	$947,576	$677,586	20,832	2.51

Figure 13.5B

In the final example, Mr. Eyeshade wants to determine the months with the highest earnings-after-tax levels over the last two years. He could use a / Data Extract command again to copy the results of the search to a separate area of the worksheet. However, he decides instead that he wants to re-sort the entire data base and perform a simple visual review of the highest values. Thus he uses the Data Sort command with the Primary-Key set to the monthly earnings-after-tax column (column F). He also specifies descending order so that the months with the highest levels of earnings after taxes will appear at the top.

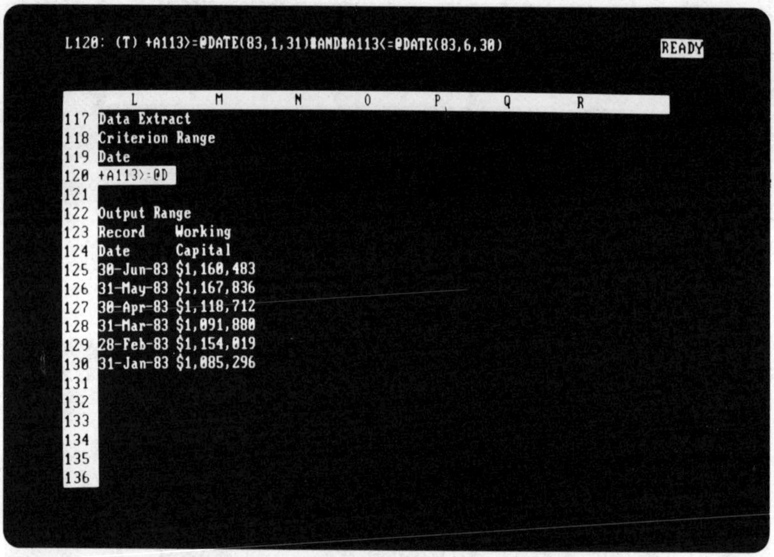

```
L120: (T) +A113>=@DATE(83,1,31)#AND#A113<=@DATE(83,6,30)          READY

         L      M      N      O      P      Q      R
117 Data Extract
118 Criterion Range
119 Date
120 +A113>=@D
121
122 Output Range
123 Record      Working
124 Date        Capital
125 30-Jun-83 $1,160,483
126 31-May-83 $1,167,836
127 30-Apr-83 $1,118,712
128 31-Mar-83 $1,091,880
129 28-Feb-83 $1,154,019
130 31-Jan-83 $1,085,296
131
132
133
134
135
136
```

Figure 13.6

Before Mr. Eyeshade executes the sort, he first double checks the
*D*ata-Range designation. He makes sure that the range is
A113..J143. He then enters *Go* from the command menu. Figure 13.7
shows the results of the *S*ort.

Graphics

Graphics is the final feature of the comprehensive model. Mr.
Eyeshade could create several different kinds of graphs. However,
in this case he decides to create and print three simple graphs: a line
chart, a bar chart, and a pie chart. This group of charts is sufficient to
give you a general idea of how graphs are created and displayed in
this integrated model.

A line chart is the first type of graph that Mr. Eyeshade creates to plot
the points for the working capital levels for the first half of 1983 that
were copied to the *O*utput range in the second data base example
above. The first thing he does in graphing the line chart is to select
*L*ine as the */ G*raph *T*ype. Next, he must set the data range. To do

A107: \= READY

	A	B	C	D	E	F	G
107	==========	==========	==========	==========	==========	==========	==========
108	Database						
109	==========	==========	==========	==========	==========	==========	==========
110					Month		
111	Record			Working	Gross	Month	
112	Date	Tot Assets	Cur Assets	Capital	Sales	EAT	Cur Ratio
113	31-Jul-83	$3,239,000	2,010,000	$1,233,000	$732,730	29,173	2.59
114	30-Nov-81	$2,889,668	1,720,860	$1,026,998	$685,821	27,259	2.48
115	31-Jul-82	$3,013,676	1,764,898	$1,059,416	$700,554	27,008	2.50
116	30-Jun-83	$3,202,976	1,907,543	$1,160,483	$729,652	26,612	2.55
117	31-Aug-82	$3,028,681	1,844,625	$1,071,413	$701,632	26,541	2.39
118	31-Mar-81	$2,737,433	1,572,624	$972,634	$675,798	26,529	2.62
119	31-Oct-81	$2,868,248	1,654,943	$972,434	$685,073	26,496	2.42
120	30-Sep-82	$3,043,640	1,867,870	$1,092,085	$704,000	26,308	2.41
121	28-Feb-81	$2,715,848	1,612,148	$958,375	$673,293	26,051	2.47
122	31-Mar-82	$2,936,500	1,675,854	$1,015,673	$690,824	26,006	2.54
123	31-May-82	$2,962,020	1,701,132	$1,006,475	$693,041	25,537	2.45
124	31-Mar-83	$3,175,632	1,875,261	$1,091,880	$717,947	25,481	2.39
125	31-Jan-81	$2,710,753	1,587,850	$985,838	$670,182	24,985	2.64
126	30-Apr-83	$3,181,407	1,843,487	$1,118,712	$722,683	24,833	2.54

Figure 13.7

this, he uses the */Graph A* command and the range M125..M130, shown in figure 13.6. If he graphs the command at this point, he will get the results shown in figure 13.8 after he selects *View*.

To dress up the graph, Mr. Eyeshade can choose graph options. For example, he might decide to use graph titles and labels for the x axis. To add the graph titles, he uses the *Graph Options Titles* command. For the main title, he sets the *First* option to "Gherkins, Inc." For the subtitle, he sets the *Second* option to "Working Capital Levels."

To set up the labels for the x axis, Mr. Eyeshade uses the range corresponding to the dates that were extracted. To enter the range, he chooses *X* from the graph menu and enters L125..L130 for the range. To avoid overlapping dates, he selects */Graph Options Scale Skip*. He chooses 2 for the skipping factor, so that every other date is shown on the graph. The results of Mr. Eyeshade's selections are shown in figure 13.9.

Notice that the order of the months displayed in the graph goes from June to January. To reverse the order of the months, Mr. Eyeshade

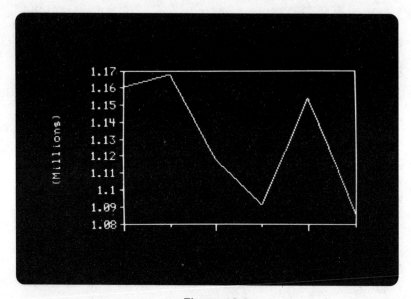

Figure 13.8

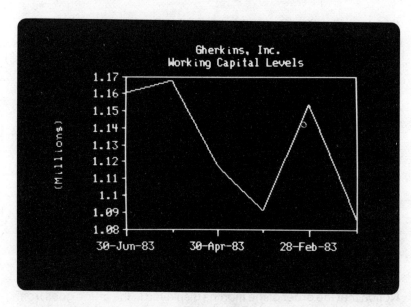

Figure 13.9

can do a /Data Sort on the Data-Range of L125..M130 with the Primary-key set to the date, e.g., L125. If he selects Ascending order for the Sort, he can get the graph to display the months from January to June as shown in figure 13.10.

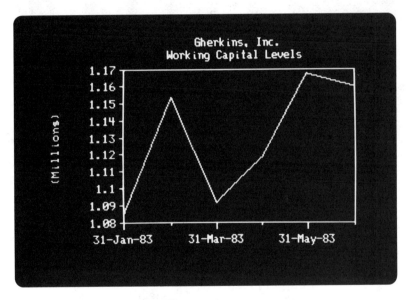

Figure 13.10

To print this graph later, Mr. Eyeshade uses the /Graph Save command. This command saves the current graph in a .PIC file so that he can print it later, after he has created all his other graphs. Mr. Eyeshade also uses the /Graph Name Create command to save the current graph settings for later use.

The next type of graph that Mr. Eyeshade might select is a bar chart of the same data. To create this chart, he simply selects Bar from the /Graph Type menu. When he enters View from the /Graph menu, the results shown in figure 13.11 appear on the screen.

Again, Mr. Eyeshade uses the /Graph Save command to save the current graph for printing and /Graph Name Create to save the current graph settings for later sessions.

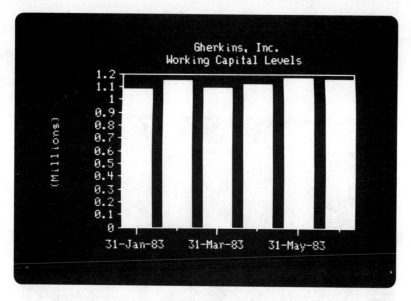

Figure 13.11

The final graph Mr. Eyeshade might create is a pie chart. For this example, let's suppose that the pie chart is called "Current Liabilities for July, 1983." The slices of the pie are Notes Payable, Accounts Payable, Accrued Expenses, and Other Liabilities.

The first step that Mr. Eyeshade must take in creating the graph is to select *Pie* as the */Graph Type*. Next, he sets the *A* range as G30..G33, corresponding to July's values for the components of current liabilities listed above. In creating the *Titles* for the graph, Mr. Eyeshade again uses "Gherkins, Inc." for the *First* title. The *Second* title that he chooses is "Current Liabilities for July, 1983." To name the slices, he uses the */Graph X* command. If he designates A30..A33 as the range for the x-axis labels, however, the labels that reside in those cells will be too long to be displayed on the screen and will, therefore, be truncated. Figure 13.12 shows what happens after Mr. Eyeshade selects *View*.

Although the labels are truncated when the graph is displayed on the screen, they are not truncated when the graph is printed. To prevent the truncation on the screen, Mr. Eyeshade sets up a special

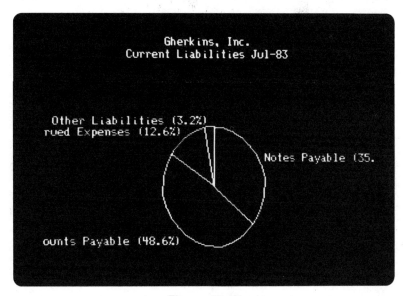

Figure 13.12

range of cells with shorter labels. To enter the range, he selects an out-of-the-way area of the worksheet and types in the labels. When the labels have been created, he uses the /Graph X command again, but this time he uses the range J41..J44. Figure 13.13 shows the new results.

Once again, Mr. Eyeshade saves the current graph for printing using the /Graph Save command. He also uses the /Graph Name Create command to save the settings for possible later use.

Printing the Graphs

To print the graphs he has created, Mr. Eyeshade must exit from 1-2-3 and enter the PrintGraph program either through the Lotus Access System or from DOS, depending on his preference at the time. One he has entered the PrintGraph program, he may select from among several different print options. For this example, we assume that he does not use any special options, but uses all standard defaults instead. Also, he selects all three graphs at once

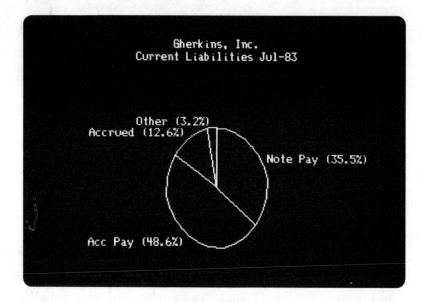

Figure 13.13

from the list of available .PIC files and prints them one after the other. The results of the PrintGraph program appear in figure 13.14.

Conclusion

The comprehensive model is an ideal conclusion for *Using 1-2-3* because it draws together all of the elements of 1-2-3 into one powerful model. It includes a spreadsheet that uses some of the techniques you learned in Chapters 3, 4, 5, 6, 7, and 8. The graphics included in this example build on the commands that are explained in Chapters 9 and 10. The financial data base was created using the tools we developed in Chapter 11. The macros in the model draw heavily on concepts developed in Chapter 12.

This book has examined every facet of 1-2-3. We hope that you have found the examples of each command and function helpful and our observations informative. It's now up to you to begin using 1-2-3 to help you solve your own problems. Remember, the model above is just one illustration of the fact that the four elements of 1-2-3—

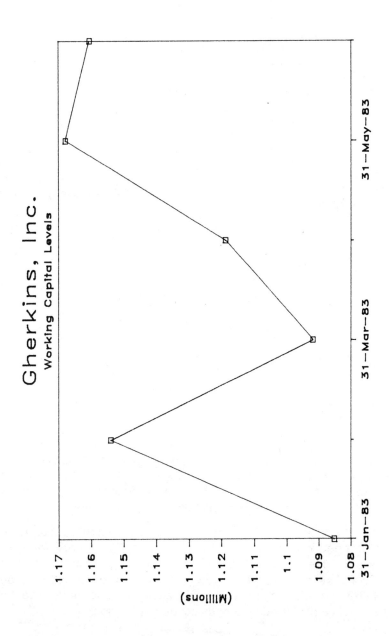

Figure 13.14A

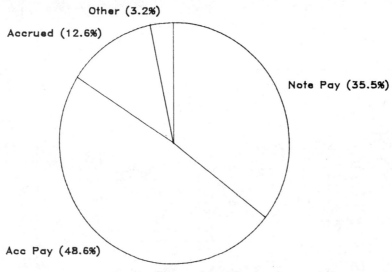

Gherkins, Inc.
Current Liabilities for July, 1983

Other (3.2%)

Accrued (12.6%)

Note Pay (35.5%)

Acc Pay (48.6%)

Figure 13.14B

spreadsheet, graphics, data management, and macros—can be merged together to form a powerful model. The possible applications for 1-2-3 are limitless. Now that you are familiar with all of 1-2-3' capabilities, you should have no trouble thinking of ways to use 1-2-3 in your business. Just use your imagination!

If you want to learn still more about 1-2-3, you should subscribe to Que's new periodical, *Absolute Reference: The Journal for 1-2-3 Users.* Edited by Geoffrey LeBlond and Douglas Cobb, *Absolute Reference* is an excellent source of ongoing information about 1-2-3. To learn more about this exciting opportunity, see the announcement inside the back cover of this book.

Appendix
Explanation of Que's Spreadsheet Feature List

Spreadsheet Characteristics

Number of rows

The number of rows in the spreadsheet. Where the number can vary, the maximum number of rows is used.

Number of columns

The number of columns in the spreadsheet.

Number of cells

The total number of row-column intersections in the sheet.

Maximum capacity of cell (characters)

The maximum number of characters of either text or formulas that can be stored in a single cell in the spreadsheet. Programs with larger numbers allow longer, more complex formulas.

RAM Memory Capacities

Minimum required memory

The amount of RAM (user) memory required for the program to function.

Maximum usable memory

The maximum amount of memory accessible by the program.

Uses virtual memory

Indicates whether the program uses virtual memory techniques to store a portion of the worksheet on diskette. Programs with virtual memory generally allow a larger model for a given amount of RAM. For its purposes, virtual memory treats mass storage and user memory the same way, allowing larger models.

Disk Capabilities

Copy protected

Indicates that the program diskette is protected from copy or backup.

Hard disk-compatible

Indicates that the program can be transferred to a hard disk-based IBM Personal Computer.

Display Characteristics

Can use a 40-column display

Indicates that the program can be run on an IBM PC with a 40-column display. These displays are typically found on television sets.

Must use an 80-column display

Indicates that the program requires the use of an 80-column display.

Uses color to highlight areas of sheet

Indicates that the program is capable of showing various parts of the sheet, such as its border, ranges, or other areas, in color on a color monitor.

Uses color monitor (on spreadsheet)

Indicates that the program can use a color display attached to the IBM Color/Graphics Adapter to display the spreadsheet portion of the program in color.

Numeric precision

The number of digits that the program uses to perform computations. This number helps to determine the accuracy of the program in complex arithmetic. Programs with higher numeric precision are better suited for scientific and engineering applications.

User-Friendliness Features

These items help to determine the user friendliness of the program: its ease of learning and ease of use.

Tutorial on disk

Indicates if the program has a diskette-based tutorial that teaches the user by simulating the operation of the program on the computer.

On-screen help

Indicates that the computer has built-in help screens that can be accessed for information at any point while the program is being used. Help screens allow the user to obtain information about what to do next without using the program's manual.

Cell editing

The ability to edit a cell after it has been defined with a label or value.

On-Screen Display

On-screen display features provide the user with a continuous status report on the condition of the program and the computer.

Window number displayed

Indicates, where a spreadsheet is capable of displaying more than one window, that the individual windows are numbered on the screen.

Model name displayed

The name of the model currently residing in the spreadsheet is displayed.

Memory counter

Provides a count of the amount of memory at the disposal of the user. Some programs use an absolute count, whereas others use a percentage measure.

"Prompted" commands

Indicates that the program prompts the user with simple instructions as the user executes worksheet commands.

Use of IBM PC Keyboard

Indicates whether the program takes advantage of the many cursor-movement and function keys on the IBM PC keyboard. Different programs use the keys for different purposes.

10 function keys (more than 1 key)

Indicates that more than one of the IBM PC's function keys are used for spreadsheet commands, functions, or cursor movement.

Keyboard status display

Some programs provide screen messages about the current status of certain keys on the IBM PC keyboard, such as CAPS, END, and NUM. This feature helps to overcome the problem of not knowing the settings of the keys.

Worksheet Formatting

Number of windows

The number of separate windows that can be opened simultaneously onto the spreadsheet.

Number of models visible at one time

Some programs allow two or more models to be viewed at the same time through different windows.

Window number displayed

For programs that allow multiple windows on the worksheet, each window is numbered on the computer's display. This feature facilitates managing multiple windows.

Column widths - Adjustable

Indicates that the widths of the columns in the spreadsheet can be altered to suit the user's requirements.

Column width - Individually adjustable

Indicates that the width of each column can be adjusted individually.

Minimum width

Specifies the minimum allowable column width for each program. Notice that some programs allow a column to have a zero width.

"Form" input feature

Allows the user to define certain cells in a spreadsheet as input cells, then to restrict the movement of the cursor so that it jumps directly from input cell to another. Programs with this feature can be easily configured for use by inexperienced spreadsheeters.

Must display border at all times

Certain programs allow the spreadsheet row-column border to be turned off; others require that it remain visible at all times.

Cell Formatting

Cell formats are specified by the user to configure the cell to the type of data desired, and the appearance of the data in the cell.

User-defined cell formatting

Indicates that the user can define special combinations of cell formats to suit particular needs.

Floating dollar sign ($)

Displays numbers with a dollar sign ($). For example, the number 2345 can be formatted to look like $2345.

Commas in numbers

Some programs allow commas to be embedded in numbers after every three digits. For example, the number 1234567 can be formatted to look like 1,234,567. In some programs this feature is part of the dollar-sign format discussed above.

Exponential

Displays numbers as an integers with trailing decimals to a power of ten. For example, the number 123456 can be formatted to appear as 1.23E5.

Percentage

Allows decimal numbers to be displayed as percentages, usually with a trailing percentage sign (%) in the same cell. For example, the number .235 can be displayed as 23.5%.

Negatives in parentheses

Programs with this feature can display negative numbers in parentheses, rather than with the minus sign (-). For example, the number -456 can be displayed as (456). In some programs, this feature is part of the dollar-sign format discussed above.

DR/CR notation

Displays all numbers with either a trailing DR (for debit) or CR (for credit). Negative numbers have the CR sign, and positive numbers have the DR sign. For example, this format displays the numbers 123 and -321 as 123DR and 321CR, respectively.

Enhanced (underline or boldface)

Marks the contents of a cell or cells for special treatment by a printer. The user can specify whether the cell should be printed as boldfaced or underlined.

Integer

The contents of a cell formatted with this feature are rounded to the nearest integer for display. Thus the number 1.4456 would be rounded to 1. Numbers formatted to appear as integers retain their full value in subsequent calculations, unlike numbers computed with a true integer format (described below).

True integer

Indicates that the integer format actually rounds the number as an integer, and that a number formatted as a true integer will not retain truncated decimals.

Fixed number of decimals

Allows the user to specify the number of decimals to be displayed. For example, the number 5.6678 can be displayed as 5.7, 5.668, or 5.6678.

Cell filler

Empty spaces in a cell are filled with filler characters, such as a *. This protects the contents of the cell from alteration. For example, the number 234 in a column 9-characters wide would be displayed as ******234.

Symbolic

Causes the contents of a cell to be displayed symbolically (graphically). For example, the number 3 could be formatted to look like ***. The symbol used can be a +, -, or *, depending on the program.

Alignment

Indicates the different ways the contents of a cell can be aligned in the cell. The possible alignments are flush-left, flush-right, and centered. Some programs allow more flexibility in aligning text than numbers.

> Align Right Text:
> > Pushes text against the right margin of the cell
> Align Right Numbers:
> > Pushes numbers against the right margin of the cell
> Align Left Text:
> > Pushes text against the left margin of the cell
> Align Left Numbers:
> > Pushes numbers against the left margin of the cell
> Align Center Text:
> > Centers text in the cell
> Align Center Numbers:
> > Centers numbers in the cell

Formula display

Causes the actual formula in a cell to be displayed instead of the results of the formula. For example, a cell containing the formula 2+2 would normally display the number 4. Under this format, the equation 2+2 would appear.

Cell protection

The contents of a protected cell cannot be changed. If the user wishes to alter a protected cell, it must first be unprotected. This format helps to prevent the accidental loss of important information.

Adjustable cell height

One spreadsheet, Context MBA, allows cells to be individually stretched to be two or more rows deep. These cells can be used as word-processing pages.

Cell/Range Names

Allows cells or groups of cells to be given a name. Once a cell is named, the name can be used instead of the cell's row and column coordinates in formulas and functions.

Print Formatting

Print formatting features allow the user to customize reports.

Headers

Headers are text messages that appear at the top of each page in a multipage report. Some spreadsheets allow dates and page numbers to be included in a page header.

Footers

Similar to headers, except that footers appear at the bottom of each page in a multipage report.

Flexible margins

Programs with flexible margins allow the user to set top, bottom, left, and right margins to suit particular needs. Some programs allow only the left and right margins to be set, whereas others allow the adjustment of all four margins.

Page numbers

Indicates that the program is capable of numbering the pages of a single- or multiple-page report at printing time.

Pause between pages

Indicates that the user can instruct the program to stop printing at the end of each page so that the paper can be adjusted. This feature is desirable if single-sheet paper is used for printing.

Printer setup strings

Some printers accept coded instructions (setup strings) that allow condensed printing, boldface printing, and other printing features. Spreadsheet software should be able to feed such a setting to the printer at the discretion of the user. Some spreadsheets allow a standard setup string to be installed in the program for automatic execution each time printing takes place.

Accepts multiple printer types

Some spreadsheet software allows the user to configure the system to work with printers other than the IBM Printer (Epson MX-80). Some will print to a printer connected to an IBM serial port.

Print cell formulas

Allows the actual contents of each cell (formulas and functions) to be printed. This feature is useful for documenting and debugging complex spreadsheets.

Printer control codes may be installed into program

Indicates that printer control codes which activate features of many different printers can be memorized by the program, so that the codes do not have to be entered prior to each printing session.

Logical printer device may be changed from program

Allows the user to print to devices other than the printer, such as a disk or a modem. For example, some spreadsheets allow the user to switch printer output between the LPT and COM1: devices.

Text Functions

These features allow the use of text entries (as opposed to numbers and formulas) in spreadsheet functions.

Justification

Allows information in a cell to be justified at the time of initial, or subsequent, entry. Justification is usually to the left, right, or center within the cell.

Text lookup

Spreadsheets with this ability can have text as the object of a lookup table. For example, with this feature a lookup table can be created with an inventory part number as the index and an inventory part description as the object.

Text in "If . . . Then" phrases

Indicates that text can serve as the object for an "If . . . Then" phrase. For example, this feature allows the user to create a formula such as "IF(SALES>1000000,"Great work","Better luck next time")."

Labels wider than columns

Labels that are wider than the width of one column automatically carry forward into the next cell (if empty) on spreadsheets with this feature.

Repeating labels

Allows the user to design single-character labels that repeat across the sheet. This feature is useful for inserting underlines beneath columns and for dividing a sheet with a solid line. The repeat is limited to a single cell on spreadsheets that do not allow text to be wider than one column. Some sheets allow a combination of characters to be repeated.

String functions

Allow the user to measure, move, and manipulate text entries.

Substring

A substring is a phrase that is extracted from another, longer phrase. For example, the phrase "bcd" is a substring of the phrase "abcdef." This feature allows the user to extract a substring from a label in one cell and move it to another cell.

String length

Returns the length in characters of a given string. For example, the string "abcde" has a length of 5.

Concatenation

This very powerful feature allows text and numbers to be concatenated, or linked together, in a single cell. For purposes of calculation, only the numeric part is used. This allows an entry such as "122 widgets" to appear in a single cell.

Recalculation

The first spreadsheets allowed only single-pass linear recalculation. Newer programs offer a wide range of recalculation options.

Manual

Allows the user to turn off recalculation while performing input or constructing a model. This feature helps to prevent long delays due to unnecessary recalculation.

Automatic

The standard state for most spreadsheets. Under automatic recalculation, the sheet computes each time an entry or a formatting change is made.

Iterative

Programs with iterative recalculation allow the user to specify the number of iterations, or repetitions, that will be performed each time the sheet is recalculated. A single recalculate command can trigger five, ten, or fifteen calculation passes through the same sheet. Some spreadsheets allow a completion test to be substituted for a specific number of passes. This feature helps to eliminate problems caused by circular references.

Natural

Topological recalculation. The recalculation algorithm identifies the most fundamental cell in a given worksheet (the cell that most other cells depend on) and calculates it first; then searches for the second most fundamental cell and recalculates it; and so on, until the entire sheet is recomputed. This method of calculation helps to eliminate problems caused by forward references.

Row wise

A form of linear recalculation. Computations are performed beginning with the top left cell in the sheet, then each cell in the top row; next the left-most cell in the second row, followed by the cells in row 2; and so on.

Column wise

Similar to row wise, except that the computations proceed in linear fashion by column, beginning with the left-most column.

Saving and Loading Files

Automatic recalculation on load

Indicates that the worksheet will automatically recalculate when it is loaded from the disk.

Partial load

Allows the user to load a specified portion of a larger model into the worksheet. This feature is used in consolidation. It allows data tables to be shared between models.

Partial save

The opposite of a partial load. This feature allows a specified portion of a larger model to be saved to the disk.

Import files from other programs

With some spreadsheets, a file from another program can be loaded directly into the worksheet. For example, Multiplan can read VisiCalc files, and 1-2-3 can read data from a dBASE II file.

Import text files

Some programs can load a text file directly into the worksheet. For example, 1-2-3 can read a WordStar file.

Save to a text file

The opposite of importing a text file. Most programs accomplish this by printing the model to the disk. This feature allows the user to save a worksheet, then edit it with word-processing software.

Format disk from within program

Indicates that a blank diskette can be formatted from within the spreadsheet (without exiting to the operating system).

Saving to communications file

Most spreadsheets allow data to be saved to a communications file with a standard format. Unfortunately, there is little standardization of the "standard" formats. Some programs save to DIF (Data Interchange Format) files, some to SDI (SuperData Interchange) files, and others to SYLK (SYmbolic LinK) files.

Sheet-to-Sheet Links

Data channels (true three-dimensional)

Indicates that a spreadsheet program can link several differently stored models together, without having to merge entire models.

Maximum number of channels

Indicates the maximum number of models that can be linked together.

Consolidation

Indicates the ability to overlay one model on another. Where cells are occupied in identical locations by the two models, either addition, or another math function is relative between the active model and the overlay model. The overlay cell locations do not replace the active contents.

Single-cell linkage

Indicates that only single-cell links may be made between the active model and linked models.

Maximum number of linkages

Indicates the maximum number of linkages that can be established between the active model and related models.

Data Base Functions

Internal to spreadsheet

Indicates that the data base is stored in the spreadsheet, like a normal model, instead of on disk. Internal data bases can be accessed faster than external ones because no disk operations are required. External data bases, however, usually are larger than internal ones.

Sorting

Indicates that the spreadsheet allows data to be sorted. Some spreadsheets allow both a primary and secondary key for the sort. Most will sort on both numeric and alphabetic keys and will allow an entire row or column, or a partial row or column, to be sorted.

Numeric:
   Allows sorting by numbers
Alphabetical:
   Allows sorting in alphabetical order
Single key:
   Allows sorting by only one criterion in a single sort
Multiple key:
   Allows sorting by several criteria in a single pass
Sort partial columns/rows:
   Sorting does not require sorting the entire data base

Criteria operations

Some spreadsheets allow the data base to be searched for records that match a set of criteria, or conditions. An example of a criteria operation is a command to delete all the records in a data base that are more than one year old. The criterion in this case is time: record date more than one year old.

Number of criteria

In a search, this function specifies the number of criteria that can be used to define records.

Deletion

Indicates that record deletion by criteria is possible.

Find

Indicates that records can be found by criteria. Finding involves moving the cursor to the cell that contains the first field of the record.

Extract

Similar to a find, except that the data is extracted from the data base into a predetermined target area. This feature allows the user to identify, then operate on, all records that meet a particular set of requirements.

Data base statistics

Spreadsheets that allow data base operations typically include a set of data base functions. These functions are similar to the normal spreadsheet functions, except that instead of providing a range for the operation (SUM(A1:A5)), the user must provide a data base range and a set of criteria for the operation. For example, a data base function can be used to find the total dollar amount (SUM) of all records in an accounts receivable data base that are more than 60 days old (criterion). Data base statistics include: SUM, AVERAGE, COUNT, MAX, MIN, STANDARD DEVIATION, and VARIANCE.

Graphics Functions

1-2-3 has built-in graphics. The following features outline the flexibility and power of the graphics element of this program.

Requires Color/Graphics Adapter

Indicates that display graphics require an IBM PC with a Color/Graphics Adapter card.

Types of graphs

The most typical types of business graphs are LINE, BAR, STACKED BAR, SCATTER, PIE CHART, and HI-LO SPREAD.

Number of ranges in a single graph

Indicates the number of different data groups that can be displayed on a single chart. An example of a graph with multiple data ranges is a line graph showing sales, cost of goods sold, and gross income.

Pie charts are always restricted to a single data range.

User-defined colors

Programs with this feature allow the user to define background and other colors in graphs.

User-defined legends

Indicates that the program allows the user to specify the legends, or labels, on graphs. The following headers are typically flexible: titles and subtitles, labels, and axis scales.

Scale definition
Allows the scale of the x and y axes to be customized by the user.

Programmability

The ability to build files of commands, sometimes called macros, that perform sequentially a number of functions.

User-defined functions

Indicates the ability to establish your own formulas, and use them as functions within the spreadsheet.

If . . . Then function

Indicates the ability to have the macro, or batch of commands, use If (condition) Then (do this) logic.

GOTO function

Indicates that macros, or batch commands, can move or apply to differing areas of the spreadsheet.

QUIT function

Indicates that macros or batch commands can perform their functions, then exit the program.

User menus

Indicates that macros or batch commands can offer you choices during processing.

Built-in Functions

Built-in functions are spreadsheet shortcuts to performing common mathematical, statistical, or financial tasks. Functions typically consist of a function name and one or more arguments.

Mathematical

Sum

Computes the total of the numeric entries in a range.

Round

Rounds off a value to the nearest integer. For example, ROUND-(5.55) results in the number 6.

Integer

Returns the integer portion of a number. For example, INTEGER-(5.55) returns the value 5.

Natural logarithm

Returns the natural logarithm of a number.

Logarithm

Returns the logarithm (base 10) of a number.

Square root

Computes the square root of a value. SQRT(4) yields the result 2.

Modulo

Computes the remainder resulting from the division of two numbers. For example, MODUOLO(14,6) yields the result 2.

Absolute value

Computes the absolute value of a number (any number changed to its positive equivalent). ABS(-93) becomes +93.

Power (X to the Y)

Computes the function XY. For example, where X is 5 and Y is 3, X^Y returns the number 125.

Trigonometric

Most spreadsheets include the trigonometric functions sine, cosine, and tangent. Others also compute the arc tangent, arc sine, and arc cosine.

All of the spreadsheet programs tested included the function pi.

Statistical

Count

Counts the number of nonblank entries in a range.

Average

Computes the mean of a range. First, the count is taken; then it is divided into the sum of the same range.

Maximum

Finds the maximum (largest) number in the range specified.

Minimum

Finds the minimum (smallest) number in the range specified.

Standard deviation

Finds the standard deviation of the range specified.

Variance

Describes the magnitude of variation between the number and the average of its range.

Linear estimation

A mathematical technique for calculating the trend of a set of numbers.

Financial

Net present value

Finds the net present value of a series of even or uneven cash flows.

Future value

Yields the future value of an annuity.

Payment

Yields the payment, given a rate and a series of cash flows.

Internal rate of return

Yields the internal rate of return, given an investment and a return, or a series of cash flows.

Modified internal rate of return

Yields the internal rate of return, given an investment, a risk rate of capital, and a return, or a series of cash flows.

Annuity

A series of cash flows. Monthly paychecks are a form of annuity.

Depreciation

Adjustment in the value of an asset over the term of its life. Depreciation demonstrates the decreasing value of an asset over a period.

Date Arithmetic

Specified date

Allows a specific date to be entered in a cell.

Today

Finds the date today as specified either from PC DOS, or from a derivative of a specified date.

Year

Year component of a specified date.

Month

Month component of a specified date.

Day

Day component of a specified date.

Time of day

Hours, minutes, and seconds, either calculated by the computer's operating system, or the hours, minutes, and seconds since the specified date, compared to the time calculated by the computer.

Julian date

The Julian date, or number of days from an arbitrary point. February 2 is the thirty-third Julian date of the year.

Logical

If . . . Then . . . Else

Evaluates the If portion as true or false. If it is true, the Then argument is returned; if it is not true, then the Else argument is returned. IF(22>23,99,11) yields 11. IF(44=44,38,0) yields 38. Cell locations may be substituted for the numbers in the preceding examples.

Nested If . . . Then

Allows more than one If . . . Then . . . Else argument statement to be linked sequentially.

AND

If two math statements are true and they are linked by AND, then their result will be true. Any other condition will be false. This is known as Boolean logic, a form of algebra. The true condition places the number 1 in the cell; a false condition places a 0 in the cell.

OR

If two math statements are linked together by OR, the overall OR statement will be true if either or both of the math statement are true. This, too, is Boolean logic. A true condition places a 1 in the cell; a false condition places a 0 in the cell.

NOT

If two statements are linked together by NOT and both their conditions are false, then the NOT statement is true. Any other condition makes the statement false. NOT is the reverse of the AND statement. A true condition places a 1 in the cell; a false condition places a 0 in the cell.

TRUE

A math statement is true if certain conditions are met. The statement must have an argument that describes the relationship between the numbers. Provided that the statement is correct, its Boolean logic evaluation is TRUE. For example, the statements 34>3 and 33=33 are TRUE, whereas 43=33 is FALSE. A true condition places a 1 in the cell; a false condition places a 0 in the cell.

FALSE

A math statement is false if the relationship between the numbers is not TRUE. As examples, 77=9022 and 16>27 are false. A true indication places a 0 in the cell; a false condition places a 1 in the cell.

ERROR

An ERROR message from a spreadsheet program indicates that an error has occurred. A math statement can also be in ERROR if certain rules of algebra are not met. For example, a number cannot be divided by zero. Also, in a spreadsheet, the user cannot refer to a formula or a cell that does not exist. Certain other conditions can cause an ERROR, such as numbers that are too large for a spreadsheet to handle, or formulas that are too complex to be evaluated.

N/A

An N/A message indicates that information is not available. For example, if a number does not meet the minimum requirement for a lookup table, the N/A message will appear. If a formula refers to a cell that is empty, N/A may appear. The N/A message appears frequently in sheets that have circular references.

ISERROR

This function allows the evaluation of an ERROR message and also allows another value to be substituted for the value that is in error. @ISERROR(B2,B9,B32) evaluates to B2. If B2 is an ERROR, then cell B9 is displayed; otherwise, B32 is displayed.

ISNA

The ISNA function is similar to the ISERROR function, except that the cell referred to is evaluated for the N/A condition.

Special

LOOKUP

The LOOKUP function allows a value to be looked up in a table. The associated value in the table is then returned. Tax, deduction, and performance tables are the most frequently used lookup tables.

Expanded lookup

Expanded lookup tables allow values to be looked up in an array of tables.

CHOOSE

Allows the nth number of a specified value to be yielded. @CHOOSE (3,9,3,2,8,1) yields 2.

Table or indexed array

A table or indexed array is a matrix of values, or text. When it is combined with relative cell references, numbers or text can be looked up in the table (in a similar way to the lookup table).

Locate text string

Finds the location of a specific combination of characters in a spreadsheet and advances the spreadsheet's cursor to that point.

This feature is useful for finding specific names or labels in a large spreadsheet.

Data table

A matrix that can be used to solve an equation for a variety of x and y values.

On-screen calculator

Allows calculation of entries without placing the results into a cell location. This feature is useful for calculating values prior to placing them into the spreadsheet array.

Other

Row

Returns the number of the row in which the calculation appears.

Column

Returns the number of the column in which the calculation appears.

Numbers to text

Allows the conversion of numbers to text to isolate them from further recalculation.

Text to numbers

Converts text strings that are legal spreadsheet numbers, formulas, or values into numeric format.

Random numbers

The ability to generate pseudorandom numbers. This feature is useful for weighting or for random iteration of statistical calculations.

	1-2-3	VisiCalc
Spreadsheet Characteristics		
Number of rows	2048	254
Number of columns	256	63
Number of cells	524288	16012
Maximum capacity of cell (characters)	254	120
RAM Memory Capacities		
Minimum usable memory128K	64K	
Maximum usable memory	544K+	256
Uses virtual memory	N	N
Disk Capabilities		
Copy protected	Y	Y
Hard disk-compatible	Y	Y
Size of test file	28672	12928
Display Characteristics		
Can use 40-column display	N	Y
Must use an 80-column display	Y	N
Uses color to highlight areas of sheet	Y	N
Uses color monitor (on spreadsheet)	N	Y
Numeric precision (to the right of decimal)	15	12
User-Friendliness Features		
Tutorial on disk	Y	N
On-screen help	Y	N
Cell editing	Y	Y
On-screen display:		
Window number displayed	N	N
Model name displayed	Y	N
Memory counter	Y	Y
"Prompted" commands	Y	Y
Use of IBM PC Keyboard		
HOME	Y	Y
END	Y	N
Arrow keys	Y	Y
PgUp	Y	N
PgDn	Y	N
TAB	Y	N
ALT	Y	N
10 function keys (more than 1 key)	Y	N
Keyboard status display	Y	N
Worksheet Formatting		
Number of windows	2	2
Number of models visible at one time	1	1
Column widths:		
Adjustable	Y	Y
Individually adjustable	Y	N
Minimum width	1	1
"Form" input feature	Y	N
Must display border at all times	Y	Y
Cell Formatting		
User-defined cell formatting	Y	N
Floating dollar sign ($)	Y	N
Commas in numbers	Y	N

	1-2-3	VisiCalc
Exponential	Y	Y
Percentage	Y	N
Negatives in parentheses	Y	N
DR/CR notation	Y	N
Enhanced (underline or boldface)	N	N
Integer	Y	Y
True integer	Y	N
Fixed number of decimals	Y	N
Cell filler	N	N
Symbolic	Y	Y
Symbol used	*-+	*
Align right:		
Text	Y	Y
Numbers	Y	Y
Align left:		
Text	Y	Y
Numbers	N	N
Align center:		
Text	Y	N
Numbers	N	N
Formula display	N	N
Cell protection	N	N
Adjustable cell height	N	N
Cell/Range Names	Y	N
Print Formatting		
Headers	Y	N
Footers	Y	N
Flexible margins:		
Top	Y	N
Bottom	Y	N
Left	Y	N
Right	Y	N
Page numbers	Y	N
Pause between pages	Y	N
Printer setup strings	Y	Y
Accepts multiple printer types	Y	Y
Print cell formulas	Y	Y
Printer control codes may be installed into program	Y	Y
Logical printer device may be changed from program (except LPT to COM1:)	Y	Y
Text Functions		
Justification	Y	N
Text lookup	N	N
Text in If...Then phrases	N	N
Labels wider than columns	Y	N
Repeating labels	Y	Y
String functions:		
Substring	N	N
String length	N	N
Concatenation	N	N
Recalculation		
Manual	Y	Y
Automatic	Y	Y
Interactive	Y	N
Natural	Y	N
Row wise	Y	Y
Column wise	Y	Y

	1-2-3	VisiCalc
Saving and Loading Files		
Automatic recalculation on load	N	Y
Partial load	Y	N
Partial save	Y	N
Import files from other programs	Y	N
Import text files	Y	N
Save to text file	Y	N
Format disk from within program	N	Note 1
Saving to communications file:		
DIF	Y	Y
SYLK	N	N
SDI	N	N
Sheet-to-Sheet Links		
Data channels (true three-dimensional)	N	N
Maximum number of channels	—	—
Consolidation	Y	N
Single-cell linkage	N	N
Maximum number of linkages	—	—
Data Base Functions		
Internal to spreadsheet	Y	N/A
Stored on disk	N	N/A
Sorting:		
Numeric	Y	N/A
Alphabetic	Y	N/A
Single key	Y	N/A
Multiple key	Y	N/A
Sort partial rows/columns	Y	N/A
Criteria operations:		
Number of criteria	32	N/A
Deletion	Y	N/A
Find	Y	N/A
Extract	Y	N/A
Data base statistics:		
Sum	Y	N/A
Average	Y	N/A
Count	Y	N/A
Max	Y	N/A
Min	Y	N/A
Standard deviation	Y	N/A
Variance	Y	N/A
Graphics Functions		
Requires Color/Graphics Adapter	N	N/A
Types of graphs:		
Bar	Y	N/A
Stacked Bar	Y	N/A
Scatter	Y	N/A
Line	Y	N/A
Pie	Y	N/A
Hi-Lo-Close	N	N/A
Number of ranges in a single graph	6	N/A
User-defined colors	Y	N/A
User-defined legends:		
Titles and subtitles	Y	N/A
Labels	Y	N/A
Scales	Y	N/A
Programmability		
User-defined programs	Y	N/A

	1-2-3	VisiCalc
If...Then function	Y	N/A
GOTO function	Y	N/A
QUIT function	Y	N/A
User menus	Y	N/A
Speed (all numbers in seconds)		
Time required to perform 1,000 iterations of:		
Simple addition	3	14
Simple multiplication	3	15
Time to load program	15	10
Time to load test file	15	58
Built-in Functions		
Mathematical:		
Sum	Y	Y
Round	Y	N
Integer	Y	Y
Natural logarithm	Y	N
Logarithm	Y	Y
Exponential	Y	Y
Square root	Y	Y
Modulo	Y	N
Absolute value	Y	Y
Power (X to the Y)	N	Y
Trigonometric:		
Sine	Y	Y
Cosine	Y	Y
Tangent	Y	Y
Arc sine	Y	Y
Arc cosine	Y	Y
Arc tangent	Y	Y
Pi	Y	Y
Statistical:		
Count	Y	Y
Average	Y	Y
Maximum	Y	Y
Minimum	Y	Y
Standard deviation	Y	N
Variance	Y	N
Linear estimation	N	N
Financial:		
Net present value	Y	Y
Future value	Y	N
Payment	Y	N
Internal rate of return	Y	N
Modified internal rate of return	N	N
Annuity	N	N
Depreciation	N	N
Date arithmetic:		
Specified date	Y	N
Today	Y	N
Year	Y	N
Month	Y	N
Day	Y	N
Time of day	N	N
Julian date	Y	N
Logical:		
If...Then...Else	Y	Y
Nested If...Then	Y	Y
And	Y	Y

	1-2-3	VisiCalc
Or	Y	Y
Not	Y	Y
True	Y	Y
False	Y	Y
Error	Y	Y
N/A	Y	Y
ISERROR	Y	Y
ISNA	Y	Y
Special:		
Lookup	Y	Y
Expanded lookup	Y	N
Choose	Y	Y
Table or index array	N	N
Locate text string	N	N
Data table	Y	N
On-screen calculator	N	N
Other:		
Sign	N	N
Row	N	N
Column	N	N
Numbers to text	N	N
Text to numbers	N	N
Random numbers	N	N

Note 1: On some Apple versions. Not available on the IBM PC.

Index

More Computer Knowledge from Que

LOTUS SOFTWARE TITLES

1-2-3 for Business $15.95
1-2-3 Tips, Tricks, and Traps 14.95
Using 1-2-3 .... 15.95
Using 1-2-3 Workbook and Disk 29.95
Using Symphony 19.95

WORD PROCESSING TITLES

Improve Your Writing with Word Processing 12.95
Using MultiMate 16.95

IBM TITLES

IBM PC Expansion & Software Guide, 4th Edition 19.95
IBM PCjr Favorite Programs Explained 12.95
IBM's Personal Computer, 2nd Edition 15.95
Introducing IBM PCjr 9.95
Networking IBM PCs: A Practical Guide 17.95
PC DOS User's Guide 14.95
Real Managers Use Personal Computers 14.95

APPLICATIONS SOFTWARE TITLES

Multiplan Models for Business 15.95
Spreadsheet Software: From VisiCalc to 1-2-3 .... 15.95
SuperCalc SuperModels for Business 14.95
VisiCalc Models for Business 14.95

COMPUTER SYSTEMS TITLES

Apple Favorite Programs Explained 12.95
Introducing the Apple IIc 12.95

Commodore 64 Favorite Programs Explained 12.95
DEC Personal Computers Expansion & Software Guide 19.95
The HP Touchscreen 19.95
MS-DOS User's Guide 14.95
TI-99/4A Favorite Programs Explained 12.95

The First Book of ADAM (Coleco) 12.95
The Second Book of ADAM: Using SmartWRITER 10.95

PROGRAMMING AND TECHNICAL TITLES

C Programmer's Library 19.95
C Programming Guide 18.95
CP/M Programmer's Encyclopedia 19.95
CP/M Software Finder 14.95
Understanding UNIX: A Conceptual Guide 18.95

Que Order Line: 1-800-428-5331

All prices subject to change without notice.

LEARN MORE ABOUT LOTUS SOFTWARE
WITH THESE OUTSTANDING BOOKS FROM QUE

1-2-3 for Business

by Leith Anderson and Douglas Cobb

Step-by-step instructions show you how to build fourteen practical business applications, using all the features of 1-2-3. The book includes models for Fixed Asset Management, Ratio Analysis, and Project Management.

The Using 1-2-3 Workbook and Disk

by David Ewing

The Using 1-2-3 Workbook and Disk guides the user through building a 1-2-3 model, explaining how to use all the commands necessary to create a practical, comprehensive 1-2-3 application. The workbook also includes a bound-in diskette that contains the workbook model at various stages of development.

1-2-3 Tips, Tricks, and Traps

by Dick Andersen and Douglas Cobb

A must for 1-2-3 users. This book explains 1-2-3's little-known features and offers advice in problem areas. Tips include shortcuts for creating macros, producing graphs, and using Data Tables. Traps help with special problems that may arise when using 1-2-3.

Using Symphony

by Geoffrey LeBlond and David Ewing

This book explains all of the basic concepts you will need to use Symphony effectively and explores the program's advanced capabilities in detail. If you decide to move up from 1-2-3 to Symphony, this book will help you master Symphony quickly and take advantage of its powerful features.

Item	Title	Price	Quantity	Extension
34	1-2-3 for Business	$15.95		
127	1-2-3 Tips, Tricks, and Traps	$14.95		
39	Using 1-2-3	$15.95		
142	Using 1-2-3 Workbook and Disk	$29.95		
141	Using Symphony	$19.95		
		BOOK SUBTOTAL		
	Shipping & Handling ($1.50 per item)			
	Indiana Residents Add 5% Sales Tax			
		GRAND TOTAL		

Method of Payment:

☐ Check ☐ VISA ☐ MasterCard ☐ American Express

Card Number _____ Exp. Date _____

Cardholder Name _____

Ship to_____

Address _____

City _____ State _____ ZIP _____

All prices subject to change without notice.

FOLD HERE

_____

_____

_____

7999 Knue Road
Indianapolis, IN 46250

Invest in

Absolute Reference™
THE JOURNAL FOR 1-2-3™ AND SYMPHONY™ USERS

today!

Call now or use this convenient form.
1-800-428-5331

fold here

- -

Please send me a ☐ one-year   ☐ two-year subscription to **Absolute Reference**.

Within the United States	Outside the United States
☐ 12 issues — $60	☐ 12 issues — $80
☐ 24 issues — $105	☐ 24 issues — $135

METHOD OF PAYMENT:

Check ☐   VISA ☐   MasterCard ☐   AMEX ☐   Exp. Date _____

Cardholder Name _____

Card Number _____

Name_____

Address _____

_____

City _____ State _____ ZIP_____

If you can't wait, call the toll-free number,
1-800-428-5331, with your credit card information.

All prices subject to change without notice.

FOLD HERE

- -

_____

_____

_____

Plac
Stam
Her

AbsoluteReference
THE JOURNAL FOR 1-2-3™ AND SYMPHONY™ USERS

Que Corporation
7999 Knue Road
Indianapolis, IN 46250